SERIAL
KILLERS

SERIAL KILLERS

True Stories of the World's Worst Murderers

AL CIMINO

This edition published in 2019 by Arcturus Publishing Limited
26/27 Bickels Yard, 151–153 Bermondsey Street,
London SE1 3HA

Copyright © Arcturus Holdings Limited

AD006211UK

Printed in the UK

CONTENTS

INTRODUCTION

Murder fascinates us all – whether it is the gentle slaughter written into existence by Agatha Christie or the choreographed butchery of Quentin Tarantino. Shakespeare's tragedies leave blood on the stage and in Dostoyevsky there would be no punishment if there hadn't been a crime – in *Crime and Punishment,* former law student Raskolnikov commits murder and sets in train his own downfall.

Murder in all its forms addresses unblinkingly the most fundamental question of human existence – the fact that we are going to die. So is everyone we know and love.

But murder is the thing we all fear more than anything. Somehow we must learn to come to terms with that. And as a writer, I know another thing about murder: no matter how gruesome, it always makes a good story. With serial killers – those addicted to murder – there is another element. Serial killers are the ultimate outlaws. They step outside not just the law, but any human norms. They are fascinating because they are almost impossible to understand.

But let's try. Say one night you accidentally killed someone and got away with it. Maybe it was an accident, but if you reported the incident to the authorities it would be impossible to escape the accusation of culpability.

If you went to jail, there would be terrible consequences for your family and children. So best keep quiet. The problem is, if you had killed once and got away with it, wouldn't there be a temptation to do it again? And again? If you got away with it each time, wouldn't it become addictive?

Some of the villains in this book slipped into serial killing that way, though rarely for the purest of motives. Usually the impulse is sexual and truly none of us are in our right minds when it comes to matters of the heart. Often they have had an almost pitiably warped childhood. Cranial trauma and other brain damage during their youth is sometimes a factor too. As they grow up, they find themselves gripped by an overwhelming urge to step outside the law. It may begin with small acts of vandalism or theft, then burglary, progressing to rape and finally murder.

Clearly, some of the perpetrators are purely evil and no excuses can be made for them. Others do seem to struggle with themselves. Many are relieved when they are finally caught, knowing that, if left at large, they would continue killing.

While studying serial killers gives us a powerful insight into the human condition, we must not forget their victims. Each one is a tragedy. Many are young and vulnerable and all of them are ruthlessly deprived of the possibilities and pleasures of a fulfilling life simply for the gratification of someone who is clearly, by any measure, inadequate. But there is nothing to be done. Those who have been murdered cannot be revived.

Then there are the families and friends of the victims to consider, who must go through the rest of their lives knowing that someone they loved has been snuffed out. They must deal with the urge for revenge, or somehow struggle with themselves to find a way to forgive. In most cases, I am sure that is impossible.

Some must ask how they did not see it coming. The parents of someone who kills, however blameless, must wonder whether it was something they did that sent their offspring down the road to murder. The children of killers even ask themselves whether they have inherited the murderous trait.

Most serial killers are single white males in their late twenties or early thirties. But not all of them. In these pages some of the serial killers are women while others are black or Chinese, and they are people of all ages. It is easy to dismiss them as monsters but better, I think, to think of them – or perhaps what they do – as monstrous. And it is comforting to know that all of the villains in this book are either dead or in jail.

As to whether, once you have killed once, you are destined to keep on doing it, the only person I know who has killed a lot of people is my mother. During World War II, she was an anti-aircraft gunner and has a medal for being in charge of the first women's battery to shoot down a German plane. And she shot down lots of them, presumably killing many young airmen. But as far as I know, since 1945 she has never had an urge to kill again. Perhaps she does not have an addictive personality. In fact, vanishingly few former soldiers, no matter how murderous the battles they have been involved in, continue killing after the war is over.

The people in this book are of a different order. It is clear that once they had killed they had to do it again. They got to enjoy it. Murder took over their lives, just the way crack cocaine or crystal meth takes over their users' lives. The killers in this book are quite literally addicted to murder.

Al Cimino

CHARLES MANSON
THE FAMILY

MURDER IN MIND

Charles Manson died in California State Prison in Corcoran in 2017 after serving forty-seven years for murder and conspiracy to murder, though he had not actually murdered anyone himself. But in 1969, on his orders, eight people were hacked to death in a meaningless orgy of violence that left America – and the rest of the world – reeling.

Born in 1934 in Cincinnati, Ohio, Manson was the illegitimate son of a teenage prostitute. Unable to support herself even through prostitution, his mother, Kathleen Maddox, left her son with his grandmother in McMechen, West Virginia. Later, he was sent to the famous orphans' home, Boys Town, in Nebraska, but he was soon kicked out for his surly manner and constant thieving. He became a drifter and was arrested for stealing food in Peoria, Illinois. Sent to Indiana Boys' School in Plainfield, he escaped eighteen times. In 1951, he was arrested again for theft in Beaver City, Utah, and served four years in federal reformatories.

Released in November 1954, he married and was then arrested for transporting stolen cars across a state line. This time he served three years in Terminal Island Federal Prison near Los Angeles. In 1958, Manson became a pimp and was arrested under the Mann Act for transporting women across a state line for immoral purposes. Then he took to forging cheques, was caught and sentenced to ten years in the federal penitentiary on McNeil Island in Washington State.

SCHOOL OF HARD KNOCKS

Being small, just five foot two inches, he had a hard time in prison. He was raped repeatedly by other prisoners. This left him with a lifelong hatred of African Americans who picked on him. To survive, Manson became shifty, cunning and manipulative. Released in 1967, he discovered that he could use what he had learned in jail on the long-haired flower children who flocked to California at the time. His contempt for authority and convention attracted them to him and he developed a taste for middle-class girls who had followed fashion and dropped out of mainstream society.

His hypnotic stare, his unconventional lifestyle and the strange meaningless phrases he babbled made him appear the perfect hippy guru. He travelled with an entourage of young women – all his lovers – and docile males who would do anything he asked. These hangers-on he called the 'Family'. Patricia Krenwinkel was a typical recruit. A former girl scout, she had had a good education and a respectable job at a Los Angeles insurance company. She was twenty-one when she met Manson on Manhattan Beach. She walked out on her job and did not even bother to pick up her last pay cheque when she moved in with the Family on Spahn Movie Ranch, a collection of broken-down shacks in the dusty east corner of the Simi Valley where they hung out.

ADDITIONS TO THE FAMILY

Twenty-year-old Linda Kasabian left her husband and two children and stole $5,000 from a friend to join the Family, where she saw her seamy life through a constant haze of LSD. Leslie Van Houten was just 19 when she dropped out of school. She then lived on the streets on a perpetual acid trip until she met Manson. A more pernicious influence was Susan Atkins, a twenty-one-year-old topless dancer and bar-room hustler. She was a practising Satanist and brought devil worship to the suggestible minds of Manson's Family. Like the others, she had to share his sexual favours. Manson tried to satisfy his insatiable sexual appetite with his female followers, one or two at a time – or even with all of them together.

One of the few men in the commune was a twenty-three-year-old former high-school star from Farmersville, Texas, Charles 'Tex' Watson. Once he had been a top student. In Manson's hands, he became a mindless automaton.

CONTROL FREAK

Surrounded by compliant sycophants, the drug-addled Manson began to develop massive delusions. His own name, Manson, became hugely significant: Manson, Man-son, Son of Man – that is, Christ, or so his demented logic demanded. He was also the Devil, or so Atkins told him.

Manson also dragged the lyrics of Beatles songs into his delusions. Unaware that a helter-skelter was a harmless British funfair ride, he interpreted the track 'Helter Skelter' on The Beatles' *White Album* as heralding the beginning of an inevitable race war. African Americans would be wiped out. Along with them would go the pigs – the police, authority figures, the rich and the famous, what Manson called 'movie people'.

Manson fancied himself as something of a rock star himself. He played the guitar – badly – and wrote a song whose lyrics consisted of the two words 'you know', repeated. Manson took his composition to Gary Hinman, a successful West Coast musician. Manson, Susan Atkins and Bobby Beausoleil – another Family member – badgered Hinman in an attempt to get the song recorded. Hinman humoured them, even letting them stay briefly at his expensive home. Manson then learned that Hinman had recently inherited $20,000. Naively believing that he kept the money at his house, Manson sent Atkins and Beausoleil to get it – and to kill Hinman for refusing to help Manson make 'You Know' a hit. Atkins and Beausoleil tied up Hinman and held him hostage for two days while they ransacked the house. The money was not there. Eventually, out of frustration, they stabbed Hinman to death.

THE WRITING ON THE WALL

To give this senseless murder some spurious significance, Susan Atkins dipped her finger in Hinman's blood and wrote 'political piggie' on the wall. The police found Beausoleil's fingerprints in the house and tracked him down. In Beausoleil's car, they found the knife that killed Hinman and a T-shirt drenched in Hinman's blood. Beausoleil was convicted of murder and went to jail without implicating Atkins.

Next Manson approached Terry Melcher. The son of Doris Day, Melcher was a big player in the music industry but, somehow, he failed to see the potential in Manson's material. On 23 March 1969, Manson drove his followers to Melcher's remote home in the Hollywood Hills to reconnoitre it. Melcher had moved out of the house in Cielo Drive in Benedict Canyon. But that did not matter to Manson. The people he saw at the house were 'movie types'.

On 8 August 1969, Manson sent Watson, Atkins, Krenwinkel and Kasabian to Benedict Canyon. Armed with a .22 revolver, a knife and a length of rope, they were ordered to kill everyone in the house and 'make it as gruesome as possible'.

The people now living at the end of Cielo Drive were indeed 'movie people'. The new tenant was film director Roman Polanski, although he was away shooting a movie in London at the time. His eight-months-pregnant wife, movie star Sharon Tate, was at home though. So was Folger's coffee heiress Abigail Folger, her boyfriend Polish writer Voyteck Frykowski and Sharon Tate's friend, celebrity hairdresser Jay Sebring.

NO MERCY

Kasabian claimed she lost her nerve at the last minute and remained outside. But the others entered the estate. The first person they met was eighteen-year-old Steven Parent, who had been visiting the caretaker. Parent begged for his life, but Watson shot him four times, killing him instantly.

Inside the house, the three killers herded Sharon Tate and her guests into the living room. While they were being tied up, Sebring broke free, but was gunned down before he could escape. Realizing that they were all going to be killed, Frykowski attacked Watson. He was beaten to the ground. Then the girls stabbed him to death in a frenzy. There were fifty-one stab wounds on his body. Folger also made a break for it. She was out of the back door and halfway across the lawn before Krenwinkel caught up with her. She was knocked to the ground, then Watson stabbed her to death.

Sharon Tate was by then the only one left alive. She begged for the life of her unborn child. Atkins stabbed her sixteen times. Tate's mutilated corpse was tied to Sebring's dead body. Then the killers spread an American flag across the couch and wrote the word 'pig' on the front door in Sharon Tate's blood.

Next day, Manson got stoned and read the lurid reports of the murders in the press. To celebrate, he had an orgy with his female followers. But soon he craved more blood.

MORE MAYHEM

On 10 August, Manson randomly selected a house in the Silver Lake area and broke in. Forty-four-year-old grocery store owner Leno LaBianca and his thirty-eight-year-old wife Rosemary, who ran a fashionable dress shop, awoke to find Manson's pistol in their faces.

He took LaBianca's wallet and went outside to the car where his followers were waiting. With them was twenty-three-year-old Steve Grogan. Manson sent Watson, Van Houten and Krenwinkel into the house with instructions to murder the LaBiancas, saying that he was going to the house next door to murder its occupants. Instead, he drove off.

Charles Manson and his followers carved an 'X' on their foreheads to show their rejection of society. Manson changed the cross to a swastika during his trial for the Tate and LaBianca murders.

Watson did as he was told. He dragged Leno LaBianca into the living room and stabbed him to death, leaving the knife sticking out of his throat. Meanwhile, Van Houten and Krenwinkel stabbed the helpless Mrs LaBianca. They used their victims' blood to write 'death to all pigs', 'Rise' and 'Helter Skelter' on the walls. Watson carved the word 'War' across LaBianca's stomach, again leaving the knife sticking in the dead man. Then the three killers had a midnight snack and took a shower together.

NO JOKE

Although the killers thought of their senseless slayings as a joke, they knew that there was a danger that they might get caught and the Family began to break up. To support herself, Susan Atkins turned to prostitution and was arrested. In prison, she boasted to another inmate about the killings. Under interrogation, she told the police that Manson was behind them. He and several other members of the Family still at the Spahn Ranch were arrested, but they were released again due to lack of evidence.

Then on 15 October 1969 Manson was arrested again. This time he was charged. Most of the Family were in custody by then. Manson and his followers took the legal proceedings as a joke and showed no remorse. Basking in the publicity that surrounded the case, Manson portrayed himself as the most evil man on Earth and boasted that he had been responsible for thirty-five other murders. He, Beausoleil, Atkins, Krenwinkel, Van Houten and Grogan were all found guilty and sentenced to death. But in 1972, the death penalty was abolished in California and the sentences were commuted to life imprisonment.

MIKHAIL POPKOV
THE WEREWOLF SERIAL KILLER

RATIONING CONFESSIONS

Mikhail Popkov was known as 'The Werewolf' in the press because he struck at night, but the authorities more prosaically called him the 'Wednesday Murderer' because that was usually when the bodies were found. Nevertheless, he is much more scary than that name suggests, for as Russia's most prolific killer he admitted to the rape and murder of more than eighty women. The final total may have been even higher than that.

Having been sentenced to life imprisonment for twenty-two murders in 2015, Popkov claimed that he stopped killing in the year 2000 after one of his victims gave him syphilis, rendering him impotent. However, in 2017 he admitted that he continued for another ten years and confessed to killing another sixty people in the Irkutsk Oblast of central Siberia. And there may have been even more victims. After quitting his job as a police officer, he travelled regularly between his hometown of Angarsk and Vladivostok on Russia's Pacific coast, over two thousand miles away, and the detectives felt that he may have killed along the way. They believed that he was rationing his confessions to delay his transfer from the relative comfort of the regular prison, where he was then being held, to a tough penal colony where he would serve out the rest of his life sentence.

KILLED THOSE OF 'NEGATIVE BEHAVIOUR'

Popkov began killing in 1992 when he found two used condoms in the rubbish at home and suspected that his wife Elena, who was also a police officer, was cheating on him. Though it seems that the condoms had been left by a house guest, one of Elena's work colleagues admitted that he had had a brief affair with her.

A few weeks after his discovery, Popkov killed 'spontaneously', he told investigators.

'I just felt I wanted to kill a woman I was giving a lift to in my car,' he said.

In 2015, he claimed that his victims were prostitutes and that his aim was to 'cleanse' his hometown. He also thought that even if they were not involved in prostitution, women who went out by themselves at night, going to bars and drinking alcohol, needed to be punished. It has been speculated that Popkov was taking psychic revenge on an alcoholic mother who abused him as a child.

'My victims were women who walked the streets at night alone, without men, and not sober, who behaved thoughtlessly, carelessly, not afraid to engage in a conversation with me, sit in the car, and then go for a drive in search of adventure, for the sake of entertainment, ready to drink alcohol and have sexual intercourse with me,' he said.

He used to have sex with them and then decide whether to murder them.

'In this way, not all women became victims, but women of certain negative behaviour, and I had a desire to teach and punish them,' he said. 'So that others would not behave in such a way and so that they would be afraid.'

The women were reassured by his police uniform and felt safe getting into a police car.

'I was in uniform. I decided to stop and give a woman a ride. I frequently did that before,' he said. 'The woman began talking to me, I offered to give her a lift, she agreed … That same morning, I drove the head of the criminal investigation to the murder scene.'

THRILL FROM INVESTIGATIONS

Popkov not only got a thrill from killing his victims, but he was also able to double his perverted pleasure by reliving every detail of the crime during the investigation. He should have been caught much earlier, as one of his victims survived and identified him. On 26 January 1998, a fifteen-year-old known as Svetlana M said a police car had stopped to give her a lift. The officer took her into some woodland where he forced her to strip naked. He then smashed her head against a tree and she lost consciousness. The next day she was found alive near the village of Baykalsk, some seventy miles from where Popkov had picked her up. Somehow she had survived the night naked in the sub-zero temperatures of a Siberian winter. When she awoke in hospital she was able to identify the officer who had tried to kill her. It was Popkov. However, his wife provided him with a false alibi. Neither she nor their daughter Ekaterina, a teacher, could believe that he was a killer. They said he was a perfect husband and father.

'I had a double life,' he said. 'In one life, I was an ordinary person … In my other life I committed murders, which I carefully concealed from everyone, realizing that what I was doing was a criminal offence.'

Popkov's colleagues in the police force also found it hard to believe that he was a killer. Nor do there appear to have been any signs of mental instability.

'I was in the service, in the police, having positive feedback on my work,' he said. 'I never thought of myself as mentally unhealthy. During my police service, I regularly passed medical commissions and was recognized as fit.'

'FASTIDIOUS'

A major clue that was overlooked was that the murder weapons were removed from the police storeroom. After wiping them to remove his fingerprints, he would throw them away near the scene of the crime.

'The choice of weapons for killing was always casual,' he said. 'I never prepared beforehand to commit a murder. I could use any object that was in the car – a knife, an axe, a bat.'

And he claimed to be fastidious.

'I never used rope for strangulation,' he said, 'and I did not have a firearm either. I did not cut out the hearts of the victims.'

However, one of his victims had had her heart gouged from her body. Others were mutilated or dismembered. One, a medical student, had been beheaded. Her body was found in a rubbish container in Angarsk, her head in another skip elsewhere.

On one occasion, the killing came close to home when he discovered that he had murdered a teacher at his own daughter's music school.

'Her corpse was found in the forest along with the body of another woman,' he said. 'My daughter asked me to give her money because the school was collecting to organize funerals. I gave it to her.'

DOUBLE MURDERS

He had another close call in 2000 when he returned to the scene of a crime. After he had left thirty-five-year-old Maria Lyzhina and thirty-seven-year-old Liliya Pashkovskaya for dead, he found that a commemorative chain he wore around his neck was missing and he went to retrieve it before investigators found it.

'I realized that I lost it in a forest glade when I killed the two women,' he said. 'I realized that I would absolutely be identified by the lost chain, and experienced the greatest stress. I realized that I should return to the scene of the crime, if the police or the prosecutor's office had not been there yet.'

But when he returned to the scene he found more than he had bargained for.

As a police officer, Popkov not only got a thrill from killing his victims, but he was also able to double his perverted pleasure by reliving every detail of the crime during the investigation.

'I found the chain right away, but saw that one of the women was still breathing,' he said. 'I was shocked by the fact that she was still alive, so I finished her off with a shovel.'

The two women had worked together in a shop. On 2 June they went to see Maria's sister and at midnight they decided they had better go home. At first they thought of taking a taxi but then they changed their minds.

It was a warm summer night and they decided to walk. On 5 June, their bodies were found in the forest near Veresovka village. Maria had a fourteen-year-old daughter and Liliya had a twelve-year-old daughter and a three-year-old son, who would now have to grow up without their mothers.

The custom in Russia is for coffins to be left open at the graveside so mourners can bid the deceased a final farewell, but the two women were buried in closed coffins because they were so badly disfigured.

Another double murder occurred in 1998 when the bodies of twenty-year-old Tatiana 'Tanya' Martynova and nineteen-year-old Yulia Kuprikova were found in a suburb of Angarsk. Tanya's sister Viktoria Chagaeva had given her a ticket for a concert, but Tanya was married with a small child and her twenty-four-year-old husband Igor begged her not to go. Ignoring his pleas, she made the mistake of stopping for a quick drink with a few friends after the show. Then the two girls accepted a lift from a policeman.

'On the morning of 29 October, Igor called me saying Tanya had not come back home,' said Viktoria. 'I got truly scared. It was the first time she had ever done this. There were no mobile phones at that time; we could only call Yulia's parents, thinking Tanya must have stayed overnight there for some reason. But Yulia's parents said she had not come home either.'

They went to the police and were told that they must wait three days before the two young women could be listed as missing. There would be no need to wait. That night a shepherd found their naked bodies near Meget, a village close to Angarsk.

'It was 1 a.m. when Tanya's husband Igor and I came to the police,' said Viktoria. 'We did not tell our mother yet. Igor was absolutely devastated and kept saying: "She was killed, she was killed." I was shocked too, but I simply could not believe it and replied: "What are you talking about?"'

Later they were told that their bodies were found next to each other. Both girls had been raped after they were dead and then mutilated.

'My elder brother Oleg went to the morgue to identify Tanya,' said Viktoria. 'He had just flown from Moscow. He felt sick when he saw the body, she was so mutilated. He was almost green when he came out of there. He just could not say a word. I did not dare to go in and look.'

The mutilation was confined to Tanya's body and the back of her head, so the coffin could be left open with her face showing. However, Yulia's coffin had to be kept closed as her face was so badly cut up.

'Many people attended Tanya's funeral,' said Viktoria. 'It felt as if the whole town was there. Our poor mother lost consciousness several times; she needed a lot of medicine to cope. Igor was in almost the same condition.'

Indeed, their mother Lubov never recovered from the loss of her daughter. 'She felt as if she had died with Tanya. Life became useless for her,' said Viktoria. 'She lived only because she was visiting various mediums one by one, looking for the killer and wasting her money. Nobody gave her any serious information but she kept doing it. She died in 2007, aged sixty-six, from a heart attack. I think her heart could not cope with the pain any longer.'

VICTIM'S SISTER KNEW THE KILLER

When Popkov was arrested in 2012, Viktoria realized that she knew him. They had both competed in a biathlon at a local sports ground.

'I was struck with horror when I saw the picture of this maniac in the paper and online,' she said. 'My sister's killer was looking into my eyes. I immediately felt as if I'd met him. Looking at him, I could hardly breathe. Some minutes later I looked at him another time and thought – oh my God, I know him! I was so shocked, I even took a knife and cut his face in the newspaper, I needed to let this horror out of me.

'I remember him as a tall slim man, he was always alone, with a slippery and shifty glance. I think such people just must not live. This beast took the life of my sister, who had so many happy years in front of her. I cried a lot that day, but it is time to be quiet and just wait. He will be punished by law and criminals in jail will punish him too. I am sure he will pay for all the murders one day.'

That a fellow officer committed these terrible crimes under their noses perturbed the police. A former police colleague said: 'When

I read about him in the press, I literally choked because I used to work with him and thought I knew him. He was an absolutely normal man. He liked biathlon; once on duty he shot a rapist during an arrest. There was an investigation and he was not punished as the chiefs considered he had taken fair action.'

Another ex-colleague said: 'I used to work closely with him for five years. He knew lots of jokes and stories, and could be the life and soul of the party.'

Popkov was caught when 3,500 policemen and former policemen were asked to give a DNA sample. His DNA matched that in sperm found on some of the victims.

'I couldn't predict DNA tests,' he told a reporter from *Komsomolskaya Pravda* in a jailhouse interview. 'I was born in the wrong century.'

When Popkov pleaded guilty to the two dozen murder charges, the judge asked him how many murders he had committed in total. In reply, the killer just shrugged.

'I can't say exactly,' he said. 'I didn't write them down.'

TED BUNDY
THE CHARMING KILLER

UNHEALTHY URGES

Ted Bundy had the power to charm women. Many of them paid with their lives. He claimed his sexual impulses were so strong that there was no way he could control them. During his first attacks, he maintained that he had to wrestle with his conscience. But soon he began to desensitize himself. He claimed not to have tortured his victims, but said that he had had to kill them after he had raped them to prevent them from identifying him.

Bundy had been a compulsive masturbator from an early age and later became obsessed by sadistic pornography. After glimpsing a girl undressing through a window, he also became an obsessional Peeping Tom. His long-time girlfriend Meg Anders described how he would tie her up with stockings before anal sex. This sex game stopped when he almost strangled her. For years, they maintained a more or less normal sexual relationship, while Bundy exercised his craving for total control with anonymous victims, whom he often strangled during the sexual act.

BIZARRE LEANINGS

His attitude to sex was often ambivalent. Although he desired the bodies of attractive young women, he would leave their vaginas stuffed with twigs and dirt and sometimes sodomize them with objects such as aerosol cans.

Some of the bodies, though partly decomposed, were found with freshly washed hair and newly applied make-up, indicating that he had kept them for necrophilia. In only one case did he admit to deliberately terrorizing his victim – or rather victims. He kidnapped two girls at once so that he could rape each of them in front of the other, before killing them.

RANDOM ATTACK

Bundy's first victim was Sharon Clarke of Seattle. He had broken into her apartment while she was asleep and smashed her around the head with a metal rod. She suffered a shattered skull, but survived. She could not identify her attacker and no motivation for the attack has been given.

Then young women began to disappear from the University of Washington campus nearby. Six vanished within seven months. At the Lake Sammamish resort in Washington State, a number of young women reported being approached by a young man calling himself Ted. He had his arm in a sling and asked them to help get his sailboat off his car. But in the parking lot they found that there was no boat on the car. Ted then said that they would have to go to his house to get it. Sensibly, most declined. Janice Ott seems to have agreed to go with him though. She disappeared. A few hours later, Denise Naslund also disappeared from the same area. She had been seen in the company of a good-looking, dark-haired young man who fitted Ted Bundy's description. The remains of Janice Ott, Denise Naslund and another unidentified young

Ted Bundy used his undoubted charm to gain his victims' trust and lure them to their doom. He decapitated many of his victims and kept their severed heads in his apartment as souvenirs.

woman were later found on waste land, where they had been eaten and scattered by animals.

Witnesses at the University of Washington came forward, saying that they had seen a man wearing a sling. Some other bodies were found, again disposed of on waste ground.

TOO MANY LEADS

The police had two suspects. Ex-convict Gary Taylor had been picked up by the Seattle police for abducting women under false pretences. Then there was park attendant Warren Forrest, who had picked up a young woman who consented to pose for him. He took her to a secluded part of the park, tied her up and stripped her naked. He taped her mouth and fired darts at her breasts. Then he raped her, strangled her and left her for dead. But she survived and identified her attacker. Both were in custody though, and the attacks continued. Bundy's girlfriend called anonymously, giving his name, but the tip-off was overlooked among the thousands of other leads the police had to follow up.

CASTING HIS NET WIDER

Bundy began to travel further afield. On 2 October 1974, he abducted Nancy Wilcox after she left an all-night party. He raped and strangled Melissa Smith, daughter of the local police chief. Her body was found near Salt Lake City. He took Laura Aimee from a Halloween party in Orem, Utah. Her naked body was found at the bottom of a canyon.

In Salt Lake City a week later, he approached a girl named Carol DaRonch. Bundy pretended to be a detective and asked her for the licence number of her car. Someone had tried to break into it, he said. He asked her to accompany him to help identify the suspect. She got into his car, but once they were in a quiet street he handcuffed her.

She began to scream. He put a gun to her head. She managed to get out of the door and Bundy chased after her with a crowbar. He took a swing at her skull, but she managed to grab the crowbar. A car was coming down the street. Carol jumped in front of it, forcing it to stop. She jumped in and the car drove away.

Carol gave a good description to the police, but Bundy continued undeterred. He tried to pick up a young French teacher outside her high school. She declined to go with him. But Debbie Kent did. She disappeared from a school playground where a key to a pair of handcuffs was later found.

FURTHER ATTACKS

The following January in Snowmass Village, a Colorado ski resort, Dr Raymond Gadowsky found that his fiancée, Caryn Campbell, was missing from her room. A month later, her naked body was found in the snow. She had been raped and her skull had been smashed in. Julie Cunningham vanished from nearby Vail and the remains of Susan Rancourt and Brenda Bell were also found on Taylor Mountain.

The body of Melanie Cooley was found only about ten miles from her home. Unlike the other victims, she was still clothed, though her jeans had been undone, convincing the police that the motive was sexual.

The Colorado attacks continued with Nancy Baird, who disappeared from a petrol station, and Shelley Robertson, whose naked body was found down a mine shaft.

BAD BREAK FOR BUNDY

A Salt Lake City patrol man was cruising an area of the city that had recently suffered a spate of burglaries. He noticed Bundy's car driving slowly and indicated that he should pull over. Instead, Bundy sped off. The patrolman gave chase and caught up with him. In his car were found maps and brochures of Colorado. Some coincided with the places girls had disappeared.

Forensic experts found a hair in Bundy's car that matched that of Melissa Smith. A witness also recognized Bundy from Snowmass

Village. He was charged and extradited to Colorado to stand trial. However, few people could believe that such an intelligent and personable young man could be responsible for these terrible sex attacks, even though Carol DaRonch picked him out of a line-up.

Bundy was given permission to conduct his own defence. He was even allowed to use the law library for research. There he managed to give his guard the slip, jumped from a window and escaped. He was recaptured a week later.

Bundy still protested his innocence and managed to prolong the pre-trial hearings with a number of skilful stalling manoeuvres. Using the time he gained to lose weight, he cut a small hole under the light fitting in the ceiling of his cell. He squeezed through the one-foot-square hole he had made and got clean away.

SHOCKING VIOLENCE

He travelled around America before settling in Tallahassee, Florida, a few blocks from the sorority houses of Florida State University. One evening, Nita Neary saw a man lurking in front of her sorority house. She was about to phone the police when a fellow student, Karen Chandler, staggered from her room with blood streaming from her head. She was screaming that she had just been attacked by a madman. Her roommate Kathy Kleiner had also been attacked. Her jaw was broken. Margaret Bowman had been attacked sexually and strangled with her own pantyhose.

Lisa Levy had also been sexually assaulted. Bundy had bitten one of her nipples off and left teeth marks in her buttocks. Then he beat her around the head. She died on the way to hospital. In another building, Cheryl Thomas had also been viciously attacked, but she survived.

The police had only a sketchy description of the attacker. But Bundy had plainly got a taste for killing again. While making his getaway, he abducted twelve-year-old Kimberley Leach, sexually assaulted her, strangled her, mutilated her sexual organs and dumped her body in the Suwannee River Park.

DESPERATE MEASURES

Bundy was now short of money. He stole some credit cards and a car, and sneaked out of his apartment where he owed back rent. But the stolen car was a giveaway. He was stopped by a motorcycle cop and arrested. At the police station, he admitted that he was Ted Bundy and that he was wanted by the Colorado police.

The Florida police began to tie him in with the Tallahassee attack. When they tried to take an impression of his teeth, he went berserk. It took six men to hold his jaw open. The impression matched the teeth marks on murdered student Lisa Levy's buttocks.

Again Bundy conducted his own defence, skilfully using the law to prolong the court case and his personality to charm the jury. But the evidence of the teeth marks was too strong. He was found guilty of murder and sentenced to death. At 7 a.m. on 24 January 1989, Bundy went to the electric chair. He is said to have died with a smile on his face. On death row, Bundy made a detailed confession. He also received sacks full of mail from young women whose letters dwelt on cruel and painful ways to make love. Even on death row, he had not lost his fatal charm.

JOHN NORMAN COLLINS
THE YPSILANTI RIPPER

FIRST VICTIM

On the evening of 9 July 1967, nineteen-year-old accounting student Mary Fleszar, an attractive brunette, was walking down the street in the small university town of Ypsilanti, Michigan when a blue-grey Chevrolet pulled over and the driver, a young man, leaned out to speak to her. An onlooker assumed that he was offering her a lift. When she refused, the man drove off. He turned at the next corner and then, moments later, sped back past the girl and into a private driveway. By this time Mary had reached her apartment block and was safe – or so she thought.

The following day, Mary's flatmate phoned the girl's parents to say that Mary had not come home. They called the police, who were unconcerned. Mary was of course nineteen and students often stayed out all night, at parties or with boyfriends. But Mary was not that sort of girl, they protested. She was a quiet, studious type who had never behaved in that way.

The following day, the police issued a missing person's report. They found a witness who had seen the young man who had offered Mary a lift, but they were unable to give a detailed description of him or the car he was driving.

Four weeks later, two boys came across a fly-covered mass of rotting meat, which they took to be a deer carcass, near a secluded lovers' lane two miles north of Ypsilanti. A pathologist identified it as human flesh. It was the body of a young woman who had been stabbed in the chest more than thirty times. The investigators also thought that she had been raped, but the body was in such an advanced state of decay it was impossible to tell. There were fresh tyre tracks beside the body and it was clear that the killer had returned to the scene repeatedly, as the body had been moved three times before it was discovered.

The corpse had also been mutilated. The feet had been cut off just above the ankle, one arm was severed at the elbow and parts of the fingers and the thumb of the other hand had been removed. These body parts were missing and an extensive search of the area failed to uncover the victim's clothes. But about fifty yards from the body the police found a sandal. Mary Fleszar's parents identified it as their daughter's.

Before Mary's recovered remains were buried, a young man turned up at the undertaker's and asked the receptionist if he could take a photograph of the body as a memento for her parents. The receptionist said that was impossible. It was only when the young man was going out of the door that she noticed he was not carrying a camera. Back then, no one had mobile phones, let alone camera phones.

INTERVIEWED AND RELEASED

Almost exactly a year after Mary went missing, twenty-year-old art student Joan Schell, who lived just three blocks from where Mary had lived, left her apartment to visit her boyfriend in nearby Ann Arbor. Her flatmate walked with her to the bus stop. They waited three-quarters of an hour and then a red car pulled up and a young man, wearing an East Michigan University sweatshirt, asked if they wanted a lift. Joan was suspicious at first, but there were two other men in the back of the car and she thought she would be safe enough. As she climbed into the car, she told her flatmate she would phone later when she arrived in Ann Arbor. She never called. Five days later, Joan Schell's body was found rotting in a storm drain with her blue miniskirt and white slip pulled up around her neck. She had been raped and stabbed to death. Although she had been dead for almost a week, the pathologist noted that she had been lying on the spot where she was found for less than a day.

Extensive enquiries revealed that Joan Schell had been seen later on in the evening she went missing, walking with a young man. The witnesses could not be certain but they thought he was John Norman Collins, an all-American boy – a fine football and baseball player, an honours student and a devout Catholic. But he had a troubled background. His father had left his mother for another woman soon after he was born, his mother's second marriage had lasted only a year and her third husband, who adopted John and his older brother and sister, turned out to be an alcoholic who beat his wife. By the age of nine, Collins had gone through a great deal of domestic strife.

Unbeknown to the police, Collins was suspected of stealing $40 from his fraternity house, as well as other petty thefts. Although he lived directly across the street from Joan Schell, he claimed he did not know her when the police interviewed him, and they had no reason not to let him go. Once again the murder investigations stalled.

METHODS BECOME MORE DRASTIC

Ten months later, a thirteen-year-old schoolboy found a shopping bag in a cemetery. His mother went back with him to the spot where he had found it and under a yellow raincoat she found a girl's body. The skirt had been pulled up and the tights rolled down. The body was that of twenty-three-year-old Jane Mixer, a law student who had been reported missing a few hours earlier. She had been shot twice in the head and then garrotted with a stocking which, the pathologist noted, was not her own. She had not been sexually assaulted – possibly because she was menstruating – and the method of murder was different from the earlier stabbings. However, she was a student, like the other victims, and it was likely that she had been abducted after accepting a lift. Earlier she had posted a note on the college notice board asking for a ride back to her hometown of Muskegon, so detectives suspected that the man the press were now calling the 'Co-ed Killer' had struck again.

Four days later, the naked body of sixteen-year-old Maralynn Skelton was found in a patch of undergrowth just a few hundred yards from where Joan Schell's body had been discovered eight months earlier. A garter belt was tied around her neck. Maralynn had been tied up and brutally beaten and then a tree branch had been jammed into her vagina. Detectives concluded that her death was the work of the same killer, whose methods were getting more drastic.

Three weeks later, the body of thirteen-year-old Dawn Basom was found among some weeds near an outlying farmhouse. The youngest victim yet, she was wearing only a white blouse and a bra, which had been pushed up around her neck. Other clothes were found in the farmhouse where her killer was thought to have tortured and murdered her.

She had been strangled with a length of electric flex and her breasts had been slashed again and again in a frenzy. The police tried to keep the discovery of the body secret. In earlier killings, the murderer had returned to the scene to move the body, so it would be their chance to catch him. But it was too late. A young reporter had already phoned the story through to his radio station.

TOWN IN A PANIC

On 9 June 1969, three teenage boys found the body of a girl in her twenties, with her clothes strewn around her, near another disused farmhouse. She had been shot in the head and repeatedly stabbed. Pathologists said that the girl had been dead for less than a day. The police were convinced that the killing was the work of the same man and again the police ordered a news blackout. But again it was too late. One of the boys who had discovered the body had called the local radio station.

The town of Ypsilanti was now in a panic. A ripper was on the loose. A $42,000 reward was offered and the police came under heavy criticism for not catching the killer. But they still had little to go on.

Then on 23 July, eighteen-year-old student Karen Sue Beineman went missing. She had last been seen in a wig shop, buying a $20 hairpiece. There were two foolish things she had done in her life, she told the shop assistant – one was buying a wig and the other was accepting a lift on a motorbike from a stranger. He was waiting for her outside.

The assistant agreed that accepting a lift from a stranger was stupid and took a look out of the window at the young man with the motorcycle. However, she had to admit that he looked decent enough.

Four days later, a doctor out for a walk near his suburban home stumbled across Karen's naked body in a gully. She had been raped and her knickers had been stuffed into her vagina. The odd thing was that there were hair clippings inside the panties.

This time the news blackout worked. The police replaced Karen's mutilated body with a tailor's dummy and staked out the area. It rained heavily that night, cutting down visibility, but shortly after midnight an officer spotted a man running out of the gully. The policeman tried to summon help, but his radio had been soaked in the rain and failed to work so the man got clean away. The chance of catching the killer was gone.

THE NET CLOSES IN

It was then that a young campus policeman put two and two together. The description that was circulating of the young man on

Only one person could have been in the house while policeman David Leik and his family were on holiday – John Norman Collins – but he refused to make a confession.

the motorbike reminded him of a member of a fraternity house who had dropped out after being suspected of stealing. The young man's name was John Norman Collins and he had already been interviewed by the police in the Joan Schell investigation.

The campus cop found a picture of Collins and both the shop assistant from the wig shop and the owner of the shop next door identified him as the man on the motorbike. The young policeman then went to interview Collins himself, hoping for a confession, but none was forthcoming. Collins even refused to take a lie-detector test. The young officer's initiative had, in fact, been counterproductive. The following night Collins emerged from his room carrying a box covered with a blanket. When his flatmate glimpsed inside it, he saw that it contained a handbag and women's clothing and shoes.

Police Corporal David Leik had been on holiday with his family and had missed the latest developments in the Co-ed Killer case. When he returned home, his wife was taking some washing down to the laundry room in the basement when she noticed that the floor was covered in black spray paint. Only one person could have been in the house while they had been away. Leik's nephew, John Norman Collins, had been given a key to let himself in to feed their dog. But why had he been painting the basement floor?

Leik soon found out. He received an urgent call, asking him to report to work. When he arrived at the station house, he was told, to his surprise and disbelief, that Collins was a prime suspect in the Co-ed Killer case.

That evening, Leik scraped some of the black paint off the basement floor with a knife. Under it there were brown stains, which Leik thought could be blood. Within two hours, lab technicians were crawling all over the basement floor. They quickly identified the brown marks as varnish stains left behind after Leik had painted the window shutters, but a more detailed examination of the basement floor revealed what later proved to be nine tiny blood stains. More significantly though, forensic experts found hair clippings on the floor next to the washing machine. Leik's wife used to cut the children's hair down there and their hair matched the hair clippings found in the panties stuffed into Karen Beineman's vagina.

ARREST BUT NO CONFESSION

That afternoon, Collins was arrested. Although he was shaken – even moved to tears – he refused to make a confession. A search of his room revealed nothing since his box of gruesome mementoes had already been disposed of.

Collins had a number of motorbikes and cars, paid for by petty theft. On closer examination, it was found that his background was even more disturbed than was thought at first. He seemed unable to express his sexual feelings in any normal way. When his girlfriend danced up close, he condemned her for inciting lust in him.

Then there was his temper. His sister got pregnant at eighteen and married the child's father. The marriage did not last, but when Collins found her dating another man he lost control. He beat the man unconscious and hit his sister repeatedly until she bled, screaming that she was a tramp.

Later, when his defence attorney was testing Collins' ability to stand up under cross-examination, he called his mother – who had another new boyfriend but had not remarried. In fact, she was a kept woman. When Collins heard this, his usually calm and detached demeanour dissolved into an apoplectic rage.

FORMER ROOMMATE ARRESTED

The police case was still flimsy, so they started a new line of enquiry. They began to hunt Andrew Manuel, a former roommate of Collins who had committed a number of burglaries with him. He and Collins had also hired a caravan, under false names, for a trip they were taking and had not returned it. It had been left in the backyard of Manuel's uncle in Salinas, California. At around that time, seventeen-year-old Roxie Ann Phillips disappeared from Salinas, after telling a friend that she had a date with a man called John from Michigan, who was staying with a friend in a caravan. Two weeks later, her naked body was found in a ravine. She had been strangled with the belt from her culotte dress and the mutilation of her corpse showed all the trademarks of the Co-ed Killer.

Manuel was found in Phoenix, Arizona. He was charged with burglary and the theft of the caravan, but he knew nothing about the murders, he said. However, he did admit leaving Ypsilanti when he heard that the police suspected Collins. He was sentenced to five years' probation for the felonies.

TRIAL DENIAL

Collins went to trial charged only with the murder of Karen Beineman. The prosecution case centred on the identification of Collins by the staff of the wig shop and the hair clippings in Karen Beineman's panties. Defence counsel questioned the wig shop attendant's eyesight and contended that the comparison of sixty-one hairs from the panties and fifty-nine from the basement floor was insufficient evidence to convict a man of murder.

The jury did not agree. After long deliberation, they brought in a unanimous verdict of guilty and Collins was sentenced to life with no possibility of parole. Throughout four appeals, his conviction was upheld. During the process, he changed his name to Chapman – the name of his biological father, who was Canadian. Then, taking Canadian citizenship, he sought a transfer to a Canadian prison where he would be eligible for parole after serving nine years. Although his request for a transfer was initially granted, it was rescinded after public protest.

He made several attempts at escape and continued to protest his innocence of the murder of Karen Beineman and the other Michigan murders. Indeed, in 2005, former nurse and convicted sex offender Gary Leiterman was found guilty of the murder of Jane Mixer. His DNA matched that found in three drops of sweat on the victim's pantyhose and a single drop of blood on her hand. However, the prosecution was forced to admit that the blood also matched that of John Ruelas, a Detroit man serving life imprisonment for an unrelated murder. He was just four years old in 1969. Leiterman also continued to protest his innocence and appealed over the DNA anomaly.

PETER MANUEL
THE BEAST OF BIRKENSHAW

Born in New York to Scottish parents, Peter Manuel longed to be an American gangster even after the family returned to Scotland in 1932, when he was six. By the age of ten he had a well-deserved reputation as a juvenile delinquent and served his first term in custody at the age of fifteen for sexual assault.

NOT YET A KILLER

In 1946 Manuel attacked a woman and was convicted of raping her. However, after reviewing the evidence for his book *Manuel: Scotland's First Serial Killer*, author and advocate Allan Nicol believes that he was wrongfully convicted. The victim had been dazed in the attack and only thought she had been raped. In addition, Nicol maintained that he was incapable of rape and only achieved sexual satisfaction from violence.

'Complete sperm [*sic*] were found on his trousers, shirt and singlet,' says Nicol. 'His dark secret meant he did not actually commit the full crime. He would have raped had he been capable.'

Manuel served nine years in Scotland's Peterhead prison in Aberdeenshire, where he pretended to be a safecracker – the glamour crime of the day. On his release in 1953 he moved to Glasgow, but he was jilted by his fiancée when she found out about his criminal record. That day Manuel took out his anger on twenty-nine-year-old Mary McLaughlan, dragging her into a field and threatening to cut her head off when she screamed for help. His eyes bulged as he groped her and forced kisses on her and he growled with rage as he described in detail what he would do.

Throughout her ordeal, Mary sobbed and pleaded and then suddenly Manuel stopped and sat back. She was the last of his victims to escape with her life. He was charged with sexual assault and she testified against him in court. A small dapper man, he defended himself and got a not proven verdict.

KILLING SPREE BEGINS

Manuel's killing spree began on the night of 2 January 1956 when he followed seventeen-year-old machinist Anne Kneilands on to a golf course in East Kilbride, not far from where he was laying pipes for the local gas board. There he smashed her head in with an iron bar and tore off her underwear, though there was no evidence of sexual interference. When Manuel turned up for work on 4 January there were scratch marks clearly visible on his face and as a known sex offender he was questioned, but he was released without charge after his father provided him with an alibi. Although he eventually confessed to Anne's murder, the case against him was dropped due to lack of evidence.

Then on 17 September 1956, Manuel broke into the home of forty-five-year-old invalid Marion Watt in the High Burnside district of Glasgow. Her husband William, a master baker who had several shops in Glasgow, was away on a fishing trip, but Marion's forty-one-year-old sister Margaret Brown and Marion's sixteen-year-old daughter Vivienne were in the house. They were shot dead in their beds and jewellery was taken.

Manuel's killing spree began on the night of 2 January 1956 when he followed seventeen-year-old Anne Kneilands on to a golf course, not far from where he was laying pipes for the local gas board.

The bodies were discovered by Mrs Helen Collison, the Watts' daily help, who turned up for work at 8.45 a.m. She was surprised to find the door still locked and the curtains drawn and then she noticed that a pane of glass in the kitchen door had been broken. When the postman, Peter Collier, arrived he put his hand through the broken pane and opened the door. Mrs Collison then went in to find the gruesome scene.

That same night a bungalow in nearby Fennsbank Avenue had been burgled and the police recognized the handiwork of local villain Peter Manuel. At the time, he was out on bail over a break-in at a local colliery. Although he was suspected of the murders he found himself off the hook when William Watt was arrested and charged with the killings. The police had interviewed a ferryman on the Clyde who thought that he had carried Mr Watt's car across the river on the night of the killings. It was a mistake, but Watt spent two months in jail before being released for lack of evidence. Nevertheless, the police continued to believe that he was the killer until Manuel was brought to book.

Manuel then served eighteen months in prison for burglary. He was released in November 1957 and quickly resumed killing. His next victim was thirty-six-year-old taxi driver Sydney Dunn, who was murdered on 8 December when Manuel was visiting Newcastle-upon-Tyne looking for work. Dunn was shot in the head and had his throat slit. His cab was found abandoned twenty miles from Newcastle and his body was dumped on moorland, but Manuel had returned to Lanarkshire by the time it was found.

He then targeted seventeen-year-old Isabelle Cooke, who on 28 December 1957 was on her way to meet her boyfriend at a nearby bus stop. They were going to a dance at Uddingston Grammar School. Over the next few days, items of her clothing were found scattered in the area, but there was no sign of the girl herself. Manuel had strangled her and buried her body in a field. Initially, Isabelle's disappearance was not tied to Manuel and her body was only found when Manuel later pointed out the spot to the police.

BECOMES CARELESS

In the early hours of 1 January 1958, Manuel broke into the Uddingston home of the Smart family, where he shot Peter and Doris Smart, a couple in their early forties, and their ten-year-old son Michael. Manuel stayed in the house for nearly a week, eating the leftovers from their Hogmanay meal and feeding the family cat. There was some money in the house, as Peter had drawn some cash from the bank in preparation for a family holiday. The notes were new. Manuel took the money and the Smarts' car and even gave a lift to a policeman looking into Isabelle Cooke's disappearance. He told the constable that they were not looking in the right place.

Passers-by noticed that the curtains at the Smarts' house were opening and closing at strange times and they felt that they were being watched. Manuel seems to have used the house as a centre of operations. At about 5.45 a.m. on 4 January, Mr and Mrs McMunn awoke to find a face peering around the bedroom door in their house in Sheepburn Road, Uddingston. Fortunately, Mr McMunn had the presence of mind to ask his wife: 'Where's the gun?' At that, the intruder fled.

Peter Smart did not return to work after the New Year break, which aroused speculation, and then his car was found abandoned. Concerned, the police visited the Smarts' bungalow. Unable to get any response, they forced the back door and immediately noticed that the door to the main bedroom was covered with blood. The bodies of Mr and Mrs Smart were found inside the room and their son Michael's was found in his own bedroom.

NEW BANKNOTES LEAD

A barman in a pub became suspicious of Manuel, who was usually broke, when he paid for rounds of drinks using new banknotes. In the days before ATMs, new notes were not a common sight. He called the police, who took the notes to the bank. After checking the serial numbers, the bank confirmed that they had been given to Peter Smart when he had cashed a cheque.

On 13 January 1958, Manuel was arrested at his home in Birkenshaw, near Uddingston. He was put on an identification parade and the staff at the pub and some of its customers confirmed that he was the man who had handed over the new notes. The Smarts' murders were conspicuously similar to the murders at the Watts' house and the police also had the letters Manuel had written to William Watt, while Watt was on remand. These contained details that only the killer could have known.

Manuel then took the police to the field where he had buried Isabelle Cooke. Asked where her body was, he said: 'I'm standing on her now.'

While in custody, Manuel confessed to eight murders, but when the case came to trial at the Glasgow High Court before Mr Justice Cameron in May 1958, he changed his plea to not guilty and withdrew his confession, claiming it had been extracted under coercion. On the ninth day of the trial, he dismissed his lawyers and proceeded to conduct his own defence.

He then pleaded insanity but was unable to convince the judge. It took the jury just two and a half hours to convict him of seven murders. Lord Cameron had directed them to acquit Manuel on the charge of killing Anne Kneilands, but it made little difference as Manuel faced a death sentence anyway.

Northumbria police attended Manuel's trial and would have charged him with the murder of Sydney Dunn had he been acquitted of the Scottish killings. A button from his jacket had been found in Dunn's abandoned cab. There were still some doubts as to whether he had done it, but a coroner's jury found him responsible at a hearing after he was dead.

EXECUTION

The original execution date was set for 19 June but this had to be postponed, pending the hearing of Manuel's appeal on 24 and 25 June. However, the appeal was dismissed so a new execution date of Friday 11 July was set. Manuel then tried to feign insanity as he sat on his bed in Barlinnie prison's condemned suite. He refused to talk to the death-watch warders and just listened to the radio he had been allowed to have. As a Catholic he was also permitted the ministrations of Father Smith, who similarly got nothing out of him. His mother, Bridget, visited him in his final days. Enraged at his play-acting, she slapped his face, telling him: 'You can't fool me!'

At 8 a.m. on Friday 11 July 1958, the hangman Harry Allen, assisted by Harold Smith, led Manuel the few paces from his cell to the gallows. Manuel's last words were: 'Turn up the radio and I'll go quietly.' His execution took just eight seconds to carry out and twenty-four seconds after the drop Manuel was certified dead by Dr David Anderson, the prison's medical officer. His body was taken down at 8.35 a.m. and placed in an open coffin ready for a 9.30 a.m. inquest before Sheriff Allan Walker. Father Smith conducted a burial service later that day, when Manuel was interred in an unmarked grave in the prison grounds near the wall of D Hall.

SHOULD HE HAVE DIED?

Little effort had been made to save Manuel from the hangman, even by those trying to abolish the death penalty. However, fifty years later, Dr Richard Goldberg of Aberdeen University's law school tried to get files on the case reopened. They had been sealed for seventy-five years. Dr Goldberg, whose father had witnessed a medical examination of Manuel while working as a consultant at the Western Infirmary in Glasgow, believed Manuel could have escaped the gallows if the court had been told the full extent of his mental health problems, which included a form of epilepsy many believe can cause criminal behaviour.

> I think there was considerable evidence that he was a psychopath, there was debate over whether there should be a reprieve, and in my view insufficient weight was given to that evidence and also to the fact that Manuel suffered from temporal lobe epilepsy. To me it is in the public

interest that we have access to this information, that the public should see that justice was done properly, and they should have access to everything in the Manuel files. I think it is remarkable that fifty years after his trial there are still files that are closed and there is still uncertainty about what evidence still lies there.

It seems that the government was eager to despatch Peter Manuel. As Dr Goldberg told BBC Radio Scotland:

When you read the files, you see the pressure from the Scottish Home Department. They look at this issue of his psychopathic personality and they say, 'We don't think he's a psychopath, but even if he is a psychopath he's a very marginal psychopath', so there is a pressure on people at the time to get him hanged. The problem is that psychopathic personality disorder still is not a basis for a plea of diminished responsibility, unlike in England, and this remains an anomaly.

Journalist Russell Galbraith, who covered Manuel's trial, said: 'I don't remember any great enthusiasm from people trying to save Manuel, I must say, although there was obviously an abhorrence at the death penalty in many places.'

JOHN WAYNE GACY
THE KILLER CLOWN

ABUSIVE CHILDHOOD

John Wayne Gacy Jr had a troubled childhood. His father was an abusive alcoholic who taunted him for being a 'sissy' and said he would probably 'grow up queer'. It is also thought that he was molested by a family friend, though he kept quiet about it to avoid further abuse from his father. Working as a mortuary attendant, he climbed into the coffin with the body of a teenage boy. Nevertheless, he married at the age of twenty-two in 1964 and went to work for his father-in-law in Waterloo, Iowa.

He and his wife had two children after his father told him, 'I was wrong about you,' before he died in 1965. However, he became interested in pornography, wife-swapping and prostitutes. Gradually, though, his taste turned to teenage boys.

ABERRANT BEHAVIOUR

In 1968, Gacy lured a youth into the back room of the fast-food franchise he was managing. He handcuffed him and tried to bribe him to perform oral sex. When he refused, Gacy tried to penetrate the youth anally, but his victim escaped. Others went through the same ordeal.

The young man reported Gacy to the police. Gacy then employed another youth to assault him in an attempt to prevent him from testifying. This failed. Gacy pleaded guilty to one count of sodomy, though he maintained that the victim had initiated the sexual encounter. This was discounted and Gacy was sentenced to ten years' imprisonment. His wife divorced him and he never saw his children again.

ON THE LOOSE

Gacy was a model prisoner and, because he had no history of serious crime, was released after eighteen months. He moved back to Chicago where he started a construction firm.

Within a year of his release, Gacy had picked up another youth and tried to force him to have sex. He was arrested, but the case was dropped when the youth did not appear in court. With financial help from his mother, he bought a house in Cook County and married for a second time. After three years of marriage, he told his wife he was bisexual. They ceased having sex and divorced by mutual consent the following year.

THIN VENEER OF RESPECTABILITY

Gacy pulled a gun on another youth who had come to him for work, threatening to shoot him if he did not consent to sex. The youth called his bluff, even though Gacy said that he had killed people before. It was true, but the youth managed to leave unmolested.

Gacy had already taken a number of teenage boys back to his home, holding them captive and sexually abusing them over a number of days. When he tired of them, he murdered them.

In 1977, Gacy was accused of sexually abusing a youth at gunpoint. Gacy admitted brutal sex with the boy, but claimed that the youth was a willing participant and was trying to blackmail him. Gacy was released with a caution.

By this time, Gacy was a successful contractor and a leading light in the local Democratic Party. And he entertained at children's parties, dressing up as Pogo the Clown or Patches the Clown. He said that dressing as a clown allowed him to regress to his childhood.

ABUSE AND TORTURE

Gacy also hung out at notorious gay bars. In 1978, he met twenty-seven-year-old Jeffrey Rignall at one of these nightspots. He invited the young man to share a drink in his car. Once inside the sleek Oldsmobile, Gacy held a rag soaked with chloroform over Rignall's face.

Rignall awoke naked in Gacy's basement, strapped to a device like a pillory. Gacy was also naked and showed Rignall a number of whips and more sinister sexual devices, and explained how he intended to use them. Gacy also told Rignall that he was a policeman and would shoot him if he raised any objection.

The abuse and torture went on for hours. At times, it was so painful that Rignall begged to die. Gacy would chloroform him again, then wait sadistically until he came round before he continued. Eventually, Rignall said that he would leave town, telling no one what had happened to him. He blacked out again, and woke up fully dressed in Chicago's Lincoln Park. There was money in his pocket but his driving licence was missing.

In hospital, it was discovered that he was bleeding from the anus, and his face and liver were damaged by the chloroform. The police were sympathetic, but had nothing to go on. Rignall could not give them a name, address or licence plate number. But Rignall was determined. He rented a car and drove the route he thought Gacy had taken him, which he vaguely remembered through a haze of chloroform. He found the expressway turn-off Gacy had taken. He waited there – and struck lucky. Gacy's black Oldsmobile swept by. He noted down the licence plate number and followed the car. It parked in the driveway of 8213 West Summerdale Avenue. Rignall even checked the land registry and found that the house belonged to John Wayne Gacy. He took everything he had found to the police.

John Wayne Gacy was overconfident and told cops, 'Clowns can get away with murder.' He even invited two of the cops stationed outside his house in for breakfast... it was a very big mistake!

When they followed up on his leads, the Chicago Police Department found that Gacy's suburban home was just outside their jurisdiction. They could not press felony charges against Gacy. Gacy agreed to give Rignall £3,000 ($3,960) towards his medical bills and the matter was dropped.

MISSING BOY

Later that year, Mrs Elizabeth Piest reported to the local police that her fifteen-year-old son Robert was missing. He was looking for a summer job and had said that he was going to visit a contractor who lived nearby. The local pharmacist said that the contractor concerned must be John Gacy, who had recently given him an estimate for the refurbishment of his shop.

The local police phoned Gacy, but he denied all knowledge of the missing boy. Robert Piest was, in fact, lying dead on Gacy's bed as they spoke. Checking the records, the police discovered Gacy's earlier conviction for sodomy. They went to see him, but Gacy refused to come down to the precinct to discuss the matter and the police realized that they had no charge on which to hold him.

DISTURBED CORPSES

They put Gacy's house under 24-hour surveillance. Nevertheless, Gacy managed to put Piest's body in a trunk and smuggle it out to his car. He jumped behind the wheel and raced off at high speed, leaving the police standing. Having lost his tail, Gacy drove down to the nearby Des Plaines River and dropped Piest's body in it.

The police finally managed to get a search warrant – quite a feat as there was so little evidence to go on. But in the house the only thing they found was a receipt from the chemist made out to Robert Piest. It wasn't much, but it was enough to justify continuing the surveillance.

Gacy was getting cocky though, even telling detectives, 'Clowns can get away with murder.' One morning, he invited two of the cops stationed outside his house in for breakfast. As they sat down to eat, the policemen noticed a peculiar smell. Gacy had inadvertently switched off the pump that drained the basement. Water flowing under the house disturbed the soil where Gacy had buried twenty-nine of his victims over the years. Armed with another warrant, the police disinterred them.

Another four bodies – including Robert Piest's – were found in the Des Plaines River. The youngest of his victims was nine, the oldest were fully grown men. Some of the victims were never identified.

IN THE DOCK

John Wayne Gacy admitted the murders but pleaded not guilty by reason of insanity. The prosecution countered this, saying that those who had survived Gacy's attacks were the 'living dead'. He was the 'worst of all murderers', and he told the jury, 'John Gacy has accounted for more human devastation than many earthly catastrophes, but one must tremble. I tremble when thinking about just how close he came to getting away with it all.' However, the defence contended that he was a 'man driven by compulsions he was unable to control'.

The jury took less that two hours to find Gacy guilty of thirty-three charges of murder, along with sexual assault and taking indecent liberties with a child in the case of Robert Piest. He was sentenced to death. Appeals lasted a further fourteenp years. In jail, despite his acknowledged homosexuality, Gacy received fan mail from women who said they admired him.

On 9 May 1994, he was executed by lethal injection, with one of the prosecutors saying: 'He got a much easier death than any of his victims.' His last words were 'Kiss my ass'. One of his defence attorneys proposed the Illinois Missing Child Recovery Act of 1984 when he realized that the investigation of Gacy had been hampered by the 72-hour period that the police in Illinois had to wait before they began the search for a missing child. Other states followed suit.

Many questions remain. There are indications that Gacy did not always act alone and there may have been more victims that those Gacy admitted to. But audiences are still fascinated by the Killer Clown. Two feature films and two made-for-TV movies have been made about him, along with a number of TV documentaries. They are unlikely to be the last.

TOMMY LYNN SELLS
THE COAST TO COAST KILLER

BIGAMOUS MARRIAGE

In early 1998, Tommy Sells rolled into Del Rio, Texas with the Heart of America Carnival. When the show moved on, he stayed on in the run-down border town and moved in with a local woman, twenty-eight-year-old Jessica Levrie, and her four young children, in the low-rent district of San Felipe. They lost their home when San Felipe Creek burst its banks in a rainstorm and the family were rehoused in a government-relief trailer at a park in the west of town.

Sells and Levrie then married, though it turned out that Sells was already married to a woman in Jonesboro, Arkansas, who had recently given birth to his child. Following his marriage, Sells got a job as a used car salesman and his boss at Amiro Auto Sales invited him and Jessica, who was a born-again Christian, to attend Grace Community Church. There he met Terry and Crystal Harris and he began to visit the double-width trailer home they lived in with their son and two daughters.

'He came to talk to my husband about marital problems and problems with his job,' said Crystal Harris.

Terry Harris was a former police officer and a nightclub bouncer, so he was more than able to look out for his family. However, on 30 December 1999, Sells bumped into Harris in a local convenience store and asked him about the luggage he had seen in the back of his car. Harris explained that he was going to Kansas to help the Surles family, who were moving from there to Texas.

While Sells pretended to be a devoted family man, he would binge on drink and drugs. That night he was in Larry's Lakeside Tavern, attempting to chat up the barmaid, Noell Houchin.

'He was obsessed with having sex with me. That's all we talked about all night long,' she said. 'At the end, he wanted just five minutes of my time.'

KILLS FRIEND'S DAUGHTER

Sometime after the bar's 2 a.m. closing time, another patron asked Sells to leave. About an hour later he turned up at the Harrises' trailer. He was carrying a 12-inch boning knife. The Harrises had a pet Rottweiler, but it knew Sells. He petted it, allowing it to get a whiff of his scent.

Unable to trip a lock on the back door, he climbed in through a window and found himself in the bedroom of fourteen-year-old Justin Harris. He was blind and thought that the intruder was one of his sisters horsing around.

During the move from Kansas the Surles children were staying with the Harrises. In the next bedroom, Sells found seven-year-old Marque Surles.

Next Sells stumbled into the master bedroom, where Crystal Harris was asleep with her twelve-year-old daughter Lori. Walking into the fourth bedroom, he found some bunk beds. In the bottom bunk, thirteen-year-old Kaylene 'Katy' Harris was sleeping. Sells lay down beside her and nudged her. Katy awoke and asked, sleepily: 'What are you doing here?'

Sells put his hand over her mouth and menaced her with the knife, then he ran the blade down her body, slicing off her bra, shorts and panties. He started to fondle her, but Katy wriggled free, stood up and screamed: 'Go get mama!'

This woke Krystal Surles who was sleeping in the top bunk. Opening her eyes, she saw a man holding Katy with a hand over her mouth and threatening her with a knife.

'She was struggling, and she told me with her eyes to stay there and not to move, so I did. I laid there but I could still see. He took the knife and slit her throat. She just fell,' Krystal said. 'She started making really bad noises, like she was gagging for air but couldn't get any breath because of all the blood.'

The man with the knife then turned on Krystal.

'I told him, "I'll be quiet. I promise. I'm not making a noise. I won't say nothing. It's Katy making the noise,"' Krystal said. The man said nothing.

INJURED GIRL PLAYS DEAD

'He reached over and cut my throat. I just lay there and pretended I was dead. If he knew I was alive, he would have come back and killed me for sure,' she said.

At his trial the prosecution showed a videotape of Sells doing a walkthrough of the Harrises' trailer after his arrest, confirming everything Krystal said. He was even seen climbing in through the window, when he said: 'I woke this girl up. I said wake up. She jumped. I cut her throat.'

Turning his attention to the top bunk where Krystal had lain, he said: 'She was awake. She just laid there. I walked over to her and cut this one's throat. I was getting a little nervous. I walked out the back door.'

When Sells left, Krystal was convinced that everyone else had been killed. After she heard a car drive off, she found her way out of the trailer and walked a quarter of a mile down the unlit road until she reached the first house. It was the home of Herb Betz, who had retired from the military. Looking through the peephole, he saw a little girl on his front porch. When he opened the door, he found her covered with blood and pointing to her throat.

'Her little eyes were saying to me, "Help me,"' he recalled. It was a few minutes after 5 a.m. when Betz called 911. 'I told them I had a little girl with a slashed throat, and that other people were hurt.'

The girl asked for a pen and paper and wrote out several messages.

'The Harrises are hurt,' said one. 'Tell them to hurry,' said another. Finally she wrote: 'Will I live?' By then, Krystal had collapsed and was going into shock.

'I kissed her on the forehead and told her several times she'd be all right,' said Betz. 'I didn't believe it. I thought she'd die on my kitchen floor.'

But she pulled through. The following day in a bed in a hospital in San Antonio, she helped the police put together a composite of the intruder. A family friend said it reminded them of Tommy Sells. After Krystal picked his picture from a photo line-up, the police got a warrant for his arrest and on Sunday morning, just over forty-eight hours after the attack, Sells was arrested. A day later and it would have been too late. Sells had sold a car and was waiting for the bank to open on Monday so he could get the money and skip town.

Sells expressed no surprise at his arrest, nor did he resist when the police handcuffed him. He then gave two written confessions that were produced in court. In one, he admitted sexual assault on Kaylene. He also said that he had considered raping Crystal Harris and killing all six people in the trailer. In the other, he claimed that he had gone to the trailer to collect $5,000 from a drug deal he had done with Terry Harris. The police found no basis for this claim.

He also admitted a string of other murders, but the Texas Rangers were wary. Some years earlier they had been duped by serial killer Henry Lee Lucas, who claimed to have murdered many more than the 350 victims that could plausibly be attributed to him. As with Lucas, some of the killings Sells claimed responsibility for were found to be bogus, but others were clearly true.

DESTINED TO BE A KILLER?

Born in Oakland, California on 28 June 1964, Sells had no clear idea of who his father was. At the age of eighteen months, his twin sister died of spinal meningitis and Sells suffered the same high fever but survived, possibly with permanent brain dysfunction. With five other children to look after, his mother sent him to live with an aunt and never once visited in three years. However, when the aunt looked into the possibility of adopting him, his mother came and took him back, never allowing him to see his aunt again.

At seven, he started to play truant from school and began sampling alcohol with his grandfather. A year later, at the age of eight, he was spending time with a man named Willis Clark, who lavished gifts on him and had him sleep over. Clark was a paedophile who was later jailed for molesting boys.

By the age of ten, Sells was smoking marijuana. At thirteen, he climbed into bed naked with his grandmother and then underwent a psychiatric evaluation after he tried to rape his mother. Finally, at fourteen, he left home to lead a nomadic life, travelling in freight wagons or stolen cars. His intake of drugs and alcohol was funded by casual labour and petty theft.

Sells served time in Wyoming for car theft and was jailed again in West Virginia after admitting a charge of malicious wounding in a plea bargain. According to the police, he had tried to rape and murder a nineteen-year-old woman. Over the years, he also spent time in a number of mental hospitals and claimed to have killed for the first time at the age of sixteen, saying that he shot a homeowner who disturbed him during a break-in in Mississippi. The following year, he said he killed a man with an ice pick in Los Angeles, but the police could find no evidence to support these claims.

In March 2000, Sells took homicide officers on a field trip to Little Rock, Arkansas, where he had lived in the early 1980s. He claimed he raped and murdered a woman nearby by pitching her body into a bauxite mine and he also claimed he shot a man during a burglary there. When he led police to the mine pit and to the burgled house,

Lapping up all the attention, Tommy Lynn Sells chats to the Texas Rangers who have brought him to Little Rock to tell local authorities about the murders he claimed to have committed in the area.

it turned out that his shot had missed the man, who was alive and well, while the mine-shaft murder remained unresolved.

One early murder seems emblematic. In July 1985, the twenty-one-year-old Sells was working at a carnival that had set up in Forsyth, Missouri when he met thirty-five-year-old Ena Cordt, who had brought her four-year-old son to see the entertainment. Cordt found Sells attractive and invited him back that evening. According to Sells, he had consensual sex with Cordt, but woke during the night to find her stealing from his backpack. Seizing her son's baseball bat, he beat her to death. He also murdered her son, in case he was used as a witness against him. The two badly bludgeoned bodies were found three days later, but by then Sells had moved on.

KILLINGS ESCALATE

Between 1987 and 1989, he said he killed a dozen people in seven states. One victim he claimed was twenty-year-old Stephanie Stroh, who was hitch-hiking across America to her home in San Francisco after spending a year travelling in Europe and Asia. On 15 October 1987 she was picked up in Winnemucca, Nevada by Sells, who was driving a stolen truck. By his account, he drove the young woman towards Reno on Interstate 80. At one point he pulled off, choked her to death and dropped her body down a hot spring, but despite a massive search Stroh's body was never found. By then Sells had moved on.

A few weeks later, hunters found the body of Keith Dardeen in a field near Ina, Illinois. He had been shot in the head and his genitals had been mutilated. In the trailer where he lived, the police found the bodies of his wife Elaine and their three-year-old son Pete. They had been bludgeoned to death. Elaine had been raped and sexually assaulted with a baseball bat that the killer had also used as a murder weapon. During the beating, the heavily pregnant Elaine had given birth prematurely and the infant was also beaten to death. Officers debriefing Sells were certain that he had committed these crimes, but no one could say why.

Other victims on his list during this period included an adolescent girl in New Hampshire; a woman and her three-year-old son killed at a bridge near Twin Falls, Idaho; a fifty-one-year-old transient named Kent Lauten, who had been knifed to death in a fight over a marijuana deal in a hobo camp near Tucson; a prostitute in Truckee, California; and a young woman hitch-hiker in Oregon.

In January 1990, in Rawlins, Wyoming, he met a young couple who needed tyres for their truck so he obliged by stealing a truck and removing the tyres. After using the profits to buy drugs, he was trying to jump a freight train when he was spotted by a policeman, who arrested him for public intoxication. Items linking him to the stolen truck were found about his person and he was jailed for sixteen months. While inside, he was diagnosed with a list of psychiatric disorders and was given medication to stabilize his condition. But it wore off as soon as he got out.

DIAGNOSED AS BIPOLAR

Sells said he killed again in September 1991, when he murdered Margaret McClain and her daughter Pamela in Charleston, West Virginia. Eight months later, he attacked a twenty-year-old woman who saw him begging and took him home to give him bags of food and clothing. He raped and stabbed her, but she managed to wrest the knife from him and slash him repeatedly, inflicting twenty-three wounds. Undeterred, he then beat her with a piano stool and left her for dead but she survived and identified him. After Sells pleaded guilty to malicious wounding, the rape charge was dropped and in June 1993 he was sentenced to two to ten years in West Virginia state prison.

In jail he was diagnosed as bipolar. He also got married. Released in May 1997, he moved with his new bride, Nora Price, to Tennessee. He continued to travel – and kill. In October 1997 he claimed to have strangled thirteen-year-old Stephanie Mahaney, whose remains were found in a pond outside Springfield, Missouri. Soon afterwards he hooked up with the Heart of America Carnival, which took him to Del Rio.

After his bigamous marriage to Jessica Levrie, Sells would disappear occasionally, saying he had work out of town or was going to visit a relative. In fact, he was out seeking victims. On 4 April 1999 he broke into the trailer home of a thirty-two-year-old woman in Gibson County, Tennessee. He raped and murdered her and then killed her eight-year-old daughter. Two weeks later, nine-year-old Mary Bea Perez disappeared at the El Mercado music festival in San Antonio. Her body was found ten days later in a creek.

Less than a month later, on 13 May, thirteen-year-old Haley McHone was playing on a swing in a park in Lexington, Kentucky when he lured her into a wood, where he stripped, raped and strangled her. He then rode off on her bike, which he sold for $20 on a housing project, getting drunk on the proceeds. Arrested for public intoxication, he spent the night in the drunk tank and left town the following morning, before her body was found.

CONFRONTED BY HIS VICTIM

When he stood trial for the murder of Kaylene Harris and the attempted murder of Krystal Surles, he was confronted by the little girl, who had a jagged pink scar across her throat. Having regained the power of speech, she gave her damning testimony with a smile.

'She wants him to die. That's exactly what she said,' her mother, Pam Surles, said.

Sells was convicted and sent to death row on 8 November 2000. From there, he boasted of his crimes on a website disturbingly devoted to mass murderers which dubbed him the 'Coast to Coast Killer'. Sells was executed by lethal injection on 3 April 2014.

LONNIE DAVID FRANKLIN JR

THE GRIM SLEEPER

FIRST ATTACK

Lonnie David Franklin Jr got his chilling nickname from a trait that makes him unique among serial killers. After being active from 1984 to 1988, he seems to have taken a fourteen-year break until 2002, when the next murder positively attributed to him occurred.

His murderous spree appears to have started in the spring of 1984, when twenty-one-year-old Laura Moore was waiting at a bus stop in Los Angeles and a man approached.

'You shouldn't be out here alone,' he said. 'Bad guys will pick you up. Let me take you where you have to go.'

Laura reluctantly agreed to accept a lift. Once in the car, the man told her to put on her seat belt and when she refused he reached under his seat, pulled out a gun and shot her six times. Miraculously she was not killed and managed to make her escape. She got a good enough look at him to recognize him thirty-two years later. Although Franklin was never charged with this assault, Laura appeared at the

After leaving the army in 1975, Franklin worked as a mechanic for the LAPD and, between 1981 and 1989, as a sanitation officer for Los Angeles, at a time when murder gripped the city.

hearing sentencing him to death for the murder of nine women and one teenage girl between 1985 and 2007. During the penalty phase of his trial, prosecutors connected him to several other slayings and attempted slayings. Detectives believe he may have killed at least twenty-five women.

MORE THAN ONE SERIAL KILLER

Born in 1952, Franklin grew up in South Central LA, where he got married and had two children. He served in the US Army until 1975, when he was given a general discharge, meaning his conduct was not up to military standard. After that he worked as a mechanic for the LAPD and, between 1981 and 1989, as a sanitation worker for the city of Los Angeles.

In the 1980s, there was a spate of murders of young women in South Los Angeles, with their bodies being dumped in alleyways and dumpsters. There had been a surge in slaying at the time, linked to the epidemic of crack cocaine that was gripping the city. Most of the victims tested positive for narcotics and some worked as prostitutes. The police set up a unit looking for the 'Southside Slayer', but it soon became clear that there was more than one killer on the loose.

Serial killers Michael Hughes and Chester Turner were also active at the time. They were caught in the 1990s, convicted and sent to death row. Both had strangled their victims, but there was another killer out there who used a gun. His victims began with twenty-nine-year-old waitress Debra Jackson, who was shot three times in the chest and dumped in an alley in the summer of 1985. Over the next three years, there were seven more killings, each using the same handgun, according to ballistics tests.

The body of thirty-five-year-old Henrietta Wright was found under a mattress in an alleyway in 1986 and twenty-three-year-old Barbara Ware was killed in January 1987. Someone called 911 saying they had seen a man dump the body out of the back of a van and gave the vehicle's licence plate before hanging up. The van was traced back to a church in the area, but that was as far as the investigation went. When detectives took up the case again twenty years later, the church had closed down. They tracked down ten men associated with the church, including the deacon who had retired to Macon, Georgia and another who was in a Florida prison. DNA samples were taken, but none matched the DNA the killer had left at the scene.

Twenty-five-year-old Bernita Sparks was the next victim in April 1987, followed by twenty-six-year-old Mary Lowe that November. It was only a short while before twenty-two-year-old Lachrica Jefferson was killed, in

January 1988, and in September the naked body of eighteen-year-old Alice Monique Alexander was found, again under a mattress, in an alley.

A few days earlier, she had visited her brother Alexander.

'We were happy to see each other,' he said. 'I asked her if she needed any money and she said no, but I gave her money anyway. I gave her $100 and a kiss. It was the last time I saw my sister.'

For over twenty years, Alexander said he had been left in the dark by the LAPD, who never told the family that Monique was the victim of a serial killer. His suspicions were closer to home.

'I knew that whoever did this, they must have known her,' Alexander said. 'Obviously, she knew him because she never would have gotten in the car with a stranger.'

WAS HE TAKING A BREAK?

The killing then stopped after an attack on Enietra 'Margette' Washington on 20 November 1988. She said she was approached by a neatly dressed black man in his early thirties, who wore a black polo shirt and khaki trousers and drove an orange Ford Pinto with a white racing stripe on the hood. He offered her a lift and when she refused, he said: 'That is what is wrong with you black women. You think you are all that. People can't be nice to you.'

But he was persistent and after some more banter she said she felt sorry for him, so she relented and got into the car. She said she was impressed by the car's interior. 'The inside was all-white, with white diamond-patterned upholstery,' she said. 'The gear-shift handle was memorable, pimped out with a ping-pong-sized marble ball.'

She mentioned that she was going to a party and he deftly invited himself, but first he had to stop briefly at his uncle's house, he said. They drove to a residential area and stopped outside a mustard-coloured house behind a high hedge. Margette did not take note of the street name. The man went into the house and returned about ten minutes later.

As they pulled away an argument broke out, at which point the man pulled a small handgun from his pocket and shot her in the chest. She blacked out but was awoken by a flash. The man had taken her picture with a Polaroid camera. Then he sexually assaulted her while she tried to fight him off. When it was all over, she begged him to take her to hospital but he refused.

He said he had shot her because she had disrespected him. Then he pushed her out of the car and left her for dead. However, she survived and the bullet taken from her chest matched those from the previous killings.

She gave a detailed description to the police and sketches were made showing a black male with pockmarks on both cheeks. Twenty years later, the police released age-enhanced versions as part of their investigation.

DNA NOT ON DATABASE

The killings began again in March 2002 with the murder of fifteen-year-old Princess Berthomieux. But she was not shot dead. Instead she was strangled. Then in July 2003 thirty-five-year-old Valerie McCovey's half-naked body was left in the street with ligature marks etched into her neck. A few years later the body of Janecia Peters was folded into a foetal position and then put into a bin bag and dumped. Someone rifling through a rubbish bin on 1 January 2007 noticed her red fingernails through a hole in the bag. On closer examination, they could see her hands and head.

'The defendant took my daughter, murdered her, put her in a plastic bag – a trash bag – like she was trash,' said her mother Laverne Peters at the trial. 'My hope is that he spends the rest of his glory days in his jail cell, which will become his trash bag.'

What linked these murders to the earlier slayings was DNA. A new task force was set up to see whether connections between the two sets of killings might render a clue. One possibility was that the killer's hiatus from 1988 to 2002 was because he was in jail, but in that case his DNA profile should have been on file. No match could be found.

Indeed, Franklin's DNA should have been on the database because he had a criminal record dating back to 1989. He had been convicted of misdemeanour assault, battery and two charges relating to stolen property, one of which he served time for. In 2003, he was convicted of a felony and was sentenced to three years' supervised probation. His DNA should have been put on the database in that period, because in 2004 California passed Proposition 69, which said that the DNA of all those charged with a felony and certain other crimes should be recorded. But unfortunately for Franklin's future victims the probation department was under-resourced and officers did not get around to collecting samples until August 2005 – and by July 2005 Franklin was on unsupervised probation.

BIRTHDAY PARTY DNA SAMPLE

However, Jerry Brown, later governor of California, was then attorney general and he took the controversial decision to allow the search for partial matches on California's DNA database. Franklin's son Christopher had been arrested for the illegal possession of a weapon – a felony – in 2009 and this provided a partial, or familial, match. What's more, the Franklins' family home was right in the middle of the area in which the murders had been committed and the bodies dumped. They had lived there for decades and neighbours described Franklin as a kind and compassionate neighbour who volunteered in the community, helped elderly residents of the block and fixed their cars for free.

What the police needed was a sample of Franklin's DNA. They got lucky when they followed him to a birthday party in an LA restaurant. There an officer took the place of a bus boy and collected Franklin's plate, cup and pizza crust. It gave the LAPD enough DNA to match that in the saliva found on one of the victims' breasts, on the clothing of some of the victims and on the zip tie of the rubbish bag Janecia Peters' body was found in.

Franklin was arrested and a search of his home produced 800 pieces of evidence, including ten guns, one of which had fired the bullet that was found lodged in Peters' spine. A photo of Peters, her breasts exposed, was found in a refrigerator in Franklin's garage.

Behind a wall in the garage, a picture of Margette Washington was also found, slouched in a car, again with a breast exposed.

Franklin had over a thousand photographs of women hidden in his house, and hundreds of hours of videotapes of women. They were usually nude, partially clothed or in overtly sexual positions. Some appeared to be asleep, unconscious or even dead.

The high school ID card of Ayellah Marshall, a high school senior who had gone missing in 2005, along with graphic pictures of her, was found. And there were photographs of twenty-five-year-old Rolenia Morris, who had also disappeared in 2005. But at least fifty-five of those women remain unidentified. This led detectives to believe that the Grim Sleeper had not been asleep at all. As a garbage worker with the sanitation department, he would have known of numerous landfill sites where he could dispose of a body with very little chance of it being found.

SERVING LIFE ON DEATH ROW

In court, defence attorney Seymour Amster challenged what he called the 'inferior science' of DNA and ballistics evidence. During his closing argument, he said that Franklin's nephew, whom he did not name, had committed the crimes because his uncle had better luck with women, though he offered no evidence to support this contention. He had based his theory on the testimony of Margette Washington, who testified that her assailant said he had to stop at his 'uncle's house' for money before the attack. Nevertheless, Franklin was convicted on each of the ten counts of murder he had been charged with.

During the penalty hearings, the prosecution presented evidence linking Franklin to at least twenty-five other crimes. Along with Margette Washington, a woman appeared who testified that Franklin, as a US Army private stationed abroad, was one of three assailants who gang-raped her in Germany in 1974.

'You're truly a piece of evil,' said Margette. 'You're a Satan representative … You're right up there with Manson.'

In a last-ditch attempt to keep Franklin off death row, Amster entered a motion calling first for a retrial due to the alleged misconduct of the prosecution and then for a sentence of life without the possibility of parole.

Superior Court Judge Kathleen Kennedy then read the names of the ten victims that Franklin had been found guilty of killing. After each, she said: 'You shall suffer the death penalty.'

Franklin then joined the other 746 inmates on California's death row. However, no one has been executed in the state since 2006, so he will probably die there of natural causes. In the meantime, while his wife Sylvia – a school employee in Inglewood – remained loyal, he attracted visits from a publicity-seeking actress-cum-author who befriends serial killers and continued to draw his lifelong LA city medical pension of about $1,700 a month.

GAO CHENGYONG
THE GANSU RIPPER

GROCERY STORE KILLER

Dubbed China's Jack the Ripper, Gao Chengyong murdered and mutilated eleven women between 1988 and 2002 and then, mysteriously, stopped. The fifty-two-year-old was arrested in the grocery store he ran with his wife in the city of Baiyin in Gansu province in northern China on 26 August 2016.

Nine of the murders had taken place in Baiyin itself, the others in Gansu in the Inner Mongolia autonomous region. According to the Ministry of Public Security, the suspect confessed to eleven murders in all.

The police said that he targeted young women with long hair wearing red clothing. He would then follow them home, where he would rape and kill them, usually by cutting their throats. He also cut off parts of their sexual organs. Usually his victims lived alone, though one was just eight years old. Reports of the attacks caused such panic that women in Baiyin would not walk in the streets without being accompanied by relatives or trusted male friends.

KILLINGS GET MORE BRUTAL

In 2004, cold-case forensic officers tied all eleven murders to a single perpetrator. Based on DNA evidence, fingerprints and footprints, he was a man aged between thirty-three and forty. The police said: 'The suspect has a sexual perversion and hates women. He's reclusive and unsociable, but patient.'

They offered a reward of 200,000 yuan (£23,000/$29,000) for information leading to his arrest. Nevertheless, no leads were forthcoming.

His first victim was a twenty-three-year-old woman who worked at the Baiyin Nonferrous Metals Company. She was found dead in her home with twenty-six wounds on her body on 26 May 1988 – around the time Gao's first son was born and Gao himself was thirty-four. Gao said that she had caught him during a break-in and he had decided to kill her.

In 1994, he killed a nineteen-year-old woman at the power supply bureau in Baiyin. The victim had been stabbed forty-three times and the wall behind her was covered in blood. Gao then cleaned himself up in a washroom in the staff dormitory. Four years later, he killed the eight-year-old in the same dormitory, stuffing her body into a cabinet. He said that he even drank a cup of tea before leaving.

That year, Gao said he had a particular need to murder and so he killed four people, throwing their severed body parts into the Yellow River. One victim was a woman whom he had met at a dance hall. The police suspected local gangsters, but their investigation led them nowhere.

As the killings went on, they became more brutal. After stabbing his sixth victim, Cui Jinping, twenty-two times before cutting her throat, he cut off her hands, ears and breasts. Her mother found her daughter's mutilated body on 11 November 1998, but despite extensive searches the missing body parts were never discovered.

On 22 May 2001 a victim managed to get to the phone and call the police, saying she was being murdered. They heard her final gasps, but she gave no name or address. Later they discovered that the scene of the crime was just a block away from the police station and had only one exit. If the caller had managed to say where she was, the police could have got there in time to catch the killer and, possibly, save her life.

LEAD FROM UNCLE'S DNA

The police were stumped because they could not match the DNA they had found on the victims to anyone living in Baiyin. That was because Gao had registered himself in Qingcheng, a town seventy-five miles from where he grew up, and had never been registered in Baiyin. Also, by remaining registered in a remote city he managed to avoid the fingerprint checks required from Chinese citizens applying for a national identity card. Relatives in Qingcheng remembered Gao as a dutiful son who looked after his ailing father in the 1980s, but after his father died he moved to Baiyin and rarely visited.

He was only caught because his uncle was arrested for bribery and his DNA was taken. Its similarity to that of the killer was noticed and this led the police to screen the DNA of his male relatives. In Gao, they found the perfect match and he was arrested.

When the police arrived, he tried to escape, but officers caught him. They asked him if he knew why he was being arrested and he said it was because he'd killed people. In the interrogation suite, he tried to commit suicide by banging his head against his chair. As a result, he needed three stitches.

After Gao calmed down he confessed to all eleven murders with a blank expression, giving details only the killer could have known. He could even remember the precise time of each murder. Asked if he ever felt regret or remorse for the victims and their families, he shook his head. His only concern was for his own family.

'My cases, will they affect my children?' he asked.

Asked why he had given up killing in 2002, he said he had gone to work as a construction worker outside town to earn money to put his

In the interrogation suite, Gao tried to kill himself by banging his head against a chair, but later he calmed down and confessed to all eleven murders he was accused of.

sons through college. Besides, he was getting old and was not strong enough to go on killing.

KILLER'S FAMILY SHOCKED

When news of his arrest spread, there were celebrations in the streets and fireworks were set off in celebration.

Gao's acquaintances said he was a quiet man who was emotionally distant but respectful of his elders. He was known to love gambling, dogs and dancing. Neighbours said Gao had once dreamt of being a pilot and had applied to an aviation college but had failed the tests, which had perhaps left him feeling disappointed.

His sons were at a loss to understand why their father had committed such horrific crimes, though one said Gao had suffered bitterly in his youth when his ambition to become a pilot was frustrated for 'political reasons'. Both had grown up, completed their education and moved away to work, only visiting at Chinese New Year. Hearing that his father had confessed, one of his sons said: 'I didn't know what to say, or how to deal with it. I've accepted the fact, but I cannot understand why he did it.'

Gao's elder son, then working in a scientific research institute, said: 'I'm shocked, but I didn't really know him. We didn't talk too much. And I just can't understand why he did those things.'

Zhang, Gao's wife of thirty years, wailed when she heard of his arrest. She said that while he had been a dutiful husband he would leave her for days at a time – she now fears that those were the times when he was killing. They had enjoyed ballroom dancing together and he had taught in an occupational college for some time.

Cui Jinping's brother Cui Xiangping said that the family had given up hope that her murder would ever be solved. He went on to say that their mother could not stop crying after hearing the news of Gao's arrest. Although eighteen years had passed, the family had never stopped thinking about his sister, he said.

'After getting the news of the arrest last night, my mother is unstable and has been crying,' he said. 'At first I couldn't believe it, but now I know the wait is over. I only hope the police can reveal more details about the case soon.'

OTHER CHINESE KILLERS

Chinese social media compared Gao to Jack the Ripper and news of his arrest also brought forth reports of other serial killers. In 2004, Yang Xinhai, known as the 'Monster Killer', was convicted and executed for the deaths of sixty-seven men, women and children in a killing spree across four provinces, according to the official newspaper, the *China Daily*. In another case in Henan in central China, a man called Huang Yong killed up to twenty-five boys before he was caught.

Yang Shubin, together with three accomplices, killed for personal gain rather than through compulsion. Posing as a rich businessman he lured numerous young women – karaoke bar hostesses, prostitutes and housewives – to his apartment. The women were then tortured until they revealed their bank account passcodes, after which they were killed.

Their bodies were then dismembered, boiled and passed through a meat grinder or dissolved in vats of acid. The killings went on for over six years, from 1998 to 2004, right across the country, from Jilin in the north-east to the southern province of Guangdong. The gang were finally arrested in 2011 in Baotou, where they had begun a new life under new identities, the English-language website Danwei reported.

POLICE SHAME

In a two-day trial in Baiyin, Gao bowed to his victims' families three times before he again confessed. He said he could not afford to give them compensation, but was willing to donate his organs.

'I felt ashamed rather than happy,' said one policeman. 'I can't believe the real killer has been living under our noses for so long while we targeted other groups of people. The cases confused me and my colleagues for so many years.'

Another former cop who had been on the case for two decades said: 'If you saw what the bodies looked like, you would want to catch the guy and put him in jail.'

It was certainly a relief to him and his colleagues. In 2011, with the case still seemingly impossible to solve, an open letter, allegedly from a policeman involved in the investigation, was posted online. It said: 'I was not able to get you in the end. I feel that I will be a guilty man for the rest of my life.'

CHRISTOPHER BERNARD WILDER
THE BEAUTY QUEEN KILLER

UNWILLING ACCOMPLICE

On 4 April 1984, sixteen-year-old Tina Marie Risico was in a clothing store in a shopping mall in Torrance, California when she was approached by a balding, bearded man who said he was a fashion photographer. She quickly fell for his offer of $100 to pose for a few test shots.

He took her to a nearby beach and after firing off one roll of film he pulled a gun, stuck the barrel in her mouth and said: 'Your modelling days are over.'

Driving her to a motel, he tied her to a bed and assaulted her. Then in another motel room he bound her spread-eagled and raped and tortured her for several days. Her assailant was Christopher Bernard Wilder, who was already on the FBI's 'Most Wanted' list.

It was a terrible ordeal, but Tina was lucky. His earlier victims had been murdered, but she was to be spared if she would help provide him with fresh victims.

EARLY SIGNS OF PERVERSION

Born in Sydney, Australia on 13 March 1945, Wilder was the son of an American naval officer and his Australian wife. It was a difficult birth and the child was given the last rites, but he miraculously survived. At two, he nearly drowned in a swimming pool. The following year, he had convulsions and fell into a coma but again he survived.

As a child, he seems to have been the victim of a paedophile and claimed to have had sexual experiences from the age of nine. At eleven, he was a Peeping Tom and when he was seventeen he and some friends gang-raped a girl on a beach. It was clear that he was the ringleader and he was given electric-shock therapy, which seems to have made him worse. Indeed, he gave electric shocks to Tina Risico and other victims.

Wilder memorized the 1963 novel *The Collector* by John Fowles, where a butterfly collector keeps a woman in his basement. He was obsessed with keeping women as slaves.

On 12 January 1965, the bodies of two fifteen-year-old girls named Marianne Schmidt and Christine Sharrock were found in a shallow grave on Sydney's Wanda Beach. The previous day they had been seen with a man answering Wilder's description. Attempts had been made to rape both girls and both had died from multiple stab wounds. However, although Wilder was one of the main suspects, no one really knows for sure if he murdered them.

At this stage his role seems to have been mainly that of a sex pest rather than a killer. In November 1969 he used nude photographs to coerce a student nurse into giving him sex. She went to the police and he fled to Florida. He then got married, but his wife left him after a week, complaining of sexual abuse. She also found that he kept pictures of naked women and other women's underwear in the boot of his car.

Then in March 1971 Wilder was caught soliciting women to pose nude for him on Pompano Beach, Florida. Pleading guilty to disturbing the peace, he escaped with a small fine.

TASTE FOR TEENAGERS

Meanwhile, he had become a successful property developer and businessman with a playboy lifestyle and was seen in the company of attractive women. However, his taste was for teenagers. Some sixty young girls said that Wilder forced them to show him their breasts and fellate him. One of them was the sixteen-year-old daughter of a family in Boca Raton, Florida for whom his company was doing some building work. In January 1976, he offered to give her a lift to a job interview and on the way he persuaded her to change her blouse. He then slapped her and forced her to perform oral sex on him. He was apologetic afterwards and it was three months before she reported the incident to the police. Wilder was arrested and charged with the oral rape of the sixteen-year-old, but was acquitted.

In another incident, on 21 June 1980, he told a young girl from Tennessee that he was taking shots for a pizza advertisement. He then asked her to pose for him while she was eating the pizza, but he had laced it with drugs. Once she was drowsy, he took her to his truck and persuaded her to take her top off. The sight of her naked breasts aroused him and he viciously raped her. The following day he was arrested and charged with rape but the girl was forced to admit that she had taken her top off voluntarily, so the charge was reduced to sexual battery. He was put on probation and given mandatory therapy. Meanwhile, he continued drugging young women and photographing them naked. Later the police found out that his victims included a number of prepubescent children.

He then joined a dating agency in an effort to find young girls. Colleagues noted that he would disappear for two or three days at a time and return disoriented, saying he suffered from blackouts and memory loss. The compulsion to take photographs was a sickness, he told a woman friend. He then advised her to leave, fearing he might harm her.

Visiting his parents in Australia in 1982, Wilder approached two fifteen-year-old girls on a beach in New South Wales. He told them he was a fashion photographer and offered them a modelling assignment. Driving them to a deserted park, he forced them to strip naked and pose for indecent photographs and then he tied them up and masturbated over them. But they got the number of his hire car and the following day he was arrested for kidnapping and indecent assault. His parents had to post bail of $350,000 before he

Wilder memorized the 1963 novel The Collector *by John Fowles, where a butterfly collector keeps a woman in his basement. He was obsessed with keeping women as slaves.*

was allowed to return to the United States. The trial was eventually scheduled for 3 April 1984, but by then Wilder was in no position to show up.

'REAL GENTLEMAN'

Back in the United States, Wilder threw late-night parties and persuaded women to pose nude in the small photographic studio he had built in his garage. But consensual sex was never enough for him. On 15 June 1983, he abducted two girls, aged ten and twelve, at gunpoint from Boynton Beach Park, Florida. He then drove them out into a wood and forced them to fellate him. The following year, when Wilder appeared on the FBI's 'Most Wanted' list, they identified him as their abuser.

Wilder then took up motor racing. On 26 February 1984, he approached twenty-year-old Rosario Gonzales, who was giving out promotional samples at the Miami Grand Prix. She left without even picking up her pay cheque and was never seen again.

Rosario had been a contestant in the Miss Florida beauty contest. Less than two weeks later, another contestant went missing. Twenty-three-year-old Elizabeth Kenyon disappeared after leaving Coral Gables High School, where she taught emotionally disturbed children. She had been a friend of Wilder's and had posed nude for him, but he was 'a real gentleman', she told her parents.

When she was reported missing, the police said they could find nothing suspicious about her disappearance. She was an adult, after all. So her parents hired a private detective who found Wilder's name in her address book. She had been seen with him at a petrol station on the afternoon she disappeared, though he denied it. They also linked her disappearance to the Gonzales case, as he had been at the track on the same day.

On 16 March 1984, the *Miami Herald* ran a story under the headline: 'Racing Driver May Be Linked to Missing Girls'. Although Wilder was not named, he slung a homemade torture kit into the boot of his car and fled.

VIOLENCE AND TORTURE

Two days later, on 18 March, Wilder approached twenty-one-year-old would-be model Terry Ferguson in a shopping mall at Indian Harbor Beach, two hours north of Boynton Beach. Sometime later he called a tow truck. His car was stuck in the sand along a dirt road near Canaveral Groves. It was a well-known lovers' lane, but Wilder was on his own. The police believe that Terry was bound and gagged in the boot when the tow truck turned up to extricate the car. After holding her for several hours, he beat her with a tyre iron and then strangled her. Four days later, her corpse was found floating in a creek in Polk County, seventy miles away, and had to be identified from dental records.

Wilder then struck again. On 20 March, he approached nineteen-year-old Linda Grober, a student at Florida State University, in a Tallahassee shopping mall. Telling her he was a photographer, he offered her $25 to pose for him and while walking to his car he showed her some magazine photographs he said he had taken. When she refused to pose for him, he knocked her unconscious, dragged her into the car and drove off. When she began to come round, he stopped and put her in the boot, choking her until she was unconscious again.

Driving across the state line to Bainbridge, Georgia, he checked into a hotel. After zipping her into a sleeping bag he carried her to his room and there he forced her to strip naked and give him oral sex. He shaved off her pubic hair and put a knife to her genitals and then he tied her to the bed, gagged her, superglued her eyes shut and raped her repeatedly.

Growing tired of that, he got out an electrical cable and administered shocks all over her body. After two hours of this torture, he dozed off. Seizing her opportunity, Linda managed to free herself, crawl into the bathroom and lock herself in. Then she pounded on the walls in the hope of alerting other guests. This awoke Wilder, who grabbed his clothes and fled.

The following day, Wilder was in Beaumont, Texas, where he approached twenty-four-year-old nurse Terry Walden and asked her to pose for him. She refused but he approached her again two days later. After she turned him down for the second time he followed her to her car, knocked her out and bundled her into the boot. Driving to a secluded spot, he sealed her mouth with duct tape and tied her up and then he stabbed her forty-three times on her breasts. He did not sexually assault her on this occasion, taking his pleasure solely from inflicting pain.

As a result of this violence, her broken ribs punctured her heart and lungs and she bled to death. Three days later her body was found floating face down in a canal.

That same day, the body of twenty-one-year-old Suzanne Logan was discovered in Milford Reservoir, near Manhattan, Kansas. She had been approached in a shopping mall in Reno. Wilder knocked her unconscious, something he had done before, and bundled her into the boot of Terry Walden's car, which he had stolen. Smuggling her into his room at a nearby inn, he cut off her hair and raped her. Then he shaved her pubic hair and bit her breasts.

Turning her face downwards, he began stabbing her. The torture continued into the following day, until he eventually administered a fatal blow above her left breast. Then he dumped her body.

WARNING POSTERS

By then, posters were beginning to appear in shopping malls warning women to beware of a man who said he was a photographer. Seeing these, he then changed tactics. In the early afternoon of 29 March, he approached eighteen-year-old Sheryl Lynn Bonaventura in a shopping mall in Grand Junction, Colorado. They were then seen together having a meal in a restaurant a hundred miles away in Silverton, where they told everyone they were heading for Las Vegas. Sheryl insisted on telling the waitress her name and other identifying information as well. She was very nervous, the waitress noticed.

Wilder tortured her with a knife for the next two days, eventually shooting her on 31 March. Her naked body was found by a tree in a beauty spot in Utah five weeks later.

On the following day, at the Meadows Mall in Las Vegas, Wilder was seen at a fashion show sponsored by *Seventeen* magazine. He approached nine of the teenage models, eight of whom agreed to meet him later to discuss a modelling assignment. They were the lucky ones. Seventeen-year-old Michelle Korfman left with him, ostensibly to see his portfolio in the parking lot, but instead he took her to a downtown motel, where he beat her, raped her and tortured her with electric shocks. Her body was found in California the following month.

TEEN HOSTAGE LURES VICTIMS

Three days later, after he had disposed of Michelle Korfman, Wilder abducted Tina Risico in Torrance. After several days of torture, she agreed to become his accomplice. On 10 April, in a shopping mall in Merrillville, Indiana, Tina introduced herself to sixteen-year-old Dawnette Sue Wilt as Tina Marie Wilder. She offered Dawnette a shop job, introducing Wilder as the manager of the store.

Taking Dawnette out to the parking lot to sign some papers, Wilder pulled a gun and pushed her into the back of the car. He then tied her up and raped her while Tina drove around looking for a motel. In a motel room near Akron, Ohio, Wilder put duct tape over Dawnette's mouth, raped her repeatedly and tortured her with electric shocks. The next day, with Dawnette in the boot of the car, Wilder and Tina drove to Syracuse, New York, where Dawnette was raped and tortured again. Throughout all of this Tina was forced to look on silently, on pain of death.

The following morning they saw Tina's mother on TV, begging for her daughter's safe return. The newspapers were full of stories about Wilder and the video he had filmed for the dating agency in Florida was being shown on the networks. Wilder told his two captives that if they tried to escape or did anything to draw attention to themselves he would kill them without compunction. He had nothing to fear as he swore the police would never take him alive.

RELEASES HOSTAGE

Wilder had developed an attachment to Tina but decided to rid himself of Dawnette. First he tried to suffocate her and then he stabbed her and dumped her body on empty land outside Rochester. But Dawnette was not dead. She managed to stagger to a nearby highway and flag down a passing motorist who drove her to hospital. Meanwhile, fearing she might not be dead, Wilder returned to the place where he had dumped her, to find she was gone.

Realizing that if Dawnette was alive she could identify the car, Wilder decided that they needed another one. Seeing a Pontiac Trans-Am he admired in the parking lot of Eastview shopping mall near Victor, New York, he carjacked the owner, thirty-three-year-old Sunday school teacher Elizabeth Dodge. While Wilder and Dodge drove out to some nearby woods, Tina followed. Wilder then shot Elizabeth Dodge, leaving her body in a gravel pit, and took off with Tina in her car.

Then in an uncharacteristic act of kindness he drove Tina to Boston's Logan airport and bought her a one-way ticket to Los Angeles, giving her a handful of money as they walked to the gate. But Wilder was not done yet. Just hours after bidding Tina farewell, he offered a lift to a nineteen-year-old woman standing by her vehicle at the roadside near Beverly, Massachusetts. As he drove away he pulled a gun on her, but when he slowed down approaching a red light she managed to jump out.

BULLET TO THE HEART

At a petrol station in Colebrook, New Hampshire, just eight miles from the Canadian border, Wilder was spotted by two state troopers, Leo Jellison and Wayne Fortier. Seeing them approach, Wilder retreated to his car to arm himself with a .357 Magnum. Jellison then grabbed Wilder from behind and in the scuffle Wilder's gun went off. A bullet entered his chest and came out of his back, hitting Jellison in the ribs and lodging in his liver. A second bullet hit Wilder in the heart, killing him instantly. Jellison was seriously injured but he made a full recovery and finally returned to duty.

After Wilder's death, at least five more victims have been attributed to him. The authorities briefly considered prosecuting Tina Marie Risico for aiding and abetting him in the abduction of Dawnette Wilt and Elizabeth Dodge, but a psychological assessment confirmed her account that she was an unwilling participant in those crimes.

CARY STAYNER
THE YOSEMITE KILLER

'WE HAD FUN WITH THIS ONE'

In February 1999 forty-three-year-old Carole Sund, her fifteen-year-old daughter Juli and Silvina Pelosso, a sixteen-year-old exchange student from Argentina who was staying with the Sund family in Eureka, California, were vacationing in the Sierra Nevadas in the north of the state. They rented a cabin at Cedar Lodge motel in El Portal, on the western boundary of the Yosemite National Park.

On 15 February, they were seen visiting the giant redwood trees in nearby Tuolumne Grove, famed for its sequoias and other conifers. That evening, they rented a couple of videos to watch in their room. They had already checked out prior to leaving the next day, so when staff found the keys on the desk in the cabin in the morning no one thought anything was amiss.

That evening they were supposed to meet Carole's husband Jens at San Francisco airport and fly to Phoenix, Arizona, but when Jens arrived at the airport there was no sign of them. He assumed they had flown on ahead but when he arrived in Phoenix they were not there either. The following day, he had still not heard from them, so he called the police, who soon discovered that Carole Sund had not returned the red Pontiac Grand Prix she had rented, nor had she contacted the car rental agency to extend the rental.

At first, it was assumed that Carole and the two girls had gone hiking in the woods and got lost but a search of the area found no sign of them, nor of the missing Pontiac. Then Carole's wallet was found in the city of Modesto, seventy miles away. Now the FBI suspected foul play.

Jens offered a $250,000 reward for any information leading to their safe return, soon upped to $300,000, while Carole's parents made an appeal on TV. It was 18 March when a burned-out Pontiac was found down a logging road off Highway 108. The licence plates were those of Carole Sund's rental car. Two charred bodies were found in the boot. They were unrecognizable, but after two days dental records revealed that they were the bodies of Carole Sund and Silvina Pelosso. As the search continued, a map showing that Juli Sund's body had been dumped near Lake Pedro, a few miles away, was sent to the police and on 25 March her badly decomposed corpse was found. Her throat had been cut. On the top of the map were the chilling words: 'We had fun with this one.'

WRONG SUSPECTS

A few weeks later, the press were reporting that the principal suspects in what they were calling the 'sightseer slayings' were in custody on other charges, along with a handful of people who were thought to have aided and abetted them. The key players included a parolee who worked at Cedar Lodge and his roommate, a sex offender who had failed to register with the local sheriff.

Others had also been questioned, including the handyman at Cedar Lodge, thirty-seven-year-old Cary Stayner, who had come to the notice of the FBI in other circumstances. In 1972, his younger brother Steven had been abducted by child molester Kenneth

Parnell and did not escape his clutches until 1980. He then became the centre of a maelstrom of media attention, before dying in a motorcycle accident in 1989.

Stayner's own claim to have been molested by an uncle was overlooked by his parents and he was still living with the uncle when the man was murdered in 1990. The following year he attempted suicide and in 1997 he was arrested for the possession of marijuana and methamphetamine, though later the charges were dropped. So when Stayner was interviewed by the police in connection with the sightseer slayings he had no criminal record and was not considered a suspect.

Then on 22 July the mutilated body of twenty-six-year-old park worker Joie Armstrong was found not far from the cabin where she lived and in the same general area where the remains of the sightseer slayings had been discovered. She had been decapitated.

BLURTS OUT CONFESSION

A blue 1979 International Harvester Scout off-road vehicle had been seen parked outside Armstrong's cabin. It belonged to Cary Stayner. The only other piece of evidence that pointed in his direction was found in his backpack. It was a copy of the novel *Black Lightning* by John Saul, which is about serial killing. The police found Stayner at the Laguna del Sol nudist camp and the arresting officer, FBI agent Jeff Rinek, started asking questions.

According to the manager, Stayner was a regular visitor who never behaved lewdly or perversely.

Once in custody, though still not a suspect, Stayner asked for a pile of child pornography in exchange for his confession. Later that day, he confessed to Armstrong's murder, saying he had 'lost control of myself and lost control of her, and when all this started out ... I had no intention of cutting her head off'.

A reporter from local television station KNTV interviewed Stayner in jail and while off camera he blurted out: 'I am guilty. I did murder Carole Sund, Juli Sund, Silvina Pelosso and Joie Armstrong ... None of the women were sexually abused in any way.'

He said that he had fantasized about killing women for thirty years, long before his brother's kidnapping and his own, claimed, molestation. Then he described in detail how he had strangled Carole Sund and Silvina Pelosso in their cabin and had then taken Juli Sund to the lake, where he killed her early the next morning.

He went on to say that he dumped Carole Sund's rental car in the woods with the bodies inside it and then returned two days later to retrieve her wallet and set fire to the car, in the hope of destroying the evidence. After that he dropped the wallet in Modesto to confuse the police, which it did. He thought he had got away with the sightseer slayings but when he fell into a chance conversation with Joie Armstrong he found he could not resist the urge to kill her.

'I am sorry their loved ones were where they were when they were,' he later said about the victims' families. 'I wish I could have controlled myself and not done what I did.'

STRANGLING IS 'NOT EASY'

The FBI said that he had already confessed all four slayings to them. In a recorded interview, Stayner had told them that only the year before he had planned to rape and murder his girlfriend and her two daughters, eight and eleven, but had chickened out as there was a male caretaker on her property. Then on 14 February he had spied on Carole Sund, Juli Sund and Silvina Pelosso, who were staying at Cedar Lodge.

He gained access to their cabin by saying he had come to fix a leak in the bathroom. Once inside he pulled a pistol and forced them to lie face down on their beds and then he bound and gagged them with duct tape.

Locking the two girls in the bathroom, he strangled Carole Sund with a length of rope. It took five minutes.

'I didn't realize how hard it is to strangle a person,' Stayner told his interrogators. 'It's not easy. I had very little feeling. It was like performing a task.'

He stuffed her body in the boot of her rental car and then he returned to strip the two girls, with the idea of forcing them to perform sex acts on each other. But Silvina's sobbing irritated him so much that he took her into the bathroom and strangled her. Then he sexually abused Juli. After that he watched TV, before meticulously tidying up – even wiping his hairs off the bedsheets.

'I watched the Discovery Channel,' he told the FBI.

'VERY LIKEABLE GIRL'

With Silvina's body in the boot of the Pontiac, he left the room as guests would when they had already checked out.

'It felt like I was in control for the first time in my life,' he said.

He wrapped Juli, still naked, in a motel blanket and put her in the front seat of the car, driving off at around 4 a.m.

'I didn't know where I was going or what I was doing,' he said. 'I just kept driving and driving.'

Along the way, he warmed to Juli.

'She was a very likeable girl,' he said, moved to tears as he confessed. 'She was very calm.'

As dawn approached, Stayner stopped near the Lake Pedro reservoir and carried Juli up a dirt path to a clearing that overlooked the water. He regretted what happened next, saying that he wished he could have kept her.

After sexually assaulting her again, he told her he loved her and fanned her hair out on the ground around her head. Then he cut her throat, but this did not kill her immediately, which distressed him.

'I didn't want her to suffer the way the other two did,' he said.

According to Stayner, she made a hand gesture which he interpreted as her begging him to finish her off. He looked away and in under twenty seconds she was dead. Then he hid her body in the undergrowth.

He drove Mrs Sund's rented Pontiac deep into the forest and took $150 from her wallet to get a cab back to Cedar Lodge. When he returned two days later with a can of petrol, he scratched on the bonnet: 'We have Sarah' – the name he said Juli had given him. Then he drove westwards for two hours and dumped Mrs Sund's wallet on a street corner in Modesto, causing the police to focus their investigations there.

After the burned-out car and the two charred bodies were found, he admitted sending the map to the police so they would find Juli's body.

'DARK DREAMS'

With Joie Armstrong, Stayner said that he had pulled up outside her cabin as she was about to leave on holiday. She was a naturalist and he struck up a conversation about Bigfoot. When she appeared uninterested, he pulled a gun and forced her back inside the cabin. He then bound her with duct tape and dragged her into his car. As he drove away across a field, she managed to open the passenger door and escape. She ran as fast as she could and was less than a hundred yards from the cabins where her co-workers lived when he caught up with her. Grabbing a knife he cut through her neck, beheading her, then he dumped her body in a ditch.

On 30 November 2000 he pleaded guilty to her murder. Before being sentenced he begged forgiveness from the Armstrong family.

'I wish I didn't do this terrible thing,' said Stayner, sobbing. 'I gave in to terrible dark dreams that I tried to subdue.'

Addressing them directly, he said: 'I'm sorry. I wish I could tell you why ... I don't even know myself. I wish Joie was here, but she isn't. I am so sorry.'

Soon after, he pleaded not guilty to the other three murders by reason of insanity, maintaining that the Stayner family had a history of mental illness, sexual abuse and obsessive–compulsive disorder. As the case proceeded, even the judge broke down in the face of the detailed evidence.

Stayner was convicted of the four murders and a slew of other connected crimes.

'The circumstances of this case are horrendous and devastating,' the judge said, before announcing the sentence. The jury recommended that Stayner be executed for his crimes.

Hearing their recommendation, the victims' families sobbed with relief. For almost four years they had been waiting for the ordeal to be over.

'He tortured my daughter,' Jens Sund told the court, while standing only feet away from Stayner. 'I know he has no trouble killing little girls in the middle of the night. I just wish he would step up and take his punishment now.'

On 12 December 2002, the judge sent him to death row at San Quentin.

PARENTS STAND BY KILLER

Stayner's parents, Kay and Delbert Stayner, maintained that their son was a sick man who was denied a fair trial.

'I stand by my son,' said Delbert Stayner. 'If he'd gotten help, there would be four people alive today.'

Carole Sund's father, Francis Carrington, exhibited some compassion.

'I feel very sorry for Stayner's mother and father,' he said. 'They've had a tough time of it. I wish them the best.'

But he felt no pity for the man who had killed his daughter and granddaughter.

'I've never seen anything so close to black and white, and evil and good, as Cary Stayner and our children,' he said.

The following month Kenneth Parnell, who had abducted Cary's seven-year-old brother Steven, was arrested at his home in Berkeley after trying to buy a young boy.

That August, the Sund family accepted a $1 million wrongful-death settlement from Cedar Lodge, contending that they had a duty to protect their guests.

JEALOUS OF HIS BROTHER

Police chief Tony Dossetti, the officer who rescued Steven Stayner from Kenneth Parnell, said: 'It crossed my mind that maybe this was Cary's way of competing with his brother's notoriety.'

Interviewed on death row by screenwriter J.P. Miller, Stayner said that he found it difficult to share a bedroom with his brother after having it to himself for seven years.

'His head was all bloated out,' he said. 'We never really got along well after he came back. All of a sudden Steve was getting all these gifts, getting all this clothing, getting all this attention.

With Silvina's body in the boot of the Pontiac, Stayner left the hotel room as normal guests would when they had already checked out. 'It felt like I was in control for the first time in my life,' he said.

I guess I was jealous. I'm sure I was. ... I got put on the back burner, you might say.'

The question remains, did he kill his uncle, Jerry Stayner, who died from a shotgun blast to the chest in the house they shared in Merced County? Then there is the case of twenty-three-year-old Sharalyn Mavonne Murphy, whose severed hands were found near New Melones Reservoir in October 1994. Her headless torso was then discovered off a mountain road in Calaveras County, near where Joie Armstrong's body was left two months later. Neither her head nor her killer has ever been found.

ANGEL RESÉNDIZ
THE RAILROAD KILLER

DEATH BY RAIL

Mexican drifter Angel Reséndiz was convicted of just one murder but was linked, by confession or evidence, to twenty-two others. They all took place near to the railroads the hobo used to train-hop around Mexico, the United States and Canada, which earned him the nickname 'the Railroad Killer' – or, in prison, 'the Choo-Choo man'.

After midnight on 17 December 1998, Reséndiz broke into an opulent suburban home in the wealthy Houston enclave of West University Place, just down the street from the railroad track, intent on robbery. Inside, he found thirty-nine-year-old paediatric neurologist Dr Claudia Benton asleep in bed. First he raped her and then he stabbed her thirty-nine times with a butcher's knife and beat her to death with a two-foot bronze statue. Grabbing any cash he could find, he fled in the victim's Jeep Cherokee. When it was found abandoned two hundred miles away in San Antonio, the police discovered

Reséndiz's fingerprints on the steering column. He already had a long rap sheet for burglary, theft, aggravated assault and various immigration offences and had been deported numerous times since he first entered the US illegally in 1973, aged fourteen.

BORDER-HOPPING RAMPAGE

Born in Izúcar de Matamoros, Puebla, Mexico on 1 August 1959, Reséndiz was brought up by his grandparents. From an early age, he ran the city streets and his mother believes that he was sexually abused by local paedophiles. He moved to Acapulco on his own while still a teenager and then went on to Florida.

In September 1976, he was arrested by a security guard when trespassing at the Chrysler factory in Sterling Heights, Michigan. After being handed over to the Immigration and Naturalization Service, he was granted voluntary departure back to Mexico. The following month, he was arrested for crossing the border illegally at McAllen, Texas, and voluntarily returned to Mexico again.

He was back in the US in 1977 when he was convicted of destroying private property and leaving the scene of a crime in Corinth, Mississippi and once again he returned voluntarily to Mexico. Two years later, he was charged with grand theft auto in Tampa, Florida, but the case was dismissed when he faced more serious charges. After breaking into a house in Miami, he ransacked it and beat the eighty-eight-year-old owner until he was semi-conscious and then fled in the victim's car. Arrested for a burglary in Clark County, Kentucky, he was extradited back to Florida, where he was convicted of burglary, aggravated battery and grand theft auto, and sentenced to twenty years' imprisonment.

Paroled after six years he was deported again, but soon afterwards he returned to the US where he began killing. The victim was an unidentified African American female, whose badly decomposed body was found in an abandoned farmhouse near San Antonio, Texas on 26 March 1986. Reséndiz said that she was from Florida and that her name may have been Norma. He had shot her repeatedly with a .38-calibre pistol three months earlier, he said, because she cast a spell on him. The victim had mentioned Santería, the religion where Yoruba deities are identified with Roman Catholic saints. He also said she had disrespected him during a motorcycle trip to the suburban community of Converse.

Soon afterwards he killed her boyfriend, a Cuban who Reséndiz said was involved in black magic, dumping his body in a creek somewhere between San Antonio and Uvalde. It has still not been found. Reséndiz confessed to both of these murders in 2001 in the hope that it would speed up his execution.

In December 1986, he was sentenced to 18 months for falsely claiming to be a US citizen and once again returned to Mexico, only to be arrested once more when trying to cross the border at Laredo, Texas by presenting a bogus US voter registration card and birth certificate. This earned him another 18 months in prison and he was again deported on 2 October 1987.

Four months later, charges against him for defrauding an innkeeper and carrying a concealed weapon in New Orleans were dropped for lack of evidence. Later that year, he was arrested for applying for a social security card with false documents. That, along with re-entering the US after being deported and being a convicted felon in possession of a firearm, earned him another thirty months in jail. These crimes had been committed under a roster of aliases.

On his release from prison in May 1991 he was deported yet again. But he was back in the US in June, when he murdered twenty-two-year-old Michael White at an abandoned house in San Antonio. He said he had done it because White was a homosexual.

The following year, he pleaded guilty to a burglary in Las Cruces, New Mexico and was sentenced to three years with eighteen months suspended. When he was released in April 1993, he was handed over to the INS for deportation. Later that year he was arrested in Albuquerque, New Mexico, for driving a car stolen two days earlier in Missouri. The Missouri authorities decided not to extradite him, so he was convicted of a misdemeanour and went back to jail.

In December 1994 he was arrested in Albuquerque again while driving a car stolen in Arizona and was released on bond. The following May he was indicted for receiving a stolen vehicle and resisting arrest. A bench warrant was issued for his apprehension. In August, he was arrested for trespassing on railroad property in San Bernardo, California and was found to be carrying a stolen handgun, which was loaded. Sentenced to thirty days in jail, he voluntarily returned to Mexico.

A warning was issued against him for trespassing at the Norfolk Southern Railroad yard in Macon, Georgia on 4 August 1996 and two days later he was arrested for illegally entering a railroad yard at Science Hill, Kentucky. Pleading guilty, he was sentenced to three days' imprisonment.

FRENZIED STUDENT ATTACK

While Reséndiz continued to hop back and forth across the Mexican border, his taste for murder grew. On 23 March 1997, he bludgeoned nineteen-year-old Jesse Howell to death with an airhose and left his body beside the railroad tracks at Ocala, Florida. His sixteen-year-old fiancée, Wendy Von Huben, was raped, strangled, suffocated and buried in a shallow grave some thirty miles away.

Then in July an unidentified transient was beaten to death in a railyard at Colton, California. Reséndiz was regarded as the prime suspect in that incident. Next it was the turn of two young people out for an evening stroll. On 29 August, he approached twenty-one-year-old Christopher Maier and his girlfriend Holly Dunn near the railroad tracks in Lexington, Kentucky. They were taking some air after a hectic university party. Wielding what looked like an ice pick, Reséndiz demanded money. They had no cash, so offered their credit cards.

Reséndiz then grabbed Maier's backpack and used the straps to tie his arms behind his back. Dunn could have run but decided to stay with her boyfriend. Reséndiz took her belt and bound her with it, then pushed them both into a ditch, where he gagged them.

While Reséndiz continued to hop back and forth across the Mexican border, his taste for murder grew. On 23 March 1997, he bludgeoned 19-year-old Jesse Howell to death with an airhose ...

While he went to see if anyone was about, Dunn worked her gag free and was working on Maier's when he returned, carrying a huge rock. Without warning he dropped it on Maier's head.

Maier was knocked out and began making a gurgling sound. Fearing that he might drown in his own blood, Dunn said: 'Turn his head to the side so he doesn't choke.'

'You don't have to worry about him anymore,' Reséndiz replied casually. 'He's gone.'

Then he pulled off Dunn's trousers. She kicked and screamed, but he pushed the ice pick into the side of her neck and raped her. Afterwards, she begged him to put her jeans back on again. Even if she was going to be murdered, she did not want to be found naked. Strangely, Reséndiz agreed, then began beating her around the head with a heavy object until she was rendered unconscious.

When she awoke, he had gone. Covered in blood, she then stumbled to a nearby house and in hospital it was found that she had a broken jaw, a smashed eye socket, an inch-deep stab wound to the neck and other cuts and bruises. Maier, of course, was dead. Fearful that the killer might return to finish her off, she changed to another university and eventually sought refuge in the UK. When Reséndiz was finally apprehended, she identified him as her attacker – the Railroad Killer.

SAVED BY COMPUTER GLITCH

On 4 October 1998, Reséndiz climbed through the window of eighty-seven-year-old Leafie Mason's house, which was just fifty yards from the Kansas City–Southern Rail Line at Hughes Spring, Texas. He then beat her to death with a tyre iron.

Next came the murder of Dr Claudia Benton and from the fingerprints her killer left in her Jeep Cherokee the police finally knew who they were after. The security at railyards was stepped up and hangouts for transients were raided. Hispanics complained of harassment by the police but still Reséndiz eluded them. It was difficult to predict where he would strike again as his path was random. He would simply jump on to a freight wagon and go where the train took him.

On 2 May 1999, Norman J. 'Skip' Sirnic, the forty-six-year-old pastor of the United Church of Christ in Weimar, Texas, and his forty-seven-year-old wife Karen, were bludgeoned to death with a sledgehammer while they slept. Karen had also been sexually assaulted. Their parsonage was adjacent to the railroad, which made them an easy target for their assassin. When their red Mazda was found in San Antonio three weeks later fingerprints found on it tied the murder to the Railroad Killer case.

A month later, on 2 June, the US Border Patrol apprehended Reséndiz near El Paso, while he was attempting to cross the border illegally. The Immigration and Naturalization Service had been informed that he was a wanted man, so while he was in custody they ran fingerprint and photo checks against their fugitive list. Unfortunately, due to a computer glitch his past was not revealed and he was simply deported back to Mexico. Two days later he was back in the US, killing again.

MADE SNACK AFTER KILLING

On 4 June, a twenty-six-year-old schoolteacher at Houston's Benjamin Franklin Elementary School named Noemi Dominguez was done to death with a pickaxe in her apartment near the railroad tracks. Again she had been sexually assaulted. Seven days later, state troopers found her white Honda Civic on the International Bridge in Del Rio, Texas.

After killing Dominguez, Reséndiz drove the ninety miles to Fayette County, taking the pickaxe with him. There, in a farmhouse at Schulenburg, Texas, he killed seventy-three-year-old Josephine Konvicka while she slept. He carelessly left the pickaxe embedded in her head and DNA linked the crime to the Dominguez murder. Reséndiz then tried to steal Konvicka's car, but could not find the keys.

Then on 15 June Reséndiz arrived in Gorham, Illinois. He bedded down in the trees behind eighty-year-old George Morber's trailer, a hundred yards from the railroad tracks and within earshot of the trains as they thundered by. When Reséndiz saw the retired prison warder and army veteran drive off, he climbed through the window but Morber soon returned with the morning newspaper and surprised the intruder. After tying him up with a telephone cord, Reséndiz killed him with a shotgun blast to the back of the head.

Then Morber's daughter, fifty-one-year-old Carolyn Frederick, who lived on the other side of the fishpond where Morber would angle for bluegill and catfish, dropped by to clean up her father's trailer. Reséndiz battered her to death with the shotgun so violently that the barrel broke. He then made a snack for himself, read the morning paper and took down the family photographs before taking a rest. After four or five hours at the crime scene, he drove off in Morber's red pickup truck.

Carolyn's husband Don Frederick discovered the carnage after one of their daughters failed to get through to her mother or grandfather on the phone. Fortunately, Morber's wife was not on hand, having been admitted to hospital with a heart complaint the day before. The television was removed from her room to shield her from the gruesome details of her husband and daughter's murders.

FBI PROFILE

The pickup was found sixty miles away and fingerprints found in the trailer identified Reséndiz as the killer. By then he was on the FBI's 'Top Ten Most Wanted' list. Wanted posters described Reséndiz as:

> 5 feet 7 inches tall, weighing 140–150 pounds; black hair, brown eyes and dark complexion; scars on right ring finger, left arm and forehead; a snake tattoo on his left forearm and a flower tattoo on his left wrist; has been known to employ any one of dozens of aliases, social security numbers and birth dates; has worked as a day labourer, migrant worker or auto mechanic.

FBI profiler John Douglas described his MO:

> When he hitches a ride on the freight train, he doesn't
> necessarily know where the train is going. But when he gets
> off, having a background as a burglar, he's able to scope
> out the area, do a little surveillance, make sure he breaks
> into the right house where there won't be anyone to give
> him a run for his money. He can enter a home complete
> with cutting glass and reach in and undo the locks.

Apparently, his main motive was theft. Sexual abuse was an
afterthought. He often left cash behind, taking jewellery that he
posted back to his common-law wife Julieta Reyes, in Rodeo, Mexico
and leaving his victim covered with a blanket. Douglas continued:

> He'll look through the windows and see who's occupying
> it. The guy's only 5 foot 7, very small … the early weapons
> were primarily blunt-force trauma weapons, weapons of
> opportunity found at the scenes. He has to case them out,
> make sure he can put himself in a win-win situation.

Two hundred agents were assigned to the case and more than a
thousand sightings were phoned in by the public. The FBI's reward
of $50,000 was upped to $125,000 when local jurisdictions chipped
in and agents brought Julieta Reyes 250 miles north to Houston,
where she volunteered to do anything she could to get Reséndiz
to surrender to the authorities. She also handed over ninety-
three pieces of jewellery he had mailed to her. Relatives of Noemi
Dominguez identified thirteen of them as belonging to her.

SURRENDERS TO AUTHORITIES

Meanwhile, enterprising young Texas Ranger Sergeant Drew Carter
contacted Reséndiz's sister Manuela, who lived in Albuquerque. She
feared that her brother might be killed in a shoot-out with the FBI,

or go on to kill again, and agreed to help. Carter promised Manuela three things – that her brother's personal safety would be assured while he was in jail, that she and his wife could visit him and that he would undergo a psychological evaluation.

On 12 July, Carter got a fax from the district attorney's office in Harris County, which covered Houston where the Benton murder had taken place, authorizing the agreement. Another relative got a message to Reséndiz, who was hiding out in Ciudad Juárez across the border from El Paso. At 9 a.m. he surrendered on the international bridge connecting the two cities.

While Texas holds the national record for sending murderers to the electric chair, Reséndiz seems to have surrendered because bounty hunters were already on his trail. He had also committed at least seven murders in Mexico, though capital punishment had not been used outside the military since 1937 and was officially abolished in 2005.

Four murder charges had been filed against him in Texas and others in Kentucky and Illinois. However, he was tried only for the murder of Dr Claudia Benton. The court-appointed defence team fought for an insanity plea, though Reséndiz refused to co-operate. Before the trial started the prosecution warned the jury that the description of the murder would be 'one of the most horrible that you will ever have the misfortune to hear'.

The trial dragged on for eight days. The only mitigating factor the defence could find was the fact that Reséndiz had handed himself in. At the end of the trial he was found sane and guilty and was sentenced to death. The appeal was then taken over by the Mexican government, who had established a fund to fight cases in which citizens face the death penalty abroad, as capital punishment was not used at home. Nevertheless, the death sentence was upheld.

'EVIL IN HUMAN FORM'

This did not worry Reséndiz, who claimed that as he was half man, half angel they could not kill him. Three days after his execution he said he would wake up in the Middle East helping the Israelis fight the Arabs. His final words were:

> I want to ask if it is in your heart to forgive me. You don't have to. I know I allowed the devil to rule my life. I just ask you to forgive me and ask the Lord to forgive me for allowing the devil to deceive me. I thank God for having patience with me. I don't deserve to cause you pain. You did not deserve this. I deserve what I am getting.

Before drawing his final breath, the killer, who claimed to be Jewish, prayed in Hebrew and Spanish. He was then given a lethal injection at 6 p.m. on 27 June 2006.

Claudia Benton's husband George, who witnessed the execution, said: 'What was executed today may have looked like a man, walked and talked like a man, but what was contained inside that skin was not a human being.' As to the crime, he said: 'This is not human behaviour, but something I can only say is evil contained in human form, a creature without a soul, no conscience, no sense of remorse, no regard for the sanctity of human life.'

He made this statement, he said, because 'people have to understand what evil really is'.

YANG XINHAI
THE MONSTER KILLER

DESIRE TO KILL

Possibly China's worst serial killer, Yang Xinhai was convicted of sixty-seven murders in a bloodthirsty spree lasting three years. He was also convicted of raping twenty-three of his female victims. Found guilty after a trial that lasted just one hour, he was unrepentant.

'When I killed people I had a desire … This inspired me to kill more,' he said. 'I don't care whether they deserve to live or not. It is none of my concern. I have no desire to be part of society. Society is not my concern.'

Yang was born in 1968 in Henan Province, central China, the youngest of four children.

His family were the poorest in the village and lived in a dilapidated house. Said to be a clever child, but introverted, he quit school at the age of seventeen and ran away from home, travelling to other regions as a hired labourer. His father only saw him twice after that.

He was sent to labour camps for re-education in 1988 and 1991 for thefts in Xi'an, capital of Northwest China's Shaanxi Province, and Shijiazhuang, the largest city in North China's Hebei Province. In 1996, he was sentenced to five years in prison for an attempted rape in Zhumadian, in central China's Henan Province.

MURDER MOVIE HOPES

Released in the year 2000, he found himself a girlfriend, who dumped him when she found out about his criminal record. He then vented his anger on society by travelling around rural China on foot or by bicycle and killing at random. His various aliases included Yang Liu, Yang Zhiya, Yang Zhiwei and Wang Ganggang.

'Yang Zhiwei harboured feelings of revenge against society,' said the newspaper *Guangzhou Daily*. 'Moreover his methods were extremely cruel. He didn't leave survivors, and more than a few families were exterminated by his hand.'

According to relatives who emigrated to Pennsylvania, there was also a perversely artistic side to his murders. He wrote them up as a series of stories taking place in the fictional 'Plato Flats'. He also made drawings and hoped to turn his murder stories into movies.

On 6 December 2002, he killed Liu Zhanwei, a thirty-year-old farmer in the village of Liuzhuang in Henan's Xiping County, along with his mother, wife, son and daughter. He would have killed Liu's sixty-eight-year-old father, Liu Zhongyuan, too had he not been sleeping in a new house the family were about to move into.

'We planned to move to the new house on 9 December,' said Liu's father. 'Who can imagine that they experienced such tragedy only three days before?'

He recalled seeing his granddaughter the morning after the attack. She was lying on the floor of a room full of blood, with a hole in her head. 'My wife could still bat her eyelids but could not speak any more,' he said.

She was the only one to survive the original onslaught, but died in hospital ten days later.

After being arrested for thefts in Xi'an (pictured) and Shijiazhuang, Xinhai was sent to labour camps for re-education. It didn't do him much good; he continued to 'vent his anger' by travelling around rural China on foot or by bicycle and killing at random.

Yang Xinhai admitted to killing the family with a hammer after breaking into their home at 1 a.m. Afterwards, he buried the hammer and threw his bloody clothes into a river. He used a new weapon for each attack and wore new clothes. His murder weapons included axes and shovels – anything he found to hand at the crime scene. He also wore shoes that were two sizes too big for him, to put the police off the scent, and white gloves, which he left at the scene. His attacks took place at night, usually when victims were asleep, and his motive was neither money nor sex.

'He committed crimes to merely hurt society,' a policeman told the *Jiangnan Times*.

An official report said: 'His girlfriend broke up with him and as a result Yang Zhiya developed a vengeful attitude towards society and committed the crimes in Henan, Anhui and Shandong.'

GRIM FACTS HUSHED UP

Despite the gruesome nature of the crimes, Yang's murders were not given much publicity. State media usually report major cases only after an arrest has been made and unsolved cases go unreported. Nevertheless, he made China's 'Most Wanted' list.

The police were making a routine sweep of the nightclubs in Cangzhou, Hebei Province, when they picked Yang up, who appeared to be acting suspiciously.

Doing a background check, they found to their surprise that he was wanted in at least four provinces. When he was in custody, *Yanzhao Metropolis Daily* reported the story. It was picked up by a few websites, though it was soon taken down.

The official media – the Xinhua News Agency, China Central Television and the *People's Daily* – did not carry any reports on the gruesome killing spree that took place in four provinces: Hebei, Henan, Anhui and Shandong. However, a great deal of attention was paid to the trial of Gary Ridgway, the Green River Killer, who was convicted of killing forty-nine people in the United States at around the same time.

When the story leaked out, one journalist said: 'There is a saying that says no wall is totally wind-proof. Some of the Cangzhou people knew about the case but the police had sealed their mouths on the report.'

It was not until the story had been published that officials from police departments in Henan, Anhui and Shandong confirmed details of the case to the English-language *South China Morning Post*, published in Hong Kong. China is unaccustomed to reading about this sort of slaying as violent crime is seen as a Western phenomenon. Poisoning motivated by revenge is more common and curiously more acceptable. The previous year a man killed at least forty-two people, many of them children, by slipping rat poison into food at a rival's shop in the eastern city of Nanjing.

'KILLING PEOPLE IS VERY USUAL'

The trial of Yang took place behind closed doors out of respect for the posthumous privacy of the women he raped. Besides those he had violated and murdered, another ten people were seriously injured. News reports described Yang as mentally unbalanced, saying he would begin rambling and shouting after a few seconds of conversation. However, it was reported that he had confessed and there was considerable DNA evidence against him. He waived his right to an appeal and was executed by gunshot in February 2004, when he was thirty-eight. While in detention in Luohe, he was positively blasé about his murders when talking to other inmates.

'Killing people is very usual,' he said. 'Nothing special.'

CHINA'S OTHER KILLERS

He proved to be correct. At around the time Yang was arrested two other serial killers came to light. Over two years, twenty-nine-year-old farmer Huang Yong murdered twenty-three boys, most of whom were local high school students between the ages of sixteen and twenty. He was only caught because one of his intended victims escaped and raised the alarm. When police visited Huang's home they found twenty-three bodies hidden around the place – including seven under his bed. And in the southern Chinese city of Shenzhen, a forty-three-year-old man, Ma Yong, and a twenty-year-old woman, Duan Zhiqun, were arrested for the robbery and murder of twelve female migrant workers, who were lured to their deaths with promises of work.

At around the same time, a Chinese man confessed to raping at least thirty-seven elderly women, some of them in their nineties, because they 'are easy to control'.

KARL DENKE
THE CANNIBAL OF ZIĘBICE

RESPECTABLE CITIZEN

Karl Denke was well liked in Münsterberg in Silesia, then part of
Prussia – now Ziębice in Poland. A teetotaller, he played the organ
in church, carried the cross at funerals and helped beggars; in the
rooming house he ran, he was known as *Vater* Denke – Father or
Papa Denke.

On 21 December 1924 one of the tenants, a coachman named
Gabriel, heard cries for help coming from Denke's room. He went
to help and found a young man named Vincenz Olivier staggering
down the corridor, covered in blood.

Before he collapsed, Olivier said that *Vater* Denke had attacked
him with an axe. The police had difficulty accepting Olivier's
story because he was a stranger and a vagabond, while Denke was
a respectable citizen. Born on 2 August 1870, he was the son of a
wealthy farmer three miles away in Oberkunzendorf in Lower Silesia,
now Kalinowice Górne, Poland.

A dull if not retarded child, Denke finished school at the age of twelve and then left home to work as an apprentice to a gardener. His father died when Denke was twenty-five and his brother took over the family farm. Denke was given some money to buy his own farm but he had no talent for farming, so he sold the land and bought a house in Münsterberg. During the inflation that followed the First World War, Denke was forced to sell the house, but he continued living there.

GORY FINDS

The doctor who examined Olivier's head wound confirmed that it had been inflicted by a heavy cutting tool and Denke was arrested. Under interrogation, he claimed that Olivier had attempted to rob him after he had given him a handout. That night Denke hanged himself in his cell and two days later the police went to search his house. They found bones and pieces of meat pickled in brine in a large barrel. A closer examination revealed hairy skin, a severed torso and large parts of a pair of buttocks. It was clear that the bodies had been cut up after the victim was dead, but the head, arms, legs and sexual organs were missing, along with slices from the buttocks. A medical examiner from the Institute of Forensic Medicine at the University of Breslau (now Wrocław), Friedrich Pietrusky, assumed they had either been eaten or sold as meat.

Other vessels were found to contain body parts and rendered human fat. Bones, cleaned of their meat and cooked, were found in Denke's shed in the backyard, in a pond that Denke had dug some years before and scattered in a nearby forest. They belonged to at least eight people and some bones were still being found in the 1940s, after the Second World War. Some of the bones had been sawn, other struck with a hammer or an axe. A knife had also been used to clean off the meat. When the police looked around the area they found three axes, a tree saw, a large wood saw, a pickaxe and three knives, all with traces of blood on them.

Denke also kept a collection of three hundred and fifty-one teeth. They were sorted according to size and stored in two tin boxes, marked 'Salt' and 'Pepper', and three paper money bags. They belonged to at least twenty people. Most were from old people, but some came from someone younger than sixteen and others from two individuals in their twenties. Some were fresh and others had been extracted long before.

The killer had experimented with making soap from human fat and turning human skin into leather. The braces he wore were made from skin flayed from one of his victims and tanned with shoe polish and he made shoelaces from human hair that he sold door-to-door, along with belts and other leather goods. He also collected small clay discs that had been moulded from then-worthless pfennig coins.

CAREFUL RECORDS

In Denke's apartment were bundles of old clothes. A closet contained garments splattered with blood, including a woman's skirt. There were also ID cards and the private papers of various individuals. Largely it seemed that the victims had recently been released from prisons or hospitals. Among his account books were a list of the names of thirty men and women, arranged chronologically with a date before each. This was assumed to be the date of their death. Only the women's first names were given, while the men's full names were followed by a date of birth and other details.

The list started at number eleven, indicating that there had been at least ten more victims beforehand. The first name on the list was dated 1921 but it was later discovered that Denke had started his murderous career with the slaughter of twenty-five-year-old Emma Sander in 1909. However, her murder was only discovered fifteen years later. Another sheet gave individuals' initials followed by a number, thought to be their weight, and a further page listed names followed by 'dead, 122, naked 107, disembowelled 83'. That last figure was repeated from the previous sheet, so the numbers seem to indicate the victim's weight in various states.

Dr Pietrusky's report noted that Denke was a good, if reclusive, citizen. He had not learned to speak until the age of six and his

Denke was well liked in the town of Münsterberg (above). A teetotaller, he played the organ in church, carried the cross at funerals and helped beggars in the rooming house he ran.

teachers had pronounced him an idiot and punished him regularly. They also noted that he was 'very obstinate and lacks respect for teachers'. His brother called him a glutton because he would eat two pounds of meat at one sitting. Generally he was humble, charitable and showed good manners. However, he was treated with suspicion because of his solitary status and his lack of interest in sex – he was said to be 'neither man nor woman'.

HUMAN FLESH EATEN AND SOLD

There was no indication that his crimes were sexually motivated. It just seems that he found murder the easiest way to obtain food. He would pick up vagrants at the railway station, take them home and murder them. Before Olivier, two other men had escaped from his apartment, injured and covered with blood, but they had failed to report the attacks to the police. Another one complained to neighbours that when Denke had asked him to write a letter for him he had suddenly felt a chain around his neck. But he was stronger than Denke and fought him off and again no one reported this to the police.

Then there was the terrible smell that came from his flat. Neighbours noticed that he always had plenty of meat even through the worst period of hyperinflation, but they thought it was dog meat, even though slaughtering dogs and selling their meat on the black market was illegal. The meat he sold, he said, was pickled boneless pork and during the economic crisis at that time it was in great demand.

No one questioned him about the buckets of blood he emptied down the drain in the courtyard, nor about the hammering and sawing that went on during the night. After all, he was preparing the dishes that he sold at the market in the morning.

He was also seen taking out heavy bags and returning empty-handed and no one asked where he got the old clothes and shoes that he sold. Perhaps they did not take any notice because no one from the town of Münsterberg, whose population was then just eight thousand, had gone missing. Denke's victims were drifters from elsewhere, people that no one would miss and that were largely unknown to the townsfolk. They did, however, notice a shortage of pork in the market the Christmas and New Year after Denke had been arrested.

A CITY REMEMBERS

Though Denke is hardly the city's favourite son, a corner of Ziębice's Muscum of Houschold Goods is given over to him. There is a table with bloody knives and a couple of axes embedded in a chopping block on it and a meat grinder is also attached.

Lucyna Biały, the curator of the archive of old printed materials in the University Library at Piasek in Wrocław, who unearthed the Denke story, put the killer in context:

> It is necessary to emphasize that since the beginning of the twentieth century, on German lands, there have been even more perverse mass murderers. Names such as Ludwik Tresnov come to mind, who raped, killed, and dismembered four children in the area of Osnabrück. Friedrich Haarmann, called the 'Butcher of Hanover', killed about fifty young people and sold their flesh as meat. He was beheaded in 1926. A bank clerk, Fritz Angerstein from Haiger killed probably seven people. He was sentenced to death in 1925. Finally, Peter Kuerten, called 'The Vampire of Düsseldorf', was accused of nine murders and seven attempted murders. He drank the blood of his victims. He was beheaded on 2 July 1931.

RODNEY JAMES ALCALA
THE DATING GAME KILLER

KILLER SEEKS DATE

Serial killer Rodney James Alcala got his nickname because in 1978, in the midst of his murderous career, he took time out to appear as a contestant on ABC's television show *The Dating Game*. The host introduced him saying: 'Bachelor No. 1 is a successful photographer who got his start when his father found him in the darkroom at the age of thirteen, fully developed. Between takes you might find him skydiving or motorcycling. Please welcome Rodney Alcala.'

This was wide of the mark. Fellow contestant Jed Mills described him as 'creepy, definitely creepy' and said he had almost immediately taken against Alcala.

'Something about him, I could not be near him,' Mills recalled.

He felt there was something wrong when they met in the green room before the take.

He was quiet, but at the same time he would interrupt and impose when he felt like it. And he was very obnoxious and creepy – he became very unlikable and rude and imposing as though he was trying to intimidate. I wound up not only not liking this guy … not wanting to be near him … he got creepier and more negative. He was a standout creepy guy in my life.

Nevertheless, the female contestant Cheryl Bradshaw picked him as her date. Later CNN asked criminal profiler Pat Brown to look at the tapes of Alcala's performance.

He was aware that he could say things that were considered sexy and funny and the girl would like that. He watched the game and he gave those answers and he won, so he learned some tricks. But a psychopath's true nature comes seeping through. … He had already committed a crime, raped a little girl. Here is a man portraying himself as a desirable young man when he is a violent sexual predator of children.

Things had been different off camera though.

He is showing his psychopathic personality in the green room. He wasn't acting at that time. Those were his enemies, and he had to beat them to get the girl and he wanted to win. This guy probably literally hated them. This guy was going on the show to prove how special and wonderful he was. And his ego was riding on it.

Although Bradshaw had picked him on the show, when the time came she then refused to go out with him. Brown thought that this rejection may have pushed Alcala over the edge.

FILM SCHOOL STUDENT

Born Rodrigo Jacques Alcala Buquor in San Antonio, Texas in 1943, The Dating Game Killer spent part of his childhood in Mexico before moving back to the US in 1954 to live in Los Angeles with his mother and sisters. At seventeen, he joined the army, but was given a medical discharge in 1964 after being diagnosed with a severe antisocial personality.

He then enrolled at the UCLA School of Fine Arts and was made a Bachelor of Fine Arts in 1968. But evil was afoot. A motorist spotted him on Sunset Boulevard luring eight-year-old Tali Shapiro into his car, so he followed them back to Alcala's Hollywood apartment and then called the police. When they arrived, they kicked the door in and found the girl lying on the kitchen floor. Alcala had raped her, beaten her with a heavy iron bar and then attempted to strangle her. They thought she was dead but when they noticed she was still breathing they applied emergency CPR. This gave Alcala the opportunity to slip out of the back door and flee.

Using the alias John Berger, he enrolled at New York University's film school where, it was said, he studied under Roman Polanski. In his spare time he pretended to be a fashion photographer, in order to get girls to pose for him. This gave him the opportunity to rape and kill.

It was not until forty years later that the police tied Alcala to the murder of twenty-three-year-old TWA flight attendant Cornelia Crilley, who had been raped and strangled. The door of her Upper East Side apartment was locked and when the police broke in they found the dead woman lying against an overturned bed, with a rope tied around her neck. Her bra had been pulled up over her head and someone had bitten her left breast. Saliva was collected, but in 1971 they did not have the technology to make a DNA profile. At the time they suspected Crilley's boyfriend, Leon Borstein, who was then an assistant district attorney for Brooklyn, and her murder remained unsolved. It was only in 2011 that a dental impression from Alcala was found to match the bite mark on Ms Crilley's body.

'I am now almost seventy-one, and this occurred forty years ago, and I am still affected by it,' Borstein said. 'I was crazy about her at the time. ... I was devastated by her death. She was beautiful, charming, with a great sense of humour. She had the Irish eyes and the Irish hair.'

PLEA BARGAIN

In the same year that he murdered Cornelia Crilley, Alcala worked at a girls' summer drama camp in New Hampshire under the alias of John Burger. It was there that two girls recognized Alcala from the FBI's Most Wanted Poster in the post office and he was arrested. Back in LA, he told Detective Steve Hodel: 'I have been trying to forget what happened. ... I have forgotten all about Rod Alcala and what he did.'

Meanwhile, the Shapiro family had returned to Mexico and they refused to let Tali testify at Alcala's trial. Although he was charged with rape, kidnapping, assault and attempted murder, without their principal witness the prosecution was forced to enter into a plea bargain. So Alcala just pleaded guilty to molesting a child, while the other charges were dropped. He was sentenced to one year to life and paroled after thirty-four months.

Within weeks, he was found with a thirteen-year-old girl who claimed he had kidnapped her. Returned to jail for violating his parole by providing her with marijuana, he was out again two years later in 1977.

Soon after his release, his parole officer let Alcala visit relatives in New York. When young socialite and daughter of the owner of Ciro's nightclub Ellen Hover disappeared, the name 'John Berger' was found written on her calendar the day she vanished. The New York police were busy with the Son of Sam case at the time, so her father hired a private detective who placed ads in the *New York Times* seeking information about a man last seen with her – a ponytailed photographer named John Burger. Burger or Berger could not be traced, but Ellen's remains were found on the wooded Rockefeller Estate.

Although he was a convicted sex offender, back in LA Alcala found a job as a typesetter for the *Los Angeles Times* at the height of the rampage of the Hillside Strangler – later found to be two people, Kenneth Bianchi and Angelo Buono, who raped and killed ten women, dumping their bodies in the Hollywood Hills.

TOYED WITH VICTIMS

Then on 10 November 1977, the half-naked body of eighteen-year-old Jill Barcomb was found in the woods off Mulholland Drive. She was posed on her knees with her face in the dirt and had been raped and sodomized before being strangled and having her face beaten in with a rock. Alcala was picked up and questioned at the same time – not for the murder of Jill Barcomb but for the disappearance of Ellen Hover, after the Burger/Berger connection was made. But Ellen's body had not been found by then, so there was nothing to hold him on.

Two days after Alcala was released, on 16 December 1977, the body of twenty-seven-year-old nurse Georgia Wixted was found in her studio in Malibu. It was the morning after she had attended a birthday party at Brennan's Pub in Santa Monica. She had been raped and sodomized before being sexually abused with a claw hammer, which was then used to smash her head in after she had been strangled with a nylon stocking. Again her body was left posed.

The following year, Alcala was interviewed at his mother's house in connection with the Hillside Strangler crimes. He was ruled out in that case, but was found to be in possession of marijuana, and so was returned to jail.

The next murder connected to him was that of thirty-three-year-old legal secretary Charlotte Lamb, whose naked body was found in a laundry room of an El Segundo apartment complex on 24 June 1978. She had been raped and beaten and then strangled with her own shoelace. Once again the body was left posed. It appeared that Alcala liked to toy with his victims, choking them until they passed out and then reviving them, only to choke them once more.

HOUSE SEARCH REVEALS EVIDENCE

That summer he appeared on *The Dating Game*. Early the following year, a fifteen-year-old hitch-hiker called the police from a motel in Riverside County in Southern California saying she had been kidnapped and raped but had escaped. Alcala was charged but his mother put up the $10,000 bail needed to release him.

While out on bail, he raped and murdered twenty-one-year-old computer keypunch operator Jill Parenteau in her Burbank apartment. His blood was found at the scene after he had cut himself breaking in through a window and he was charged with murdering Jill, but the case was dismissed.

Six days later, on 20 June 1979, twelve-year-old Robin Samsoe disappeared. She had been with her friend Bridgett Wilvert at Huntington Beach when a man asked them to pose for pictures in their swimsuits. A neighbour intervened and the photographer took off. Bridgett then lent Robin her yellow bike to go to her afternoon ballet class. She was never seen alive again.

Detectives circulated a sketch of the photographer to the media and Alcala's parole officer recognized him immediately. On 2 July 1979, US Forest Service rangers found Robin's remains dumped near Sierra Madre in the foothills of the San Gabriel Mountains. Her body had been scavenged by animals and there was little more than her skeleton left but it was clear that her front teeth had been knocked out by her assailant.

Arrested at his mother's house in Monterey Park on 24 June, Alcala claimed that he had been applying for a job as a photographer for a disco contest at Knott's Berry Farm at the time of Robin's disappearance. However, in a search of Alcala's house the police found a receipt for a locker. In it were a number of photographs, some of young girls Alcala appeared to be stalking. One was a picture of Lorraine Werts, who was posing for him on Huntington Beach, near where Robin and Bridgett had been approached. They also found earrings that belonged to Robin Samsoe and Charlotte Lamb.

In a search of Alcala's house, the police found a receipt for a locker in which there were pictures of young girls he appeared to be stalking. They also found earrings that belonged to his victims.

AMERICA'S MOST PROLIFIC KILLER?

In 1980, Alcala was convicted of Robin Samsoe's murder and sentenced to death, but the conviction was overturned by the California Supreme Court because the jurors had been improperly informed of his prior sexual offences. A second conviction was thrown out in 2001, because a witness was not allowed to back up Alcala's claim that the park ranger who found Robin's body in the mountains had been hypnotized by the police.

However, by 2003, DNA in the semen found on the bodies of Jill Barcomb, Georgia Wixted and Charlotte Lamb was matched to Alcala's. At his third trial, the charge of the murder of Robin Samsoe was joined with those for the murder of Jill Barcomb, Georgia Wixted, Charlotte Lamb and Jill Parenteau. He pleaded not guilty by reason of insanity. This time Alcala elected to act as his own attorney, even cross-questioning himself in the witness box. He was convicted on five counts of first-degree murder. During the penalty stage of the proceedings, Tali Shapiro made a surprise appearance and Alcala was sentenced to death once more.

Some 120 of the photographs in Alcala's locker were published in case they showed other possible victims. Twenty-one women came forward to identify themselves and other people recognized family members who had disappeared, while another nine hundred photographs were held back from publication as they were too sexually explicit. Alcala was charged with the murder of Christine Thornton in Sweetwater County, Wyoming in the summer of 1977, after she was recognized from one of the photographs.

In 2012, Alcala was extradited to New York where he was convicted of the murders of Cornelia Crilley and Ellen Hover and given another twenty-five years to life. Alcala is also thought to be responsible for murders in San Francisco and Seattle and is under investigation for more cold cases in California, New York, New Hampshire and Arizona. There is speculation that there were hundreds of victims, possibly making Alcala America's most prolific serial killer.

RICHARD CHASE
THE VAMPIRE OF SACRAMENTO

DRANK VICTIM'S BLOOD

At around 6 p.m. on 23 January 1978, twenty-four-year-old laundry-truck driver David Wallin returned to his modest suburban home in north Sacramento to find his twenty-two-year-old wife Terry, who was three months pregnant, dead and horribly mutilated. Screaming in horror, he ran to the house of a neighbour, who called the police.

It appeared that Terry Wallin had been attacked in the living room of her house while she was preparing to take the rubbish out. She had been shot with a .22 calibre firearm and had been stabbed repeatedly before and after she was dead. The perpetrator had then raped her corpse, cut off her left nipple and slashed open her belly. Some of her body parts were missing and there was a yoghurt carton beside her body which the killer appeared to have used as a cup to drink her blood. He had also collected dog faeces from the yard and forced them down her throat.

PROFILE OF A KILLER

The local police called Russ Vorpagel, a veteran cop with the FBI's Behavioral Science Unit on the West Coast. He in turn contacted Robert Ressler, a pioneer in psychological profiling at the FBI's Training Academy in Quantico, Virginia. It was clear to both of them that such a killer was not going to be satisfied with one homicide. Unless he was caught quickly, he was bound to kill again. Ressler flew out to California as soon as he could.

Psychological profiling was in its infancy and normally the cases that got referred to the BSU were cold. This one gave them the chance to try out profiling techniques on a case that was hot. Ressler immediately came up with a profile of the suspect:

> White male, aged 25–27 years; thin, undernourished appearance. Residence will be extremely slovenly and unkempt and evidence of the crime will be found at the residence. History of mental illness, and will have been involved in use of drugs. Will be a loner who does not associate with either males or females, and will probably spend a great deal of time in his own home, where he lives alone. Unemployed. Possibly receives some form of disability money. If residing with anyone, it would be with his parents; however, this is unlikely. No prior military record; high school or college dropout. Probably suffering from one or more forms of paranoid psychosis.

It proved extraordinarily accurate but was of no immediate use.

ORGANS REMOVED

While the investigation got under way, there were more horrifying murders. Just four days after the slaughter of Terry Wallin, three bodies were found in another suburban house in north Sacramento, not far away. Thirty-six-year-old mother of three Evelyn Miroth, her six-year-old son Jason and fifty-two-year-old family friend Daniel J. Meredith had all been shot with a .22 firearm. Evelyn had been babysitting her twenty-two-month-old nephew David Ferreira, who was missing. It was assumed that the killer had abducted the child.

While Jason and Meredith had just been shot and were otherwise unmolested, Evelyn Miroth was found nude on her bed. She had been sodomized and there were multiple stab wounds all over her body, including cuts to the face and around the anus. As with Terry Wallin, her belly had been slashed open and organs removed. Blood, brains and faecal matter had been thrown into the bath.

In the playpen where David Ferreira would have been there was a blood-soaked pillow and an expended bullet, so detectives did not expect to find the child alive. Meredith's wallet and car keys were missing. The killer had used the keys to make his getaway in Meredith's red station wagon, which was found abandoned nearby with the driver's door open and the keys in the ignition. Ressler concluded that the killer was a 'disorganized' type and that he would live within half-a-mile to a mile from where he had left the car. He also believed that the perpetrator had committed 'fetish burglaries' in the area – that is, he had stolen jewellery of little marketable value or articles of women's clothing for autoerotic purposes.

Armed with an updated profile, sixty-five police officers began a manhunt in the immediate area. Ressler appeared to be on the right track when it was discovered that a dog had been shot and disembowelled at a nearby country club.

A woman then came forward to say that she had seen a man she had known at high school in the shopping centre that Terry Wallin had visited on the morning of her murder. She had cashed a cheque there. He was thin and dishevelled, with sunken eyes, a yellow crust around his mouth and blood on his sweatshirt. He had tried to engage her in conversation and had pulled on the door handle of her car. She then took fright and drove away.

Aerial view of Downtown Sacramento: Richard Chase became the 'Vampire Killer of Sacramento' after a murder binge in which he claimed six lives.

BRAIN TISSUE IN FRIDGE

The man's name was Richard Trenton Chase. He had graduated from her high school in 1968 and lived just a block from where the station wagon had been abandoned and a mile from both the shopping centre and the country club. The police phoned his apartment, but there was no answer. They knew that the killer had a .22 pistol so they staked out Chase's apartment and waited for him.

When he emerged, he was carrying a box. Seeing the officers, he made a dash for his truck but they gave chase and brought him down. As they grappled with him on the ground, a .22 pistol fell from the shoulder holster he was wearing. A quick search revealed Daniel Meredith's wallet in his back pocket and the box he was carrying was full of bloody rags.

His truck was a wreck and full of empty beer cans, newspapers and other litter. There was a twelve-inch butcher's knife locked in the toolbox, along with a pair of rubber boots with blood on them. His apartment was also a mess. In it, the police found newspaper articles about Terry Wallin's murder, bloodstained clothing, pet collars and leads and food blenders with blood in them. In a kitchen drawer, there were knives taken from the Wallins' house and in the fridge they found dishes containing brain tissue and other body parts. On the wall of the apartment was a calendar with the word 'Today' scrawled on the days of the murders. The same word appeared on forty-four days spread out over the rest of the year. Clearly, he intended to kill again.

Soon after Chase was arrested, it was found that he had committed another murder. The bullets from his gun matched the one taken from the body of fifty-one-year-old Ambrose Griffin. On 28 December 1977, Griffin had just returned from the supermarket with his wife. They were unloading the groceries from their car when Chase drove by and fired two shots. One of them hit Griffin in the chest and killed him. Not only that but the decapitated body of the missing infant David Ferreira was eventually found not far from Chase's apartment.

Chase also fitted the description of a thief responsible for a number of fetish burglaries in the area and the collars and leads found in his apartment belonged to dogs and cats that had gone missing in the vicinity. He also had a criminal record. The previous August, he had been arrested near Lake Tahoe by an Indian agent. He had blood on his clothes but explained that he had been hunting rabbits. In his truck were a number of guns and a bucket of blood, which turned out to be bovine. However, his father rode to the rescue and he was released after paying a fine.

BIT HEADS OFF BIRDS

Born in 1950, Chase was said to have been a sweet and co-operative child, though he wet the bed until the age of eight. When he was about twelve, his parents fell out. His mother accused his father of being unfaithful, taking drugs and trying to poison her. Ressler described Mrs Chase as the classic mother of a schizophrenic – 'highly aggressive ... hostile ... provocative'. The fighting went on for ten years until the couple divorced and his father remarried.

Chase was unremarkable at school, lacked any ambition, had no close friends and was unable to keep girlfriends when they found he could not sustain an erection. He then began drinking heavily and smoking marijuana. Caught in possession, he was sentenced to community service. Unable to hold down a job, he dropped out of junior college and lived alternately with his mother and father, who supported him.

In 1972 he was arrested for drink driving and stopped drinking afterwards. The following year he was arrested for carrying a gun without a licence and resisting arrest. He was then thrown out of a party after trying to grab a girl's breast and, when two men restrained him after he returned, a .22 fell out of his waistband. The police were called and he was fined $50.

He got ill in 1976 after injecting himself with rabbit blood. Sent to a nursing home, he frightened other patients by biting the heads off birds he had caught in the bushes. He described his pleasure in killing small animals and was often found smeared with blood, so the staff called him Dracula. Apparently he believed he was being poisoned and his blood was turning into powder, so he had to drink another creature's blood to replenish it. Even so, Chase was discharged in 1977.

His mother then found him an apartment. At this point he became obsessed with flying saucers and thought a Nazi crime syndicate was out to get him. After his arrest at Lake Tahoe in August, his mental state rapidly disintegrated. The following month, he killed his mother's cat after an argument with her and in October he bought two dogs from an animal shelter for $15 each. Also in that month he tried driving out of a petrol station without paying his petrol bill for $20, but after being stopped and questioned he was allowed to drive on.

He soon bought more dogs and tormented a family who had placed an advertisement in a newspaper asking if anyone had seen their missing pooch. Meanwhile, police reports of missing pets backed up.

ABLE TO BUY GUN

He then bought a gun, swearing on the form that he had never been in a mental institution. While he waited the ten days required before he was allowed to pick it up, he followed the doings of the Hillside Strangler in the newspaper and looked at small ads offering dogs for sale. Once he had the gun he shot at the side wall of the home of the Phares family. Next a bullet went through a kitchen window which, according to Ressler, parted the hair of Mrs Polenske. A few days later Ambrose Griffin was killed. He lived across the street from the Phares. Chase kept a cutting from the *Sacramento Bee* about the murder.

On 23 January, before he killed Terry Wallin, he tried to enter the home of a neighbour but when she saw him through the kitchen window he sat motionless on her patio, escaping before the police arrived. He then entered a nearby house, stole a few things, urinated on clothes in a drawer and defecated in a child's cot. An hour later he was at the shopping centre where he met the woman who had known him at high school. She did not recognize him until he asked her whether she had been on the motorcycle when her boyfriend, a friend of his, had been killed. She said she had not and asked who he was before making her escape. Immediately after that he left the shopping centre, entered the nearby Wallins' home and killed Terry.

WORKINGS OF A KILLER'S MIND

Although Chase was unco-operative with the police, he confessed all to a prison psychiatrist, saying:

> The first person I killed was sort of an accident. My car was broken down. I wanted to leave but I had no transmission. I had to get an apartment. Mother wouldn't let me in at Christmas. Always before she let me come in at Christmas, have dinner, and talk to her, my grandmother, and my sister. That year she wouldn't let me in and I shot from the car and killed somebody. The second time, the people had made a lot of money and I was jealous. I was being watched, and I shot this lady – got some blood out of it. I went to another house, walked in, a whole family was there. I shot the whole family. Somebody saw me there. I saw this girl. She had called the police and they had been unable to locate me. Curt Silva's girlfriend – he was killed in a motorcycle accident, as a couple of my friends were, and I had this idea that he was killed through the syndicate, that he was in the Mafia, selling drugs. His girlfriend remembered about Curt – I was trying to get information. She said she was married to somebody else and wouldn't talk to me. The whole syndicate was making money by having my mom poison me. I know who they are and I think it can be brought out in a court of law if I can pull the pieces together like I've been hoping.

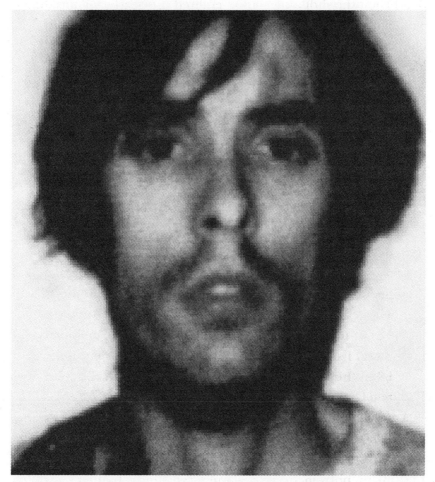

Richard Chase: 'It was his eyes that really got me,' said FBI profiler Robert Ressler. 'I'll never forget them. They were like those of the shark in the movie Jaws. *No pupils, just black spots.'*

'HIS EYES GOT ME'

On 6 May 1979 he went on trial on six counts of first-degree murder. The *Sacramento Bee* reported:

> The defendant has a totally lustreless quality. Dull, limp brown hair, sunken opaque eyes, a sallow complexion and scarcely a spare ounce of flesh clinging to his bony frame. For the past four and a half months Richard Trenton Chase, just a couple of weeks short of his twenty-ninth birthday, has sat hunched in his chair, toying with papers in front of him or staring vacantly at the fluorescent lights of the courtroom.

The defence argued that he was not guilty by reason of insanity but the jury found him guilty on all counts and he was sentenced to death. While he was on death row in San Quentin, Ressler visited him. Ressler voiced his thoughts:

> It was his eyes that really got me. I'll never forget them. They were like those of the shark in the movie *Jaws*. No pupils, just black spots. These were evil eyes that stayed with me long after the interview. I almost got the impression that he couldn't really see me, that he was seeing through me, just staring.

Again he admitted the murders. His excuse was that he was being poisoned via his soap dish. The toxin pulverized the blood so he had to drink more fresh blood to stay alive. Again he rambled on about the Nazis and UFOs, claiming that he had murdered in self-defence. He also claimed that his victims had left their doors unlocked, which invited him in. Otherwise he would not have entered their homes. On death row, the other inmates taunted him and his paranoia got the better of him. He saved up his anti-depressant pills and killed himself with an overdose.

THE MAD BUTCHER OF KINGSBURY RUN

THE CLEVELAND TORSO MURDERER

HEADLESS CORPSES

The Cleveland Torso Murderer was neither caught nor identified. He was active during the 1930s in Kingsbury Run, which is a prehistoric river bed some sixty feet deep that runs across the east side of Cleveland. It was once a beauty spot but as the city grew up it was pitted with quarries that provided stone to build the city. Rapid industrialization in the nineteenth century polluted the clear waters of the Cuyahoga River. During the Great Depression, the railroads that ran through Kingsbury Run brought itinerant workers. Most of them ended up in a squalid shanty town next to an area called 'The Roaring Third', the home of bars, brothels, flophouses and gambling dens. This backed on to the hobo jungle in Kingsbury Run itself.

On the afternoon of Monday 23 September 1935, two teenage boys found a headless corpse at the foot of an embankment known locally as Jackass Hill. When the police were called, they found not one headless corpse, but two. Both victims were white men and they were naked, though one still had his socks on. The men's penises had been cut off and their heads were found nearby.

Curiously, the bodies had been washed and drained of blood. Clearly the murders had not taken place where the corpses had been found. The flesh appeared scorched, either by acid or some corrosive chemical – or perhaps oil had been poured over them in an attempt to set them on fire. A bucket of oil and a torch were found nearby.

BEHEADED WHILE ALIVE

The first victim was thought to be in his forties. One of his testicles was missing and the clean edges of the incision showed that a sharp instrument had been used. Also the muscles of the neck were retracted, indicating that the man had been beheaded while still alive. According to the coroner's report the skin appeared leathery and tanned as if it had been processed using acid. The conclusion was that the body had been treated with a chemical preservative after death and then dowsed with oil and set on fire. Coroner Arthur J. Pierce's verdict was: 'Homicide by person or persons unknown.' The advanced state of decomposition prevented fingerprints from being taken and Victim One remained unidentified.

Victim Two had only been dead for two or three days. He was younger than the other man, being in his twenties. Again the cause of death was decapitation. There were rope marks on his wrist, indicating that his hands had been tied behind him while he was castrated and beheaded. Fingerprints identified him as Edward A. Andrassy of 1744 Fulton Road. He had been arrested several times for being drunk and had spent time in Warrensville Workhouse after being arrested for carrying a concealed weapon. At one time he had worked at Cleveland City Hospital, but when he died he had no job or visible means of support and was known to associate with unsavoury company in The Roaring Third. His mother told detectives that a middle-aged man came to the house two months before her son's death and said he was going to kill him for 'paying attentions to his wife'.

Strange stories circulated about Andrassy. According to one, he had once claimed to be a gynaecologist and had offered to examine a childless acquaintance's wife. He had then used the opportunity to sodomize her. Others said that Andrassy was gay or bisexual and that he smoked marijuana, dealt in pornography and possibly had

Detectives examine the bones of two murder victims found at the East 9th Street Lakeshore Dump in 1938. The bodies were the 11th and 12th confirmed victims of the Cleveland Torso Murderer.

gangster connections. He had told his sister that the mob were after him because he had stabbed an Italian in a fight.

THE LADY OF THE LAKE

The two murders appeared to be related to an incident that had occurred a year earlier. On 5 September 1934 the lower half of a woman's torso had washed up on the shore of Lake Erie, just east of Cleveland, and according to the coroner the remains had been in the water for three to four months. The skin was discoloured, as if it had been treated with the same chemical preservative as the other two corpses. The upper half of the torso had been washed up earlier, some thirty miles away, but it was so badly decayed that it was not immediately identified as part of a corpse and the head was never found.

Aged about thirty, the victim did not fit the particulars of any missing person's report and was never identified. The newspapers called her 'The Lady of the Lake', but to the police she became 'Victim Zero'. They believed that her body had been dumped in Kingsbury Run and had then floated down the Cuyahoga River into Lake Erie.

TATTOOED MAN

On Sunday 26 January 1936 parts of a woman's body wrapped in newspaper were found on Central Avenue and detectives found further body parts in hessian sacks. The victim had been dead for two to four days. It appeared that she had been killed elsewhere, as before, and the cause of death was again decapitation. A sharp knife had been used and the killer appeared to be expert at cutting flesh.

Her right arm was intact and fingerprints revealed that she was forty-two-year-old Florence Polillo, a waitress and barmaid who had been arrested a couple of times for prostitution. A heavy drinker, she had slipped inexorably to the bottom of society and at the time she died she was living in a rooming house on the edge of The Roaring Third.

On 5 June 1936, two young boys out on a fishing expedition took a shortcut through Kingsbury Run, where they saw a pair of trousers rolled up under a bush. When they poked the garment with a fishing rod, a man's head rolled out. The following morning the naked, headless body of a man in his twenties was found dumped in front of the building occupied by the police who had been hired by the railroad company. Their job was to keep hobos out of the freight cars.

Although he had been found in Kingsbury Run, this victim was certainly not a hobo. His clothes, which were found nearby, were expensive and new and he was clean shaven and well fed. Again, the body had been drained of blood and washed clean. No blood had soaked into the ground so, once more, the victim had been killed elsewhere.

On the body were six distinctive tattoos, so detectives visited tattoo parlours and went to bars frequented by sailors. Hundreds traipsed through the morgue to view the body and pictures of the tattoos and a plaster cast of the victim's head were put on display at the Great Lakes Exposition of 1936, which was visited by seven million people. Nevertheless, the 'Tattooed Man' was never identified.

Then on 22 July 1936, the naked headless corpse of a forty-year-old white man was found near a hobo camp in the woods to the west of Kingsbury Run. The man's head was found fifteen feet away. His hair was long and his clothes were cheap. This time blood had soaked into the ground, indicating that he was killed where he lay. But again, the butchery showed the same expert hand.

ELIOT NESS CALLED IN

Less than two months later, on 10 September 1936, a hobo tripped over the upper half of a man's torso while trying to hop a train in Kingsbury Run. The head and hands were never found and the victim could not be identified. By now the press had dubbed the killer 'The Mad Butcher of Kingsbury Run' and panic spread through the area.

Eliot Ness, whose Untouchables had rid Chicago of Al Capone, had been called in to clean up Cleveland. He was pulled off the largest corruption case in the city's history and put on the investigation and every hobo in the area was brought in for questioning.

Twenty detectives were assigned to the case. They interviewed more than 1,500 people in what would be the biggest murder investigation in the history of Cleveland. These included a crazed giant who stalked Kingsbury Run carrying a large knife, a 'voodoo doctor' who claimed to have a death-ray and 'Chicken Freak', who hired prostitutes to strip naked and behead chickens while he masturbated.

Newspaper speculation ran wild. Some said that the killer was a religious maniac who was bent on ridding the world of prostitutes, homosexuals, wastrels and hobos. Others thought he was a wealthy doctor who killed lower-class people for sport.

Eliot Ness held a 'Torso Clinic' to piece together what they knew about the killer. It was agreed that one perpetrator working alone was responsible for all of the murders. He was strong because he overpowered his victims and carried their bodies considerable distances over rough terrain. And while the killer was clearly a psychopath, he was not obviously insane. Some of the mutilation had been done to thwart identification, while some was purely gratuitous.

EXPERT DISMEMBERMENT

Beheading is necessarily a messy business as blood spurts all over the place. The killer would need private premises where the victims could be slaughtered and stored until they could be dumped. They would have to be near Kingsbury Run and the killer clearly had an intimate knowledge of the area.

The expert dismemberment meant that the killer could be a doctor. But a butcher or a hunter who cut up game would have enough anatomical knowledge to do the job. While there was speculation that the murderer dumped the bodies in Kingsbury Run to scare off the hobos who lived there, picking victims from the lower strata of society also made them more difficult to identify.

In November 1936 Pierce was replaced as coroner by Samuel Gerber. Qualified both in medicine and law, he would make the Mad Butcher case his own. His first crack at the case came on 23 February 1937, when the upper half of a woman's torso washed up on the beach in virtually the same place as The Lady of the Lake had surfaced. She had only been dead for between two and four days. Three months later the lower half of her torso washed ashore. Again the question was asked whether she had been washed down the Cuyahoga River into Lake Erie from Kingsbury Run.

The victim's head, arms and legs had been removed with the murderer's usual expertise but the bisection of the torso was more amateurish and she had not been killed by decapitation. Instead, her head had been cut off after she was dead and the killer had inserted the pocket from a pair of trousers into her rectum. Her identity was never discovered.

BOTH SEXES MURDERED

Gerber set about writing up his conclusions, which were published in March 1937. He deduced that the killer was right-handed and used a sharp, heavy knife rather than a medical instrument. As to motive, Gerber believed the killer to be a sexual psychopath, the first on record to have murdered both sexes. Because of his own knowledge of anatomy, Gerber believed that the killer was a medical student, a male nurse, a surgeon or a veterinary practitioner.

On 6 June 1937 a human skull was found under the Lorain-Carnegie Bridge. Nearby was a rotting hessian bag containing skeletal remains. They were wrapped in a newspaper from June 1936. The victim was a petite woman around forty years old with a wide nose and kinky hair. Gerber concluded she was an African American. This time, though, there was 'considerable hacking and cutting of the 3rd, 4th and 5th cervical vertebrae', indicating that the perpetrator had not demonstrated the Mad Butcher's normal level of skill. Dental records indicated that the victim was a prostitute named Rose Wallace who had disappeared in August 1936, though the identification remained in dispute.

On 6 July 1937, the upper part of a man's torso was seen bobbing in the water in the wake of a passing tugboat near the West Third Street Bridge. Over the next few days, police recovered other body parts from the Cuyahoga River, though the head remained missing. The victim was a man in his mid to late thirties with well-groomed fingernails and the cause of death was decapitation. All of the internal organs had been ripped out and none of them were ever found. The victim was never identified.

DOCTOR BECOMES SUSPECT

Detectives now combed the records for doctors that had a weakness for drink, drugs or illicit sex – particularly of a homosexual nature, as it was still illegal then. They soon happened upon Dr Francis E. Sweeney, who was large and physically strong. He had grown up in the Kingsbury Run area and at various times had run his practice from there.

He had been a resident surgeon at St Alexis, a hospital close to Kingsbury Run, but had lost his job because of drunkenness. Violent when drunk, he was divorced and there were rumours that he was bisexual. However, Dr Sweeney had an alibi. He had been at the Sandusky Soldiers' and Sailors' Home, a veterans hospital fifty miles west of Cleveland, when the Mad Butcher was at work. Moreover, he was a first cousin to Democratic Congressman Martin L. Sweeney, who was a fierce critic of Cleveland's Republican mayor and 'his alter ego, Eliot Ness'. He said Ness spent all of his time persecuting cops who took $25 bribes from bootleggers while doing nothing to catch The Mad Butcher of Kingsbury Run.

In mid-March 1938 a severed leg was found in a swampy area near Sandusky. Lieutenant David L. Cowles, head of the crime lab, drove out there but found that the leg was part of hospital refuse that had not been properly disposed of. While he was there, Cowles decided to check out Dr Sweeney's alibi.

He quickly confirmed that Dr Sweeney had admitted himself to the Sandusky Soldiers' and Sailors' Home to treat his alcoholism at times when the Mad Butcher was at work. However, there was little security and it would have been possible for Sweeney to travel back to Cleveland, commit the murders, dump the bodies and return without his absence being noticed.

MURDERS START AFTER MARRIAGE BREAK-UP

The veterans' hospital shared some of its facilities with the Ohio Penitentiary Honor Farm. There Cowles met a burglar named Alex Archaki, who supplied Dr Sweeney with liquor while Sweeney wrote Archaki prescriptions for drugs. What's more, Archaki believed that Sweeney was the Mad Butcher. He said that every time Sweeney returned from one of his unexplained absences a new body turned up in Kingsbury Run.

They had met in a bar in downtown Cleveland a few years earlier. When Sweeney approached Archaki he asked him a lot of personal questions. Where was he from? Was he married? Did he have any family in the city?

By making sure he had no close friends or relatives in the area Sweeney was clearly sizing him up as a victim.

When Cowles returned to Cleveland, he discreetly renewed the investigation of Dr Sweeney. He discovered that Francis Edward Sweeney had been born in 1894 into a poor Irish immigrant family who lived on the edge of Kingsbury Run. After his father had been crippled in an accident he took to drink and died of alcoholism in a mental hospital. Then his mother had died of a stroke when he was just nine.

Sweeney served in the First World War and was injured in the head. After working his way through medical school, he married and had two sons. In 1928 he took a surgical post at St Alexis hospital and rose quickly through the ranks. However, in 1929 he began drinking heavily and St Alexis sacked him. His wife left him in 1934 and when she filed for divorce two years later she requested a restraining order to prevent him 'visiting, interfering, or molesting her'. The break-up of their marriage coincided with the first Torso Murders.

Sweeney certainly had the ability to expertly decapitate and dismember the victims. He was also strong enough to carry the bodies to where they were dumped in Kingsbury Run. And his alleged bisexuality could explain why the victims were both male and female.

CORPSES DUMPED NEAR NESS'S OFFICE

Cowles was just putting the finishing touches to his case when, on 8 April 1938, the lower half of a woman's leg appeared in the Cuyahoga River. A month later the police pulled two hessian sacks out of the same river. They contained the nude torso of a woman, which had been cut in half. The head was missing, along with the hands, and the young woman was never identified.

Sweeney was put under surveillance, but he soon spotted he was being followed. Then his lodgings and his office were searched and his mail opened. Meanwhile, the activities of the Mad Butcher continued. On 16 August 1938, the torso of a woman was found on a rubbish dump within sight of Eliot Ness's office. It had been dismembered with a sharp knife. The head was found nearby and, uncharacteristically, the hands were also present. Most of the body was so badly decomposed that it was impossible to determine the cause of death, but some parts were remarkably well preserved as if they had been kept in a refrigerator.

More bones were found nearby. These belonged to a white male whose corpse had also been dismembered with a long, sharp knife. But, again, the cause of death could not be determined.

There was some doubt that these two were the victims of the Mad Butcher as they did not conform to his developing MO. He had not left the hands and heads with the bodies of his victims since 1936 and he usually dumped them in the Cuyahoga River or in Kingsbury Run, where they would be found easily. These two corpses had been discovered by accident – though leaving them in sight of Eliot Ness's office smacked of the audacity the killer had shown before.

POLYGRAPH TESTS

Desperate for action, Ness staged a raid on the hobo shanty towns of Kingsbury Run. He arrested sixty-three men, fingerprinted them and sent them to the workhouse. After the shacks had been searched, they were burned to the ground. But this only brought about an adverse press reaction since it did nothing to help catch the Mad Butcher.

Ness only had one course left open to him. He pulled in Dr Sweeney. But instead of taking him to police headquarters, Sweeney was held discreetly in a suite at the Cleveland Hotel. It was made clear that if he did not co-operate he would be marched downtown through a howling mob of reporters.

Sweeney was left to dry out for three days and then on 23 August 1938 the interrogation began.

It was conducted by Ness, Cowles and Dr Royal Grossman, a court psychiatrist. In an adjoining room Dr Leonarde Keeler, co-inventor of the polygraph, set up his equipment. Two hours of cross-questioning yielded nothing, but after Sweeney was hooked up to the polygraph, Keeler said: 'He's your guy.'

'Well?' Sweeney asked Ness. 'Are you satisfied now?'

'Yes,' said Ness. 'I think you're the killer.'

'You think?' said Sweeney. Then, with his face inches from Ness's, he hissed: 'Then prove it!'

JEERING POSTCARDS

Polygraph tests were inadmissible and the only evidence they had was Sweeney's absence from the Sandusky veterans' hospital at the times of the murders, which was circumstantial at best. Besides, it had been provided by a convicted criminal, who could hardly be regarded as a credible witness.

Two days after the interrogation Dr Sweeney checked back into the Sandusky veterans' hospital and instructions were given that if he left the hospital grounds the police were to be informed. From 25 August 1938 until his death in 1965, Sweeney remained confined voluntarily to various veterans' and state mental hospitals, taunting Ness with a series of jeering postcards.

Then on 5 July 1939, fifty-two-year-old alcoholic Frank Dolezal confessed to the murder of Florence Polillo. They had lived together for a while, Dolezal said, and he and Polillo also drank in a tavern frequented by Edward Andrassy and Rose Wallace.

Dolezal claimed that Polillo attacked him with a butcher's knife and in self-defence he hit her and she fell against a bathtub. He cut up her body and dumped it in the alley where she was found. Her head and other missing parts were thrown into Lake Erie.

The transcript of Dolezal's 'confession' was incoherent and before he could go to trial he was found dead in his cell. Apparently, five-foot-eight Dolezal had hanged himself from a hook that was only five feet seven inches from the floor. Gerber's post-mortem revealed that he also had six broken ribs, presumably obtained while in the sheriff's custody. To this day no one thinks Frank Dolezal was the Torso Murderer.

RONALD DOMINIQUE
THE BAYOU STRANGLER

DERIDED AS A LOSER

On 3 October 1998, twenty-seven-year-old hustler Oliver LeBanks went to Rawhide, a popular gay bar in New Orleans. There he met Ronald Dominique, a thirty-four-year-old man who had been constantly derided as a fat slob, a loser and 'a fag' when he was growing up. Nobody liked him – even when he did his Patti LaBelle drag act.

Dominique offered to pay LeBanks for oral sex and they went out to his car. After some mutual fellatio, LeBanks attempted to sodomize Dominique. Dominique did not like being sodomized as he had been brutally raped in jail. When he felt LeBanks trying to penetrate him, he grabbed a tyre iron and beat his brains out, then strangled him with his belt just to make sure.

Now with a body to dispose of, Dominique drove out into the suburb of Kenner. He looked for a place quiet enough to dump the body without being caught, but busy enough for the body to be found easily. Dominique had killed before and reading about the discovery in the newspapers was part of the kick.

On the Earhart Expressway, Dominique passed a state trooper and took care to obey the speed limit. Stopping on a deserted freeway ramp, he pushed LeBanks' body out of the passenger door, dragged it over to the parapet by the belt that was still around its neck and let it drop. Then he headed home. The following day, the body was spotted by a passer-by, who reported it to the sheriff in Jefferson County. The murder was soon linked to that of David Mitchell, a nineteen-year-old African American who had disappeared in nearby St Charles Parish on 13 July 1997. He had been sodomized and drowned before his body had been dumped in a similar fashion. Then on 14 December 1997 the body of twenty-year-old African American Gary Pierre had also been found in St Charles Parish. This time the victim had been raped and strangled.

FBI PROFILE NARROWS SEARCH

Dominique took a break from killing for a while, but on 31 July 1998 thirty-eight-year-old Larry Ranson went missing in St Charles Parish. His body was found dumped and it was found he had been raped and strangled. As the bodies were found close to one another down the same road, the police figured they were the work of the same killer. But there were no clues to work on – no fingerprints, no hairs or fibres and no DNA as the rapist-killer had used a condom. Even a criminal profile – that the killer was poor, white, between his mid-twenties and mid-thirties, ill-educated with poor social skills – was of little help.

However, with the murder of LeBanks in Jefferson Parish Dominique had left some clues. There were tyre prints in the soft sand nearby and there were marks of a ligature around LeBanks' wrists. He had been tied up.

During the post-mortem, it was noted that he had Caucasian hairs on his body. These were collected with tweezers and put into a sealed bag so any DNA would not be contaminated. LeBanks, who had a criminal record of his own, was identified by his fingerprints. Interviews with friends and family led detectives to Rawhide, but no one recalled seeing him.

Two weeks after LeBanks was killed, the partially clothed body of sixteen-year-old African American Joseph Brown turned up in St Charles Parish. A month after that eighteen-year-old Bruce Williams was dumped in Jefferson. Both had been sodomized and strangled. Like LeBanks, Williams had been a hustler and had gone missing from New Orleans. The FBI were called in and their profiler concluded that the killer lived near the airport – which narrowed the search down to around a million men. But he was right. Dominique lived less than fifteen miles from New Orleans International (now Louis Armstrong International).

True to form, the next half-naked body – that of twenty-one-year-old African American hustler Manuel Reed – was found in a rubbish container in Kenner, the New Orleans suburb that is home to the airport, on 30 May 1999. He had been raped and strangled.

Another twenty-one-year-old African American hustler, Angel Mejia, went missing on 30 June 1999. His partially clothed body was found dumped in front of a rubbish bin that night and again he had been sodomized and strangled.

PRESS COVERAGE

While the corpses rendered precious few clues, the press got wind of a serial killer on the prowl. On the mistaken idea that all the bodies had been bare-footed, headline writers dubbed him the 'Shoeless Serial Killer'. In fact, some victims were found wearing shoes and in cases where they weren't the shoes were usually found nearby.

The killer appeared to be goading the police when he dumped the body of thirty-four-year-old African American Mitchell Johnson just feet from where LeBanks had been found. Johnson had last been seen in Kenner on 1 November 1999 and witnesses said that a suspicious-looking white guy in his thirties, with puffy cheeks and receding hair, had been seen cruising the area at the time. A sketch

It was in New Orleans that Ronald Dominique met hustler Oliver LeBanks in a gay bar called Rawhide. Nobody liked Dominique – not even when he did his Patti LaBelle drag act.

of the suspect was drawn up and distributed to both the gay and the mainstream media.

After it was published in the *Times-Picayune,* New Orleans' major newspaper, Dominique quit his job and moved the trailer he lived in from Boutte, fifteen miles west of New Orleans, to Houma, sixty miles to the south-west. He parked it in the yard of his sister Lainie's place on Bayou Blue Road and then he got a job as a labourer and bought a second trailer, which he parked next to the first. Although it was a rundown rural city in the backwoods of Louisiana, Houma had two gay bars.

While Dominique kept a low profile in case someone had seen the sketch in the newspapers, he could not help but advertise his activities. On 1 January 2000, the body of small-time African American criminal Michael Rydell Vincent, aka Chris Vincent, was found hanging from a barbed-wire fence on Highway 7 in neighbouring Lafourche Parish. He had died from asphyxia. There were ligature marks on his wrists, but the autopsy report did not record that he had been raped, though there were abrasions to his scrotum.

ESCAPES JAIL

Dominique had been brought up in Thibodaux, the county seat of Lafourche. At school, he had been ridiculed for being gay, though he had remained firmly in the closet. He claimed that a priest had molested him, but his parents did not believe him. At the age of twenty-one, he pleaded guilty to making dirty phone calls and at thirty he was charged with drunken driving. Two years later, a half-naked young man jumped from Dominique's bedroom window, screaming: 'He's trying to kill me.' The police were called and Dominique was arrested.

During the three months Dominique spent in custody awaiting trial, he claimed to have been raped by other prisoners, splitting his anus. This had to be stitched up, which left him particularly sensitive in that area. A conviction would have meant spending long years in Louisiana's notorious state penitentiary Angola, but Dominique got lucky. The young man who had escaped through his bedroom window could not be found and he was released in November 1996.

While Dominique did not kill again for two years after the murder of Michael Vincent, he did get into trouble with the police. In May 2000, he pleaded guilty to disturbing the peace after a loud public altercation and paid a fine to avoid going to court. He was arrested again in February 2002 for slapping a woman in a Mardi Gras parade and once more he avoided standing trial, this time by signing up for community service. He then took a job as a pizza delivery man with Domino's and spent weekend afternoons calling bingo numbers for senior citizens at the Lions Club. However, preparing to kill again, he towed one of his trailers out to a remote spot in the bayous.

JOB AS METER-READER

Dominique's next victim was a serial sex offender himself. Kenneth Fitzgerald Randolph Jr, a twenty-year-old African American and near neighbour of Dominique, had been arrested three times for having sex with a minor. Although he had a felony conviction, he was on parole when his body, naked except for his socks, was found in the cane fields on 6 October 2002. There were ligature marks around his wrists and throat.

Less than a week later, on the evening of 12 October 2002, small-time criminal Anoka 'Noka' T. Jones told his girlfriend he was going out to smoke a cigarette. The next morning his partially clad body was found in Dominique's old stamping ground of Boutte. He was identified by his fingerprints and an autopsy concluded he had been raped and strangled with a ligature.

The police interviewed his friends and criminal associates, some of whom he owed money to. A couple were picked up, but they were released when the link between the Jones and the Randolph killings was noted. It was becoming clear that a serial killer was at work.

On 24 May 2003, two young men out dirt-track riding found the body of a black man, partially stripped, in a cane field outside Houma. Fingerprints identified him as teenager Datrell Woods, who had repeatedly been in trouble with the law. It was clear he had been dumped there, because there was no dirt on the soles of his socks and his bicycle, jettisoned nearby, had no dirt on the tyres – nor were there any tyre tracks. However, the previous day a witness had seen a white or cream-coloured car coming down the dirt road in the cane field. It had turned on to Highway 56.

Interviews with Datrell's family and friends led nowhere and it soon became clear that he was another victim of the serial killer in the area. Dominique then took another break from murder and was careful not to attract attention, which made things difficult for the police. Meanwhile, he took a job as a meter-reader, which made him familiar with the backroads.

Then under cover of Tropical Storm Matthew, which struck the Louisiana coast on 10 October 2004, Dominique dumped the body of another black male near a pond in the Des Allemands area, twenty miles away. Fingerprints identified him as Larry Matthews, a drug dealer from Thibodaux. Again there were signs that he had been strangled, though he might also have overdosed with cocaine, but the rain from the tropical storm had washed any other clues away.

FIRST WHITE VICTIM

Soon afterwards the naked body of a middle-aged man was found in a storage unit, though none of the fifty people who rented other units at Gator Storage had noticed anything out of the ordinary. The *Houma Daily Courier* quickly linked this corpse with the others. A dragon tattoo on his arm identified the deceased as Michael Barnett, and dental records confirmed this, but what made him different from the other victims was that he was white.

On 20 February 2005, some dirt-track riders came across a body near the small airport the oil companies used outside Houma. The detective who came to the scene recognized the victim as Leon Lirette, a friend of Noka Jones. He had been very drunk when he was strangled. A white guy with a maroon car was seen near where the body had been dumped.

Another body was found in a wood in Lafourche Parish on 9 April 2005. The victim was identified as thirty-two-year-old African American August Terrell Watkins from Houma, who was homeless after being forced to move out by his former girlfriend, Elizabeth Jones. She said that a white man in a white truck had been looking for him. His brother said that the white man was a friend of Terrell's. Jones said that she had later seen Terrell's new girlfriend Winter Lewis in the white truck with the white man, but this line of investigation went nowhere.

Up until that point all of the State of Louisiana's resources had been used to track down Derrick Todd Lee, aka The Baton Rouge Serial Killer. He was a black man killing white co-eds, which commanded media attention, whereas a white man killing black, mainly gay, men did not – even though his body count was more than double. Nevertheless, with bodies spread across the jurisdiction of four parishes, the authorities finally agreed to form a police task force. Fourteen cops drawn from the parishes, the state and the FBI were put on the case.

POLICE TASK FORCE FORMED

Reviewing the fifteen murders, it was clear that the killer was currently operating in Terrebonne Parish, whose parish seat was Houma. As the police got to work the partially clad body of twenty-three-year-old Kurt Cunningham was found floating in a ditch in Lafourche Parish. He was white and lived in Thibodaux. Last seen in Houma on 8 April, he was not found until twenty days later. The body was so badly decomposed that the cause of death could not be established.

Then on 2 July 2005 the body of twenty-eight-year-old African American Alonzo Hogan was found in a cane field in St Charles Parish off Highway 306. He was fully clothed, but the autopsy ascertained that he had been sodomized and strangled. The body of seventeen-year-old African American and Houma resident Wayne Smith was then found fully clothed in a ditch off Grand Caillou Road. The cause of death could not be determined.

The task force was hard at work on these cases when they were closed down by Hurricane Katrina, which hit on 28 August 2005. When the flood waters subsided, the body of African America Chris DeVille was found fully clothed in a ditch off Highway 1 in Assumption Parish. He was forty years old. Unlike the other victims, who had all been involved in crime in one way or another, DeVille came from a 'respectable' family. His brother was even a cop. The body had been eaten by rats.

'When we found him he was nothing. Nothing but bones,' said his sister. 'We had to bury bones.'

PAROLEE ESCAPES KILLER

Then the police got lucky. After serving time for a minor drug offence, John Banning was out on parole and by chance his parole officer Tom Lambert was a member of the task force. Banning was walking along when Dominique pulled up beside him and asked if he wanted a beer. Then he pulled out the picture of an attractive white woman.

'How'd you like to f**k this white girl?' he asked. 'She'd really like to make it with a guy like you.'

This was Dominique's standard practice with a straight guy. There were six or seven of them among his victims. Banning got in and Dominique drove him to Bayou Blue Road.

'Don't be surprised that I want to tie you up,' said Dominique. Then he volunteered: 'There's a stigma about being gay.'

Dominique pulled into his sister's yard and they went into his trailer there.

'I'll tie you up now,' Dominique told Banning. 'Take off your clothes.'

He would say that the woman the man was to have sex with had been raped, hurt, so he had to be tied up before they started. Normally, when Dominique got the man bound hand and foot, he would tell them that it was not true, that there was no woman. Then he raped and murdered them.

Banning was suspicious. He looked around and saw the trailer was a mess, full of old clothes and stacks of gay porn, so he made a dash for the door. Dominique did not attempt to stop him.

DNA MATCH NOT CLOSE ENOUGH

Lambert figured that some of his parolees had a similar profile to the killer's victims, so he questioned them for clues. Banning told him of his encounter with a mysterious white guy who had wanted to tie him up. He led the police to Bayou Blue Road and the trailer that belonged to Ronald J. Dominique.

Dominique agreed to accompany them to their headquarters, where they told him of Banning's complaint, but he said the bondage was just part of a sex game. Nevertheless, he consented to provide DNA samples. Then they drove him back to his trailer. Back at headquarters, detectives pulled up his record. Among the charges that had been dropped were two counts of sodomy with men. But while they were building a case there would be more victims.

Twenty-one-year-old Nick Pellegrin was working on his house when Dominique arrived to read the meter. Pellegrin, who was short of money, agreed to go out with Dominique after he had finished work, to have some 'fun'. His body was found on 9 November 2005. He had been raped and strangled, and there were ligature marks around his wrists. The police had had the killer within their grasp, yet he had killed again.

A few days later, the lab called saying that they had a DNA match between Dominique and the chest hairs found on Oliver LeBanks' body. But it was a mitochondrial match. Mitochondrial DNA is inherited solely from the mother, so it narrows the match only to members of the family and not to a specific individual. Even so, Dominique was put under 24/7 surveillance.

There was another DNA match with semen left in Angel Mejia's rectum, but again it was a mitochondrial match – so not enough to convince a jury 'beyond reasonable doubt'.

EIGHT LIFE SENTENCES

Short of funds, the local cops took to following Dominique on their own time, but on 15 October 2006 he managed to shake his tail. That day twenty-seven-year-old Christopher Sutterfield disappeared after visiting friends in Houma. His body was dumped along Highway 69 in Iberville Parish near Baton Rouge. It was clear from the marks on his body that Dominique had killed again.

Frustrated, the police asked a judge to issue an arrest warrant on Ronald J. Dominique for two first-degree murders – those of Oliver LeBanks and Manuel Reed. By this time, his sister was fed up with the surveillance and wanted no trouble with the police, so Dominique had to move to the Bunkhouse, a flophouse in Houma used by oil-rig workers. He was arrested there on 1 December 2006.

Dominique quickly confessed to the two murders – and to the murder of Michael Vincent – and then he agreed to take the police to all twenty-three dump sites. He pleaded guilty to eight of the murders, in exchange for a life sentence rather than suffer the death penalty, and he also admitted that he had raped all of his victims before he had strangled them, though he released those who did not consent to being tied up.

On 23 September 2008, Ronald Dominique was sentenced to eight life sentences and was sent to the Louisiana State Penitentiary at Angola – the very last place he wanted to end up – where he will remain for the rest of his life.

SEAN VINCENT GILLIS
THE OTHER BATON ROUGE SERIAL KILLER

DERRICK TODD LEE FAN

Gillis was a great fan of murder. On the internet, he graduated from watching porn to viewing crime-scene sites that showed the bodies of dead women. He also followed the murderous career of his rival Derrick Todd Lee, whom the press dubbed 'The Baton Rouge Serial Killer'.

Lee had a long rap sheet that included being a Peeping Tom, stalking, vandalism, drunk driving, disturbing the peace, robbery, burglary, criminal trespass, domestic violence, assault and even attempted murder, which brought him regularly into contact with the authorities. Meanwhile, after 1992, when he was aged twenty-four, Lee began a series of murders that included at least seven white women. The killer was mistakenly thought to have been white, because most serial killers were white males. At that time, it was mistakenly thought in the United States that serial killers were racially selective – that is, white killers killed white victims, black killers killed black victims. However, skin left under the fingernails of twenty-one-year-old Geralyn Barr DeSoto, found stabbed to death on 14 January 2002, convinced the cops they were looking for a black man. DNA also linked the perpetrator to other murders.

In July that year, Lee was disturbed during the beating and attempted rape of Dianne Alexander. Having survived the attack, she was able to describe her attacker to a police sketch artist, but Lee continued killing. On 3 March 2003, twenty-six-year-old Carrie Lynn Yoder was abducted and her body was found ten days later. Suspected of murdering twenty-eight-year-old Randi Mebruer, Lee was forced to give a DNA sample, but he then fled. On 27 May 2003, he was arrested in Atlanta. Convicted on two counts of murder, Lee was sent to death row in Angola jail, but he died of heart disease before he could be executed.

ANGRY YOUNG BOY

While Lee was in custody Gillis continued killing, so he became 'The Other Baton Rouge Serial Killer'. Born in 1962, Gillis was said to have been an exemplary child until one day his mother returned home to find his alcoholic father holding a gun to his head and threatening to kill them both. Disarmed, he was remanded to a mental hospital.

Although his father was out of the picture, his mother took him to see his paternal grandparents regularly and he had a good relationship with them. But while his mother described him as a normal boy, who was very well-behaved, he gave the other kids in the neighbourhood 'the willies'.

At school he found good friends and his gang began smoking marijuana and became interested in Satanism. He enjoyed having a secret life, hidden from his doting mother, but others noticed disturbing signs. Neighbour Carolyn Clay recalled:

> About three in the morning, I awoke to a loud noise coming from their yard. Sean was in the front yard beating wildly on some garbage cans. He told another neighbour that he was frustrated because he didn't have a girlfriend.

He was prone to fits of anger like that. He was an angry young boy.

His mother did not see that side of him. At seventeen he was reunited with his father and was disturbed to discover that he was a homosexual and even more horrified by his collection of gay pornography. After that, he refused to visit his father in his new home in California. Soon he began to build a rap sheet of minor crimes.

GIRLFRIEND MOVES IN

In 1992, his mother took a job with a TV company in Atlanta, Georgia, but Gillis refused to accompany her and stayed behind in their house in Baton Rouge. Neighbours again remarked on his peculiar behaviour. He was once seen in the garden on all fours, howling at the moon, and was found peeping into a local lady's house pretending to be looking for his cat. The police were then called.

Terri Lemoine, who worked in a local convenience store, knew nothing of this. She was attracted to him, though she found him a little nerdy, and she decided that if she was going to have a serious relationship with him she must put him to the test. One day, during an argument, she seized the chance to slap his face. With tears in his eyes, he insisted that violence should play no part in their relationship. He had no such reservations outside it.

At around this time, Gillis broke into a nearby retirement home with the intention of raping eighty-two-year-old Ann Bryan. When she started screaming, he cut her throat, stabbed her forty-seven times in the face and then began slashing her breasts, body and genitals. The nurse who came to administer her medication the next morning found her nearly decapitated and disembowelled.

When Terri moved in with Gillis she noticed that he was addicted to pornography and was appalled when he tried to show her websites featuring the victims of sex killers. What she did not know was that when she was out working at night he was cruising Baton Rouge's rough north side, looking for women.

Gillis spotted fifty-two-year-old Hardee Moseley Schmidt out jogging on the south side of Baton Rouge and began stalking her. It would be three weeks before he pounced. He ran into her with his car and knocked her into a ditch.

BODY ON BACK SEAT

On 4 January 1999 he picked up thirty-year-old prostitute Katherine Hall. Once she was in his car, he lassoed her with a plastic cable tie, stripped her, stabbed her, had sex with her corpse, mutilated her and dumped her bloody body in plain sight under a 'dead end' sign.

Four months later, he spotted fifty-two-year-old Hardee Moseley Schmidt out jogging on the south side of Baton Rouge and began stalking her. It would be three weeks before he pounced. Then at 6.30 a.m. on Sunday 30 May, he ran into her with his car and knocked her into a ditch. With a cable tie around her neck, he dragged her into his car, drove her to an isolated spot, raped her, killed her and mutilated her body, which he loaded into the boot of his vehicle. When he went to pick up Terri from work, she said she noticed a funny smell, but Gillis said that he had run over a squirrel and would wash the car. Later he dumped Hardee Schmidt's naked body in a bayou near the highway, where it was spotted by a cyclist the next day.

On 12 November 1999, he picked up thirty-six-year-old Joyce Williams in the Scotlandville district of Baton Rouge, took her across the Mississippi and strangled her in a cane field near Port Allen. He took her body home to dismember it, eating some of the skin and her severed nipples. Liking the look of her legs, he cut one of them off and kept it. When he picked up Terri from work Joyce Williams' body was on the back seat, but he disposed of it the next day.

Though he liked to dump his victims' bodies in plain sight, hers was not found until January 2000. That same month, he killed fifty-two-year-old Lillian Robinson. He did not have time to mutilate her body before Terri finished work, but he toyed with it and put his penis in her mouth. Again, her naked body was dumped in a bayou, where it was found by an angler a month later.

KILLS SOMEONE HE KNOWS

Some months later, in late October 2000, he was visiting his god-daughter in Lafayette when he saw thirty-eight-year-old prostitute Marilyn Nevils. After picking her up, he strangled her, took her body home and had a shower with it. He then dumped the body on a levee on the banks of the Mississippi, three miles from his home, where it was found by a man walking in the woods.

Gillis then took a break from killing, though his interest did not diminish. He kept a file on his computer named 'DTL', which contained everything he could find on the doings of Derrick Todd Lee, whom he feared might outdo him.

Meanwhile, Gillis renewed his friendship with a forty-five-year-old divorcee named Johnnie Mae Williams and her three children. Ten years earlier, she had been the cleaner at the Gillis house and now she was a crackhead who supported her habit by prostitution. It is rare for a serial killer to kill someone they know, but in October 2003 he drove her to a secluded area where he beat her, raped her and murdered her, cutting off her hands. Then he posed her mutilated body in various positions and photographed it, leaving it exposed on top of a bank.

On 26 February 2004 Gillis picked up yet another hooker, forty-three-year-old prostitute Donna Johnston. She, too, was a mother and crack addict and that night she was drunk and in no state to put up any resistance. They were near his home when he strangled her, before going about his butchery. He slashed her breasts and cut off a nipple, which he ate, and then he excised a tattoo as a souvenir and cut off her left arm at the elbow. It thought he took this home with him in order to use the hand as a masturbation aid. He took fifty photographs of her body and then took it to another location, where he left it in an obscene pose.

PARTNER KNEW NOTHING

With Lee now under lock and key, the police formed a new task force to hunt The Other Baton Rouge Serial Killer. When dumping two of his victims he had left tyre tracks and with the help of Goodyear the police were able to identify the tyre, getting a list of everyone in Baton Rouge who had bought similar ones. DNA swabs were taken from everyone on that list, including Gillis. When his DNA matched samples from the crime scenes, Gillis was arrested at home in front of Terri, who insisted that they had got the wrong man.

'Don't you realize that you are living with a serial killer?' a policeman asked.

She could not believe that the man she had taken to be a mild-mannered nerd had killed eight women – until he admitted it, that is. All Gillis could find to say to Terri was 'sorry'.

Searching their home, the police took away large knives, a machete, a fourteen-inch bayonet, a hacksaw and several other saws, along with photographs of his victims and four computers. On the hard drives, they found files named 'Best of Snuff', 'Beheading and Hangings', 'Manson Murders' and 'DLT'. He also kept a library of books about serial killers.

In addition, the police had written evidence. Gillis had written to Tammie Purpera, a friend of Donna Johnston's who was dying of AIDS, saying:

> Your friend died quickly. She was so far gone that night that I really do not think she even knew what was happening to her. She was so drunk it only took about a minute and a half to succumb to unconsciousness and then death. Honestly, her last words were, 'I can't breathe'. I still puzzle over the post-mortem dismemberment and cutting. There must be something deep in my subconscious that really needs that kind of macabre action.

'I WAS PURE EVIL'

He went on to say that he really didn't 'know what the hell is wrong with me. ... I was in a real bad place. I was pure evil that night. No love, no compassion, no faith, no mercy, no hope.'

Under interrogation, he admitted that he knew that what he was doing was wrong but he went ahead anyway, perhaps because he had 'hated God for a long time'.

In August 2007, Gillis pleaded guilty to the second-degree murder of Joyce Williams and was sentenced to life. Then in July 2008 he was found guilty of the murder of Donna Johnston and was sentenced to life in prison without parole, after the jury was deadlocked over the death penalty.

On 17 February 2009, Gillis also pleaded guilty to the murder of Marilyn Nevils and was given another life sentence. She had disappeared in Lafayette and the Baton Rouge police did not even know she was missing until Gillis admitted murdering her.

JOEL RIFKIN

THE LONG ISLAND SERIAL KILLER

TERRIBLE SMELL

At around three o'clock on the morning of 28 June 1993, a battered black and tan Mazda pickup truck was travelling down the Southern State Parkway in Nassau County, Long Island. It had a bumper sticker that said 'Sticks and Stones May Break My Bones, but Whips and Chains Excite Me', and its rear licence plate was missing, a minor traffic violation.

This was spotted by two state troopers, Sean Ruane and Deborah Spaargaren. They flicked on their flashing lights and followed the truck, but its driver did not speed up, nor did he pull over. He simply ignored them. The siren did not help, nor did an order to stop over the loudhailer.

After ten minutes' low-speed pursuit, Ruane and Spaargaren called for backup. When three more patrol cars joined the pursuers, the pickup suddenly speeded up, then veered off the road and into a utility pole.

Out of the crippled truck stepped Joel Rifkin with his hands up.

'I know I had a plate on when I left home,' he told Ruane. 'It's always a 25-cent part.'

But Ruane and Spaargaren were not concerned so much with that. It was the terrible smell. 'I've smelled it before,' said Ruane. 'It's not something you can forget.'

Under a tarpaulin in the back of the pickup, they found the dead body of a woman. Rifkin explained: 'I picked up this hooker near Allen Street in Manhattan. We had an arrangement for sex, but things got out of hand. I strangled her.'

Later asked why, he said: 'I don't know.'

The victim was twenty-two-year-old methadone user Tiffany Bresciani, whom he had picked up several days earlier. Once he had a detailed confession, senior investigator C. Thomas Capers asked Rifkin if he had killed any more people. Rifkin did not reply.

'More than ten? More than twenty?' asked Capers.

'One or a hundred, it doesn't make any difference,' said Rifkin.

Capers changed tack.

'You want these people to have a proper burial, don't you?' he said. Then Rifkin opened up. Over the next few hours he admitted to seventeen murders, giving details of the victims and drawing maps showing where he had dumped their bodies.

Evidence had piled up in his home, where he kept bras, panties, jewellery, credit cards, driving licences and other mementoes, along with cuttings about Arthur Shawcross, the Genesee River Killer, who killed some fourteen people in upstate New York between 1972 and 1989. There was also a book about the Green River Killer, who had yet to be apprehended in Washington State. None of his family or neighbours had suspected a thing.

BULLIED AT SCHOOL

Born in 1959, Joel had been adopted when he was just three weeks old. His adoptive father Bernard Rifkin was a structural engineer and his wife Jeanne was a homemaker and keen gardener. They were so pleased with their new child that, three years later, they adopted another one – a daughter named Jan.

Although Joel had an IQ of 128 he was dyslexic, leading his teachers to believe that he was mentally impaired. He was no good at arithmetic or sport either and as his father was good at both it made him feel inferior. Bernard was a pillar of society and a war hero, having been a GI who had fought in the Second World War, though he never talked about it. Then at the age of eleven Joel learned that he was adopted, which made him feel further alienated.

At school he was bullied mercilessly and classmates called him 'The Turtle', because of his hunched posture and slow gait. Shunned by his peers, he became a loner. His only friend was his mother. He joined her in the garden and learned the Latin names of the plants, becoming an avid collector of rocks and fossils and sharing her passion for photography. But from an early age he had secret graphic sexual fantasies that involved violence.

ADDICTION TO PROSTITUTES

While his peers went off to university, he went to the local community college, which offered nothing in the way of student life, leaving him more isolated than ever. Girlfriends were a problem. Determined to have some sexual experience, he began patronizing local prostitutes.

When he went on to college at Brockport, near Rochester in upstate New York, he lived briefly with a girlfriend. However, he was depressed and lethargic and she soon got tired of his slovenly ways and moved out, even though she had no idea that he was still using prostitutes behind her back. Unprotected sex was common in that period and he caught herpes, which was endemic at the time.

Although he showed promise as a photographer, Rifkin dropped out of college and returned home to Long Island. He went to work in a warehouse, but his inability to handle figures meant that he missed out on promotion and he was eventually fired.

After that he moved into a squat with a middle-aged prostitute, who was both a drunk and a junkie. The relationship, such as it was, ended when she stole money and a camera from him. Rifkin moved back home again and, at his father's insistence, went back to college to study biology, learning dissection as part of the course. But he dropped out once more after his father, who had been diagnosed with terminal cancer, committed suicide.

Rifkin's addiction to prostitutes got him into trouble when he was arrested for soliciting a plain-clothes cop. Nevertheless, he continued using hookers, though it drove him deep into debt. They frequently ripped him off by asking him to front money to buy drugs and then they disappeared or had someone purporting to be their boyfriend turn up while they were still undressing. Sometimes the same girl would con him in the same way more than once.

FIRST MURDER

By the time he started killing prostitutes, he reckoned that he had been with over three hundred of them – and had left them unharmed, though he did spice up the sex by fantasizing about strangling them. One night in March 1989, when his mother was away on holiday, he picked up a hooker called Susie in the East Village and took her home. After they had had sex, she wanted him to take her out to buy drugs, which annoyed him. He picked up an old howitzer shell he had recently bought at a flea market and beat her with it until he thought she was dead.

Sudden she rose up and bit his finger to the bone. He pinned her down until she died – he was not sure if it was from smothering or strangulation – and then he tidied up and went to bed. Waking after a few hours, he stuffed Susie's body into a large plastic bag and dragged it into the cellar, where he cut her up. He pulled her teeth out with a pair of pliers and pushed her head into an empty paint can. The other body parts were collected in rubbish bags, which he threw into the back of his pickup before taking off. He left the head and some of the body parts spread around in a wooded area in New Jersey and then he drove back to Manhattan and dumped the rest in the East River.

Rifkin's addiction to prostitutes got him into trouble when he was arrested for soliciting a plain-clothes cop. By the time he started killing prostitutes, he reckoned he had been with over 300 of them.

A week later, Rifkin heard on the radio that Susie's head had been found. He panicked, but despite an extensive investigation the police found nothing to connect her murder to him. Regardless of the danger, he took the risk of returning to the East Village to pick up more prostitutes, but vowed not to kill again.

IRRESISTIBLE URGE TO KILL

Eighteen months later, his mother went on holiday once more and he took another hooker back to the house. She stole some of his mother's jewellery and he then had to admit what he had done when his mother returned. Another hooker named Charlene retrieved some of the stolen jewellery from a crack house. They became friends and he drove her to detox and to see her kid.

Next time his mother went away he took another hooker named Julie Blackbird home and spent the night resisting the urge to kill her. In the morning, they went to the ATM so he could pay her, but it would not let him withdraw the funds. They would have to wait until the bank opened. Back at the house he could resist no longer, so he grabbed a heavy piece of wood and bludgeoned her to death.

He put her body in the basement before going to sleep and, when he woke, he went to a DIY warehouse and bought some cement. Resisting the urge to have sex with the corpse – he had read of the exploits of Ted Bundy and the Green River Killer, who were both necrophiliacs – he cut the body up and encased the parts in cement, before dumping them in the Hudson River. While he was determined that Julie would never be found, he kept some of her jewellery and other property and even her diary. From then on, he kept souvenirs from most of his victims. On his way to dump Julie, he stopped to talk to other prostitutes, debating whether he should pick one up even though he had body parts in the car.

REALIZED HE HAD A PROBLEM

After Julie Blackbird's murder he took other women home, who left in the morning unharmed. But then in July 1991 it was the turn of thirty-one-year-old Barbara Jacobs. Once he got her home, he spent time debating whether to kill her. Deciding that he would, he began clubbing her but she fought back. In the struggle he strangled her and then dragged her into the basement, but he found that this time he could not cut the body up. Instead, he wrapped her corpse in plastic, put it in a cardboard box and dumped it in the Hudson. On the way home he stopped in the city to pick up a prostitute for oral sex.

Driving back out to Long Island, he heard on the car radio that Barbara Jacobs' body had been found. This time he didn't panic but instead he was reflective.

'After the third, I realized that this was a problem,' he said later. 'It's not gonna go away.'

He had got away with three murders, but sooner or later he was going to slip up and get caught. Curiously, his main concern was the shame that this would bring on his dead father. The victims themselves, as far as he was concerned, were not human beings but rather like casualties in a war. He briefly considered counselling, but realized that admitting murder fell outside the ambit of the normal doctor–patient privilege.

VICTIM 'WANTED TO DIE'

On Labor Day weekend in 1991, Rifkin had no particular urge to kill, though it was in the back of his mind as he visited the areas of Queens, Brooklyn and Manhattan, where he usually picked up prostitutes. After finding no one of interest in his price range, he was heading home when he spotted Mary Ellen DeLuca, a twenty-two-year-old junkie. He picked her up for quick sex before he finished for the night, but she wanted drugs, so he drove her around several crack houses, spending $150 on her over the next ten hours. When he finally got her to a motel, she wanted to get high again before they had sex and, while this was going on, asking whether he had finished. Afterwards, she said she hated her life and wanted to end it. He asked if she really wanted to die and when she said she did he got on top of her and strangled her.

Buying a trunk from a nearby store, he put her body in it. Then he drove upstate and dumped it, naked except for a bra, at a picnic site near West Point. The badly decomposed corpse of a Jane Doe was found weeks later, while the DeLuca family fretted and the police visited crack houses looking for Mary Ellen.

DUMPS BODIES IN RIVER

Rifkin continued entertaining himself with prostitutes without harming them, though murder was always in the back of his mind. One afternoon, just an hour after having one woman, he picked up thirty-one-year-old Korean-born Yun Lee, whom he had been with before. Normally he was content with oral sex, but that day he wanted full intercourse. They drove to a parking lot on the East River, but he found he could not maintain an erection – possibly because he had had sex only an hour before. This made him angry and he grabbed Yun Lee by the throat and killed her.

He drove back to Long Island with her dead body on the passenger seat beside him, even though it was daylight. At the time he was running a failing landscape gardening company, so he got the trunk he had used for Mary Ellen DeLuca out of the store there and put Yun Lee in it. With the trunk on the back of his pickup, he drove to the South Bronx and dropped it in the Harlem River. The trunk with the body in it was found floating in the river in late September.

Perhaps disturbed by killing a woman he had known, Joel checked his stride, but only briefly. Just before Christmas, he picked up a woman whose name he did not recall and strangled her in his truck while she was performing oral sex. He later pleaded guilty to murdering this particular Jane Doe. He then drove back to Long Island with her body on the front seat. After storing his anonymous victim's body under a tarpaulin on his landscape gardening lot overnight, he stuffed it into an oil drum and dropped it in the river. He was then confronted by two patrolmen who thought he was doing some illegal dumping, but he insisted that he was scavenging parts from the cars dumped in the area.

On the day after Christmas he spotted twenty-eight-year-old Lorraine Orvieto, a former cheerleader with mental health issues and a crack habit, in Bay Shore, Long Island. Again he strangled her while she was performing oral sex. In her handbag he found a bottle of the anti-HIV drug AZT, which he kept as a memento. The fact that he might have contracted AIDS did not bother him. Her body was also stuffed into an oil drum and this time he dumped it in an inlet at Coney Island, where it was found by a fisherman in July 1992. He felt no guilt about her murder, saying that her life was not worth living and he had saved others from catching AIDS from her. He even blamed her parents for her mental health problems.

MURDERS IN DOUBLE FIGURES

In early January 1992 he picked up thirty-nine-year-old Mary Ann Holloman and took her to the parking lot where he had killed Yun Lee. By now, strangling a girl while she was giving him oral sex had become automatic. She fought back, punching and scratching, but he overpowered her and her body went into the customary oil drum, which was dumped into Coney Island Creek.

The next girl he picked up fought him off when he tried to strangle her – and she even chastised him for trying to hurt working girls. Then twenty-five-year-old Iris Sanchez lost her life on the back seat of his mother's car on Mother's Day weekend. Rifkin insisted that he ejaculated during the act of strangulation, not after his victim was dead, because he was determined not to be thought a necrophiliac like Bundy. Men were fishing in the creek behind Kennedy airport, so instead of dumping Iris Sanchez in the water he left her body hidden under a mattress, after taking her ring, watch and bracelet.

The next to die was thirty-three-year-old mother of three Anna Lopez, on 25 March 1992. Troubled since adolescence, she had attempted suicide before sliding into crack addiction. Rifkin left her body on the front seat of the car while he searched for somewhere to dump her, even stopping for petrol along the way. He then dumped her body in a wood north of New York, where it was found a week later. Rifkin had taken an earring as a souvenir and the other one was left with the body. This would eventually link him to the murder.

With twenty-one-year-old Violet O'Neill he reverted to his earlier pattern – taking her home to Long Island before strangling her after sex and dismembering her. Bits of her body were found in the Hudson.

Rifkin had seen thirty-one-year-old Mary Katherine Williams, a cheerleader and actress before succumbing to drugs, twice before he killed her and had had 'a great time'. But somehow, on their third meeting, she bent the gear stick in his mother's car, so he decided that she had to die. He then had trouble starting the car and sat there for a time with her dead body. Eventually the car started and her body was found in the snow in a cul-de-sac in Yorktown. Again he kept some jewellery.

Though the murders were now well into double figures, Rifkin claimed that he had tried to stop killing. He reckoned that if he got girls' phone numbers and arranged to have sex with them at their home or somewhere else it was more likely that there would be someone to protect them, so it would be safer for them. However, he did not have the money for this kind of service and the junkies he went with were seldom that organized. As it was, he did not always have to kill. One night he planned to murder one of his regular girls, but after sex in a secluded spot he drove her back to where he had found her.

MOTHER TAKES CORPSE SHOPPING

Like Mary Williams, twenty-three-year-old Jenny Soto had ambitions which were hobbled by her involvement in drugs. Rifkin picked her up in November 1992, had sex with her in his pickup and then strangled her. She fought back ferociously, breaking all her fingernails before he broke her neck and this time he took a haul of mementoes – her bra and panties, ID card, gold earrings and syringe. Her body was dropped in the Harlem River where it was found a few days later and initially her boyfriend, who had recently been paroled, was blamed.

In New York, Rifkin picked up twenty-eight-year-old Leah Evans, who unusually for him had no record of prostitution or drug addiction. She did not want to have sex in the car park where he took her so suggested going to a girlfriend's house. Thinking he was getting the runaround, he strangled her and then buried her in a shallow grave in a wood at the eastern end of Long Island. Four months later, nature lovers spotted her hand sticking out of the soil.

Twenty-eight-year-old mother of two Lauren Marquez was an advanced drug addict. Rifkin had talked to her before but her addiction had left her in such a bad state that he had never picked her up. When he did, he did not bother having sex with her but just strangled her and dumped her body near where Leah Evans had been buried.

The discovery of these two bodies close together merited coverage in the Long Island newspaper *Newsday* and on the local TV station, but this did not discourage Rifkin.

In June he picked up Tiffany Bresciani in the East Village. Her ambition to be a serious dancer had slipped when she became addicted to cocaine and methadone and she then went to work as an exotic dancer at the Big Top Lounge on Eighth Avenue, where Rikfin had seen her, turning tricks on the side.

She agreed to take $20 for straight sex and he drove her to the *New York Post*'s parking lot. First he found he could not get an erection and then they were disturbed by a man parking next to them, so he strangled her, even though the man was doing tai chi just feet away. He drove back to Long Island with her naked body on the back seat, even stopping to pick up a patio window on the way, and then visited a store. After wrapping Tiffany's body in a tarpaulin, he put it in the boot and then his mother took the car to go shopping. When she returned Rifkin drove her to work and then put Tiffany's body in the garage, where it was nearly found by his sister who was looking for a wheelbarrow. He then set about fixing his truck, which had broken down.

200 YEARS IN JAIL

After three days, Rifkin had decided on a place to dump the body. It was about fifteen miles from his home. He was on his way there when he was spotted by state troopers Ruane and Spaargaren. Then more police turned up and the high-speed chase began.

In custody, Rifkin admitted murdering seventeen women. He only stopped talking when a lawyer arrived and halted the interrogation. Otherwise, it was thought, he would have confessed to more. As it was, his confession to sixteen of the murders was inadmissible as a lawyer had not been present. Nevertheless, Rikfin had volunteered that he had killed Tiffany Bresciani, so that charge stood. He then pleaded not guilty but the jury disagreed.

At subsequent trials in different jurisdictions Rifkin did not contest the charges and pleaded guilty. He would have to serve two hundred years before he was eligible for parole. In prison, he was kept in solitary confinement for his own protection.

LOREN HERZOG AND WESLEY SHERMANTINE

THE SPEED FREAK KILLERS

KILLERS IN THE MAKING

California's Central Valley is an agricultural area of the state that has little to do with Los Angeles and Southern California, or San Francisco and the Bay Area. In the 1970s, as well as producing fruit and vegetables, it became known for the production and distribution of crystal meth. With it came an attendant wave of crime.

Loren Herzog was born to a middle-class family in the town of Linden on 8 December 1965. He was a good-looking young man, who was rarely without a girlfriend. In the 1980s, he married and started a family, but there was another side to him. The words 'Made and Fueled by Hate and Restrained by Reality' were tattooed along his left leg and 'Made the Devil Do It' appeared on his right foot.

His friend Wesley Shermantine, born on 24 February 1966, came from a well-off family who spoiled him. The two friends went through elementary and high school together. While Herzog was docile and compliant, Shermantine was loud and aggressive. He would fight with other boys, or intimidate them, and answer back to teachers. Herzog claimed to have been bullied by Shermantine since nursery school and to have lived in fear of him ever since. Nevertheless, the bond between them endured, because if anyone else tried to bully mild-mannered Herzog, Shermantine would intervene in his defence.

The Shermantine clan had quite a reputation in the area. They relished conflict and those who accused them of intimidation or assault usually dropped the charges. Wesley's mother was a prime example. When one of her husband's customers was late paying a bill, she took a bulldozer and knocked down the debtor's house. The victim did not file a complaint and though the police knew who was responsible the matter ended there.

Mrs Shermantine was also a drinker and often heaped verbal abuse on her children, although she was not above hitting them too. But a particular punishment was devised for Wesley. He was made to stand still while his parents shot at his feet, even for trivial offences.

At sixteen, when Shermantine got his driving licence, his parents bought him a new car. The first thing he did was go around to pick up Herzog and they drove around San Joaquin County showing off the shiny vehicle. Both boys had a love of the outdoors and Wesley's father had taught them how to hunt. This was commonplace for boys brought up in rural California, though Shermantine would sometimes talk about the 'ultimate kill' – hunting humans. They also collected guns and knives.

As they grew up they began drinking heavily in the nearby Linden Inn, where they soon progressed to crystal meth. They then became drug dealers and earned a reputation as a couple of thugs. Shermantine's sister Dolly said Herzog had entered her bedroom one night when he was drunk and raped her. No one in the family would listen to her. Later she said Wesley had raped her too, but that also fell on deaf ears.

California's Central Valley is an agricultural area. In the late 1970s, as well as providing fruit and vegetables, it was known for producing crystal meth and the wave of crime that came with it.

CRYSTAL METH-FUELLED KILLINGS

By the time they left high school in 1984 both Shermantine and Herzog were addicted to crystal meth. They had graduated from snorting the powder to smoking it and those around them noticed the change in their behaviour. Their increasing consumption brought them into contact with high-level drug dealers and prostitutes, who were offered drugs free or at a knock-down price for their services. The women were then supposed to do whatever the men demanded once they got high. It is thought that this was when they started killing. If a woman refused them, she would be killed and disposed of by being dropped down an old well. This killing spree was said to have started in September 1984, though some suspected that Shermantine started killing on his own two years earlier.

That September, Herzog and Shermantine went up to the new casino at Lake Tahoe, but they lost all their money and ran out of meth. They knew no one they could score off up there, so after they had scraped together enough money for a drink they set off back to San Joaquin County. On the way, they came across forty-one-year-old Henry Howell, a drunk driver who had pulled over to sleep it off.

According to Herzog, Shermantine pulled over, took a rifle from the boot of the car, shot Howell dead and then robbed him – though it might have been Herzog himself who had pulled the trigger. The body was found soon enough, but there were few clues on which to build an investigation.

A couple of months later, on the night of 26 November, Herzog and Shermantine were taking a drive after drinking and getting high on meth when they saw a 1982 Pontiac parked on a rural road, with two men in it. They pulled up behind and the two of them got out with shotguns. Shermantine then blasted one of the men, killing him. Herzog said that after that Shermantine pulled the other man from the car and then killed him using his friend's gun. It was thought unlikely that Shermantine would have switched guns like that, so they must have killed one man each. The two then celebrated the killings with more beer and meth.

When the bodies were found the next day, the victims were identified as thirty-one-year-old Paul Cavanaugh and thirty-five-year-old Howard King. At the time, the investigation seemed to stutter to a halt, but the killers had left behind a crucial clue – a tyre print from Shermantine's truck, which would eventually be used in evidence against them.

The killers' next victim was nineteen-year-old Kimberly Billy, who went missing from Stockton, ten miles from Linden, on 11 December 1984. It is thought that Herzog approached her and then Shermantine raped and killed her, after which her body was dropped down one of the mine shafts that pockmarked the surrounding area.

Some months later, on 29 August 1985, sixteen-year-old JoAnn Hobson disappeared from San Joaquin. No one suspected that the Speed Freak Killers, as they became known, were involved until Shermantine, then on death row, wrote to her parents saying that Herzog and an accomplice named 'Jason' had killed her and thrown her body down a well.

He later wrote to a reporter, saying that they would find JoAnn's body with that of an unidentified pregnant black woman. Shermantine also said that Herzog hung out in Modesto, twenty-five miles from Linden, and it was thought that they may have killed others in that area. Of course, the letters could have just been a cruel hoax, designed to distress JoAnn's family.

MURDER ANNIVERSARY CELEBRATION

The following month, Herzog and Shermantine wanted to celebrate the anniversary of their first murder together. High on booze and meth they drove into Stockton, where they met twenty-four-year-old Robin Armtrout, who supported her drug habit with prostitution. In a field outside Linden they all did drugs. Herzog said that Shermantine started stabbing Armtrout while he was having sex with her. Others think that it was Herzog who killed her. They left her naked and mutilated body face down in a creek. Although they had left biological evidence, Herzog and Shermantine were never considered serious suspects and were not even interviewed.

Although sixteen-year-old Chevelle 'Chevy' Wheeler seemed to have grown out of her rebellious phase, on 7 October 1985 she told friends she was going to skip school and hang out with a boy at Valley Springs in Calaveras County. She was overheard talking to a 'Wes', so it was clear that her date was with Wesley Shermantine. They had started seeing each other several months earlier and Shermantine supplied her with drugs. Her parents did not approve, particularly when they saw that he carried a gun.

When Chevy did not return home that day, Shermantine turned up at the Wheelers' house and asked where she was. He appeared to be smirking. The Stockton police investigated and when they interviewed Shermantine he denied seeing Chevy on 7 October. Nevertheless, they got a search warrant for Shermantine's car and the family's hunting cabin in Calaveras County. There they discovered drops of blood that matched Chevy's blood type. It was the best they could do as DNA profiling had not been introduced back then. Later DNA testing confirmed that it was Chevy's blood and Herzog then admitted that he was with Shermantine when he stabbed her to death. Again her body was disposed of in a mine shaft.

FAMILY MEN

By the mid-1980s Herzog was married with three children and was said to be a good father. Shermantine was also married, and had fathered two boys, but he was said to have physically abused his wife and children, although his wife only asked for a divorce when he was on death row. Meanwhile, the families socialized and occasionally the two men would go off on a hunting trip, fuelled with drink and crystal meth.

Although Shermantine had been the prime suspect in the disappearance of Chevy Wheeler, they began killing again in the summer of 1986. No one is sure how many people they murdered in the next twelve years. When they were finally arrested in 1999, Herzog told the police that the body count was twenty-four – though he said Shermantine was to blame.

On 3 June 1986, thirty-one-year-old Sylvia Lourdes Standley was abducted in Modesto. She was raped and murdered and her body was consigned to a mine shaft or cave. The following year, sixteen-year-old Theresa Ann Bier disappeared after going to a store in Fresno. The same fate befell her. Two more murders took place in 1988. On 18 October, eighteen-year-old Gayle Marks disappeared from Stockton and then, on 19 November, nine-year-old Michaela Garecht was seized in Hayward. The description given by a witness to the abduction fitted Herzog.

Michaela was never seen again. Later from death row Shermantine said that Herzog was responsible, but then withdrew the accusation.

The Speed Freak Killers then appear to have taken a break. They may have been busy with family responsibilities. It was nearly five years before forty-seven-year-old Phillip Martin went missing from Stockton on 30 September 1993. Fuelled by crystal meth, Herzog and Shermantine were thought to have subjected him to a lengthy torture session before killing him and disposing of his body.

Then on a hunting trip to Utah in 1994, when the game grew scarce, Herzog said that Shermantine lined up another hunter in his sights and shot him dead. Shermantine denied it, blaming Herzog. Circumstantial evidence indicates that they may have killed others outside California.

HIGH-PROFILE MURDER

In 1997, in the small town of McCloud, California, 200 miles north of Linden, two people went missing. First Karen Knechtel Mero disappeared from her front porch, though it was not reported for some months. At first it was thought that she had left of her own accord, until it was realized that she had not taken vital medication. Then on 4 June 1997, fifteen-year-old Hannah Zaccaglini also disappeared.

When Herzog and Shermantine were arrested, it was discovered that they had been on a hunting trip in the area at the time. Two more men were arrested for the abduction and murder of Hannah Zaccaglini, but Herzog and Shermantine remained suspects in the Karen Mero case.

Although Shermantine and Herzog had somehow got away with killing Chevy Wheeler – someone known to them – the Speed Freak Killers were about to make the same mistake again. Twenty-five-year-old Cyndi Vanderheiden was the daughter of John Vanderheiden, owner of the Linden Inn. She had worked there as a cook and a barmaid and had also learned to drink there. In her twenties, she moved on to marijuana and crystal meth and had a bad time with money and men, but by 1998 she had straightened out. She returned home, worked as a computer technician and saved money.

On Friday 13 November 1998, she dropped by the Linden Inn for a drink. Shermantine and Herzog were there, already a little high, and Herzog invited Cyndi to sit with them, which she accepted. She knew them from the bars in the area and, while others shunned them because of their wild talk, she considered their murderous boasts empty braggadocio. For a time, Herzog had even been the lover of Cyndi's sister Kim.

The Speed Freak Killers had been rejected by several women that evening and were determined to even up the score. Although Cyndi had been free of crystal meth for some time, the alcohol lowered her inhibitions and she agreed to meet them in a nearby cemetery for a smoke.

At first things were pleasant enough. Then Shermantine made his move on Cyndi. When she refused his overtures, he punched her repeatedly then forced her to give him oral sex at knifepoint. Afterwards he cut her throat. The two men loaded her body into the boot of Shermantine's car and dropped her body down a decommissioned mine in Calaveras County and then they returned home to their families like any other evening.

The following morning John Vanderheiden grew concerned when he saw his daughter's car parked outside the cemetery, which was an infamous drug haven. A quick ring around her friends established that no one had seen her since the Linden Inn the previous evening, when she had been sitting with Herzog and Shermantine, two notorious thugs.

After a couple of days, her parents filed a missing person's report, but given Cyndi's troubled background the police took little notice at first. However, when they learned that she had been seen with Shermantine – still the prime suspect in the disappearance of Chevy Wheeler thirteen years earlier – they put him and his sidekick Herzog under twenty-four-hour surveillance.

Meanwhile, the Vanderheidens plastered the area with missing persons' posters, offering a $20,000 reward, and organized a hunt that attracted over five hundred people.

ADVANCES IN DNA PROFILING

While the killers tried to maintain a low profile, the police reopened the Chevy Wheeler case that had been cold for over a decade. In the meantime, there had been considerable advances in forensic science. DNA profiling had first been used in Britain in 1986, but large samples were needed. However, during the early 1990s methods of amplification were developed that allowed reliable profiles to be built from small or badly degraded samples. Even so, it was still an expensive process and the Department of Justice Crime Lab in Washington, DC, discouraged police departments from sending samples unless they had a firm suspect.

The police upped the surveillance on Herzog and Shermantine's homes and also increased the pressure on them. When the two men were called in for interviews, Shermantine refused but Herzog complied. He was clearly uncomfortable during the interview. Although he admitted seeing Cyndi on the night of her disappearance, he said he had only talked to her for a short time. Witnesses, however, said they had been together for an extended period, but he could not be cajoled into a confession and the police had to let him go.

Meanwhile, Shermantine had fallen behind on the repayments for his car and it had been repossessed. This gave the police the opportunity to make a forensic examination of the vehicle. They found spots of blood on the passenger headrest and in the boot, which provided them with enough evidence to bring Shermantine in. Under interrogation, he said that he had not talked to Cyndi on the night she had gone missing, but witnesses said that he had. This, along with the blood found in the car and the cabin, was enough for the police to arrest Shermantine for the murders of Chevy Wheeler and Cyndi Vanderheiden.

While there was little evidence against Herzog, the police picked him up and read him his rights. Waiving his right to see a lawyer, he told investigators what had happened to Cyndi, saying that he had begged Shermantine not to kill her but had not intervened because he was afraid of him. Herzog went on to clear up a number of missing persons' cases in the Central Valley from the 1980s and 1990s, along with the murder in Utah in 1994, blaming Shermantine in each case. He also admitted being with Shermantine when he killed Chevy Wheeler.

Despite Herzog's confession, Shermantine continued to deny everything – even when he was told DNA profiling matched blood found in his car with that of Cyndi Vanderheiden. When pressed, he turned on Herzog.

EQUALLY GUILTY

The two men were tried separately. Shermantine's lawyers blamed Herzog, but on 14 February 2001 Shermantine was found guilty on four counts of first-degree murder, including those of Chevy Wheeler and Cyndi Vanderheiden. Shermantine now faced the death penalty, but the district attorney offered him life without parole if he revealed where the two women's bodies were. He agreed – provided he received the $20,000 reward the Vanderheidens had offered. He said he was going to use the money to compensate the victims' families under a restitution order made by the judge, with the remainder going to his two sons. The Vanderheiden and Wheeler families rejected the deal and Shermantine was sentenced to death.

The only substantial evidence against Herzog was his confessions. However, when forensic investigators reconstructed the murders of King and Cavanaugh, it showed that two shooters had been involved. Herzog's attorney's defence that his client was only guilty of 'having the world's worst friend' did not work. He was found guilty on three counts of first-degree murder and was sentenced to life imprisonment, though with the possibility of parole.

In jail, Herzog was stabbed and his life was constantly under threat. An appeal court found that the questioning that had elicited his confession had violated his Fifth Amendment rights against self-incrimination and a new trial was ordered. He was offered a plea bargain – a sentence of fourteen years if he pleaded guilty to the voluntary manslaughter of Cyndi Vanderheiden. Taking into account the time he had already served, he was paroled in 2010, but the only accommodation that could be found for him was a trailer in the grounds of the High Desert State Prison, miles from the nearest town, where he was kept under tight security.

On 16 January 2012 he was found hanged from a homemade noose. A few days before a bounty hunter had contacted him, telling him that he was dealing with Shermantine in an effort to find the remains of Chevy Wheeler and Cyndi Vanderheiden. Shermantine then provided a hand-drawn map showing a location he called 'Herzog's Boneyard'. The authorities found human bones there, belonging to three women and a foetus.

Next Shermantine revealed that Chevy Wheeler had been buried in the backyard of his parents' house. Her remains were quickly found. Then he told the authorities the location of the mine shaft in Calaveras County where he had dumped Cyndi Vanderheiden.

DANIEL CAMARGO BARBOSA
THE SADIST OF CHANQUITO

PARENTAL ABUSE

It is thought that Daniel Camargo Barbosa killed as many as 150 people – and probably raped many more. Like many serial killers it was the peculiar circumstances of his childhood that perhaps set him on his course.

Born to a relatively prosperous family in the small town of Anolaima in the Colombian Andes in 1930, he was the son of a local businessman named Daniel Camargo Briceño. His mother, Teresa Barbosa, was his father's second wife and he had an older half-sister from his father's first marriage. When Camargo was two years old his mother died and his father remarried shortly afterwards.

Camargo was very intelligent and did well in school, but his father remained distant and would dismiss the boy as useless and a lost cause. His upbringing was left to his stepmother, Dioselina Fernández, who was a mere adolescent at the time of her marriage and wanted to have a daughter of her own. When she found she was unable to have children she doted on her stepdaughter but abused her stepson. Her cruelty for minor infractions extended to forcefully undressing him from his waist down and beating his bare buttocks with a bullwhip.

Understandably, Camargo developed violent tendencies. After he got into a fight at school, his stepmother punished him by taking away his trousers and forcing him to wear girls' clothes. Schoolmates were invited to witness this humiliation and he became the victim of bullying. From then on, Camargo came to despise women and everything feminine.

In the early 1940s, his father sent him to a prestigious, all-male Catholic boarding school in the Colombian capital, Bogotá. Camargo excelled academically, but any plans for him to continue his studies were curtailed when his family was hit by the economic downturn caused by *La Violencia*, Colombia's civil war that started in 1948. He was then forced to work as a door-to-door salesman to support them. Despite the hardship the country was suffering, he was charming, convincing and relatively successful.

LOVER LURES YOUNG GIRLS

In 1957, he began a relationship with a young client named Alcira Castillo. After a few dates, he rented a house and they moved in together. Soon they had a growing family and to make ends meet he took to crime. On 24 May 1958, he was arrested for robbing a shop owned by another client. Convicted of petty theft, he was sent to a minimum-security prison, but he was not there long. Taking advantage of the confusion caused by the widespread mass arrests, Camargo simply walked out with the staff, clutching a clipboard. He then returned home and seemingly there were no repercussions.

In 1962, Camargo fell in love with another woman named Esperanza and decided to leave Alcira, even though they had two children. He intended to marry Esperanza, but when they got engaged he discovered that she wasn't a virgin. Then he found her in their bed with another man. Angry at first, Camargo soon realized that he could manipulate the situation to his own advantage. He insisted on Esperanza bringing him young girls, so he could take from them the virginity she had denied him.

Esperanza reluctantly complied and lured five young girls to their apartment. She then drugged them with sleeping pills, so Camargo could rape them while they were unconscious. However, the fifth child realized what had happened to her and reported the couple. Esperanza and Camargo were arrested and on 10 April 1964 Camargo was convicted of sexual assault. Initially he was sentenced to three years but a second judge increased this to eight years. He served the full term but remained angry at what he saw to be an injustice.

LUST FOR VIRGINS

When he was released he moved to Brazil, but in 1973 he was arrested for being an undocumented immigrant and was deported back to Colombia. He used this as an opportunity to adopt a false identity. It is thought that he then resumed raping young girls, possibly as many as eighty, and murdering them so that they could not go to the police.

In the northern town of Barranquilla, Camargo went to work as a street vendor selling televisions. On 2 May 1974, he was walking past a school there when he saw a nine-year-old girl who took his fancy. He lured her to a secluded area, then raped and strangled her. The following day, Camargo returned to dispose of the body and retrieve the TV set he had left there and was arrested. He was then convicted of the girl's rape and murder. Sentenced to thirty years in prison, he was sent to the island of Gorgona, Colombia's 'Devil's Island', situated some twenty miles off the country's Pacific coast.

Ten years into his sentence, Camargo found a rowing boat that had been washed up on a beach. For years he had been studying the currents in the hope of escape, so he jumped in and after a few hours' paddling made landfall in Ecuador. Even though he was reported as a fugitive, the currents were particularly treacherous

In the 1940s, Camargo's father sent him to a prestigious, all-male Catholic school in the Colombian capital, Bogotá. When young, Barbosa had been abused by his stepmother. She punished him for getting into a fight by taking away his trousers and forcing him to wear girls' clothes.

there and it was assumed he had died at sea. The Colombian press even reported that Camargo had been eaten by sharks. In fact, he was the first man to escape from the Colombian Alcatraz.

Ten years on Gorgona had not quenched his lust for virgins. On 18 December 1984, he abducted another nine-year-old girl in Quevedo, then raped and killed her. He went on to commit at least fifty rapes and murders of girls and young women between 1984 and 1986.

His modus operandi was to target peasants, maids and students transitioning from primary school to college, though younger schoolgirls were also easy prey. He would approach them pretending he was a foreigner who was trying to find a Protestant pastor in a church on the outskirts of town, where he was to deliver a large sum of money. This was all the more convincing because he was fluent in English and Portuguese and was adept at adopting an accent. There would be a reward, of course, to any girl who would show him the way – a small part of the money or something as trivial as a pen. Younger girls would be given sweets while older victims were lured with the possibility of a job at the church. The journey often involved a bus trip. He insisted they alighted in a wooded area and then made off into the forest, claiming that he was now familiar with the area and remembered a shortcut. If the victim got suspicious and refused to follow him, Camargo would let her go and find someone new.

MEMORIZED VICTIMS' DETAILS

If the girl followed, Camargo would lead her to a secluded spot then rape her at knifepoint. Afterwards he would strangle her, stab her or cut her up with a machete. One adult woman hit him on the head with a rock while he was raping her, which enraged him so much that he decapitated her and threw her head away. Another victim was found dissected with all her internal organs removed. The bodies would be left to be stripped by scavengers, while he made off with their clothes and any valuables. He would urinate on his hands to wash off the blood and he always carried a clean shirt to change into. Before he left, he liked to memorize as many details about the victims as possible, such as scars, tattoos and moles, so he could relive the experience later. In some cases he even obtained the phone number of their families, so that he could call and taunt them about their missing daughters.

EXECUTED BY FELLOW PRISONER

Most of the murders happened in the Guayas province, but Camargo roamed all over Ecuador, following in the footsteps of Pedro López – 'The Monster of the Andes' – another Colombian serial killer active in Ecuador. In 1983, he was convicted of the murders of 110 girls in Ecuador and confessed to another 240 murders in Colombia and Peru.

As with López, Camargo's killings were so numerous that the police did not believe that the abductions were the work of one man. Organized crime must be involved, they thought, or perhaps white slavers or a Satanic ring.

Camargo was arrested on 26 February 1986 by two Quito policemen, minutes after he had murdered another nine-year-old girl named Elizabeth Telpes. He was found in possession of a bag containing bloody clothes belonging to his final victim, along with a copy of Fyodor Dostoyevsky's *Crime and Punishment*.

After a local woman named María Alexandra Vélez survived an attack by a man matching his description, he was then taken to Guayaquil, where she identified him. Camargo admitted killing seventy-one victims in Ecuador following his escape from prison. He told investigators that he picked virgins 'because they cried'.

In 1989, he was convicted and sentenced to sixteen years in jail, the maximum sentence in Ecuador. He was imprisoned at Quito's García Moreno Prison, the same penitentiary that was home to Pedro López. On 13 November 1994 Camargo was sitting in his cell when a new inmate, twenty-nine-year-old Giovanny Arcesio Noguera Jaramillo, came in and forced him to his knees. After saying 'it is the hour of vengeance', he stabbed Camargo eight times, killing him, and then he cut off one of his ears as a trophy. Noguera showed the ear to the guards, maintaining that his aunt was one of Camargo's victims and he had avenged her. Because nobody claimed Camargo's body, he was buried in a mass grave located in Quito's El Batán cemetery. He was sixty-four years old when he died.

López was released in 1994 but was deported back to Colombia, where he faced further murder charges. Found insane, he was committed to a mental hospital in Bogotá. Discharged in 1998, he was arrested again in 2002, but absconded.

IRINA GAIDAMACHUK
SATAN IN A SKIRT

VODKA HABIT

Since the collapse of the Soviet Union in 1991, life had become hard in Russia. While the oligarchs plundered the economy and siphoned the money out of the country through London, most ordinary people were left living on the breadline. They comforted themselves with vodka, which was readily available, so heavy-drinking housewife Irina Gaidamachuk appeared to be nothing out of the ordinary. A wife and mother, she was charming, kind and seemingly harmless. Then it was discovered how she paid for her booze. She did it by beating in the heads of elderly women and stealing what little money they had.

Born on 26 September 1972 in the town of Nyagan in Western Siberia, Irina became a heavy drinker at an early age. At twenty-one she had a baby daughter named Alina but, unable to cope, she handed the child over to a state-run orphanage and visited rarely. In the early 1990s, she moved 500 miles away to Krasnoufimsk in the Urals, which is 760 miles from Moscow. There she married and had two more children.

EXCEPTIONALLY BRUTAL

Gaidamachuk's murder spree began in 2002 when she was thirty. Her victims were between sixty-one and eighty-nine years of age and they were bludgeoned to death with repeated blows for the small amounts of cash they had in their purses or hidden around their apartments. In the worst attack, she staved a victim's head in with twenty-four blows.

Sometimes Gaidamachuk would garner as little as £20 and she only made a total of some £1,000 ($1,260) from her victims. In one case, she had trouble finding where the victim had hidden her savings, so she spent the night with the corpse, covering the dead woman's bloodstained face with a pillow. After finding the money, she then trashed the flat to make it look like a burglary. In another case, she set the apartment on fire after smashing an eighty-two-year-old woman's skull to pieces, in an attempt to cover her tracks.

During their eight-year investigation, the police said they fingerprinted 15,000 women, questioned 3,000 witnesses, conducted more than 2,000 forensic examinations and travelled as far as the Central Asian republic of Turkmenistan, 1,300 miles away, in pursuit of leads. In 2008 they arrested a woman named Irina Valeyeva, who under interrogation confessed to the murders of several of Gaidamachuk's elderly victims. She was held for several months until her innocence was established.

One of the problems with the investigations was that the police initially thought they were looking for a man. Gaidamachuk surprised them all. According to one of the detectives on the case:

> She's an exceptionally brutal woman. I was convinced we were dealing with a man. After all, how could a woman smash a head with twenty-four blows? For a while, when

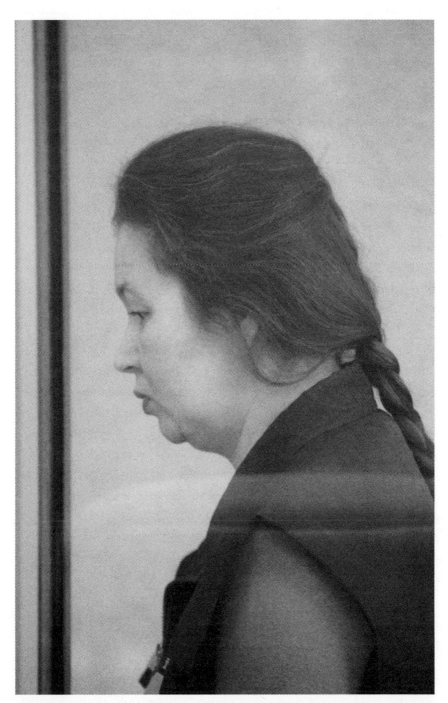

Irina Gaidamachuk was charming, kind and seemingly harmless. Then it was discovered how she paid for her booze. She did it by beating in the heads of elderly women and stealing their money.

witnesses began talking about a woman, we even suspected a man dressed up as a woman.

She said she'd lost count of how many people she'd killed after the tenth murder. She's very cold-blooded but also charming and even attractive. She even tried flirting during our questioning.

GAINED VICTIMS' TRUST

In a single week, shortly before she was captured, Gaidamachuk killed three women in the same street in Krasnoufimsk. She picked on elderly women who lived alone. The police said she had managed to get hold of a regional list of pensioners. For several days, she would keep watch on her potential victims to find out when they left home, where they went and whether they were visited by any relatives.

Armed with this knowledge, she set out to befriend them by offering to redecorate their flats or carry out household chores, then once she had gained their trust she would strike.

After getting away with murder for so long, she eventually grew careless. The net closed in after one of the victims survived an attack and was able to help police draw an artist's impression. Neighbours recognized Gaidamachuk as the woman who had painted the victims' flats shortly before they were killed.

'At some point, Gaidamachuk decided she would never be caught, and started searching for victims among the people she knew,' investigator Kirill Melenkov told *Komsomolskaya Pravda.* 'Her last victim hired her to make repairs. That's how we managed to find the killer. She also started leaving notes, "Be home at 11.00, a social worker will visit." A simple handwriting test helped identify the murderer.'

When she was finally caught it was found that fingerprints at three murder scenes in 2010 matched those at an earlier crime scene, linking her to a whole series of killings.

Confessing to the police, she said: 'I did it for money. I just wanted to be a normal mum, but I had a craving for drink. My husband Yuri wouldn't give me money for vodka.'

However, Gaidamachuk also told the police that her main motive was to send money to Alina, the child she had sent to the orphanage. Detectives believed she felt guilty at having abandoned her daughter.

FAMILY DISBELIEF

Her mother-in-law said she knew all along that her daughter-in-law had a drink problem. She would also behave strangely sometimes, she said – pretending to take a call and then speaking to herself on the phone – but she had never thought her capable of murder. Indeed, even when Gaidamachuk was arrested she did not believe it.

'We're all in a state of shock,' she said, 'still hoping the police have made a mistake.'

Husband Yuri, who had moved in with a new partner, said: 'I lived with her for fourteen years but never suspected anything.'

Their twelve-year-old daughter Anastasia, who lived with her mother, was equally disbelieving.

'She was always good to me and helped me do my homework and even write poetry. I don't believe what people are saying about her can be true,' she said.

A friend said: 'I simply cannot believe Irina is a mass murderer. She was a kind and gentle mother, always eager to help.'

Gaidamachuk was found to be mentally competent and was convicted of seventeen counts of murder and one of attempted murder. She was sentenced to twenty years in prison. This meant she would only be the age of her youngest victim when she was released. The judge said he had deducted five years from the maximum sentence of twenty-five years because she was a mother.

While her lawyer demanded greater leniency, saying he would appeal the sentence, the families of the victim were outraged. One family member said: It's little more than one year for each murder. She never deserves to be freed.'

The police also came in for criticism. 'It's scandalous that it took eight years to catch the killer,' said Elena Golovenkina, whose sixty-six-year-old mother was murdered in 2002 in a rain of blows from a bronze bust of Lenin. 'How could someone kill a frail and defenceless old lady in such a savage way?'

RIVAL GRANNY-KILLER

But Gaidamachuk was not the only granny-killer at large. Modelling herself on Andrei Chikatilo – 'The Rostov Ripper', who killed between fifty-two and fifty-six children in a period from 1978 to1990 – Tamara Samsonova was captured in 2015 after killing Valentina Ulanova, a friend whose carer she was supposed to be. They had fallen out over dirty teacups.

'I came home and put the whole pack of phenazepam – fifty pills – into her Olivier salad,' Samsonova told the police. 'She liked it very much. I woke up after 2 a.m. and she was lying on the floor. So I started cutting her to pieces. It was hard for me to carry her to the bathroom; she was fat and heavy. I did everything in the kitchen where she was lying.'

She dumped the body parts outside the flat they shared in St Petersburg, where the limbs were found by dogs. CCTV footage showed Samsonova going in and out seven times carrying body parts in bags and a saucepan containing Ulanova's head. The internal organs were not found and it is thought she may have eaten them.

When police searched the apartment they found diaries that showed that Samsonova had killed up to eleven people over twenty years. The torso of a man thought to have been one of her victims had been found in the street twelve years earlier.

In the diaries, Samsonova said: 'I killed my tenant Volodya, cut him to pieces in the bathroom with a knife, put the pieces of his body in plastic bags and threw them away in the different parts of Frunzensky district.'

Forty-four-year-old Sergei Potynavin was killed after an argument on 6 September 2003. She then dismembered his body and dumped the body parts in plastic bags. It was also suspected that she had killed her husband, whom she reported missing in 2005. Her mother-in-law also disappeared.

While admitting to murdering Mrs Ulanova and others, Samsonova refused to co-operate with the police over other suspected killings.

'We may never know the extent of this granny's killings,' one source close to the investigation said.

At the time of her arrest Tamara Samsonova was sixty-eight.

JOANNA DENNEHY
THE PETERBOROUGH DITCH MURDERS

CHANGED BY DRUGS

Violent and unpredictable, Joanna Dennehy claimed to have killed her father for raping her. She also savagely beat the father of her two children and threatened to kill anyone who annoyed her. Then she killed her flatmate and got a taste for murder, killing two more men she knew and going out to hunt strangers. She was quite unapologetic about it and if she had not been stopped she would have kept on doing it – just for fun.

Until she was fifteen, Dennehy lived with her parents in their pleasant, four-bedroom family home in St Albans, England. According to her mother Kathleen, she was a sympathetic child when growing up, and loved hockey and netball.

'She was very sensitive,' Kathleen told the Crime and Investigation Channel. 'If she stood on a worm or something she would be really upset if it died – she used to take them to bed with her. So she was a loving girl. She was polite to everybody. Teachers always said that she was a nice girl.'

Her ambition was to be a lawyer and her parents even paid for extra lessons for her. But everything changed in her mid-teens when she started skipping school, drinking and taking drugs.

'There was cannabis and drugs involved,' said her sister Maria. 'She became a bit of a rebel.'

'My daughter was the fourteen-year-old who never came home,' Kathleen said.

UNWILLING MOTHER

In 1997, she met John Treanor, five years her senior, who was walking his Alsatian in the park.

'She approached me,' he said. 'She had a thing for dogs – it just went from there. She'd fallen out with her parents and she was a bit of a free spirit but I liked her – in fact I loved her.'

They became inseparable. Her parents did not approve.

'She had been in trouble at school for drinking. She was also stealing. At fifteen her mum kicked her out and told her not to come back,' he said.

His family did not approve either and they slept rough for about a year. When they eventually found a place in a shared house in Luton, they had to flee after tipping off the police about a drug dealer in the house. They then moved to Milton Keynes, where Joanna had her first baby when she was seventeen.

'She never wanted the kids,' said Treanor. 'She always said she wanted it to be just me and her. We took a photo of her, holding the baby. You could see in her face, she was not interested.'

The couple soon split up.

'She cheated on me with a neighbour and she was using cocaine,' Treanor said. 'I was out working seventeen hours as a security guard and she was drinking at friends' houses till God knows what time.'

Treanor moved to King's Lynn in Norfolk, taking their daughter with him. They were soon reconciled though, finding a council house in Wisbech, a quiet market town in Cambridgeshire. Neither of them worked, but Dennehy would spend her benefits on drugs and alcohol. Elderly neighbours heard them arguing and once she armed herself with a cricket bat.

'She went berserk, she was shouting and swearing and kept on hitting him with the bat,' a neighbour said. 'I liked John, he was nice and polite, but Jo was a nightmare, she was trouble from the start. She hit him all the time. He would have black eyes and marks on his face. Jo was forever drunk and on drugs, even when she was out walking with her oldest daughter. On one occasion she shaved the little girl's head until she was completely bald. She told us it was because she had nits but nobody was convinced.'

They had a second daughter, but Treanor did all the parenting.

'It was John who took the older daughter to school in the morning and picked her up later,' the neighbour told the *Daily Express*. 'When Jo was with her daughter, she was usually stumbling around either drunk or on drugs. Other times I would come home from town through the park and I'd pass Jo in the wooded area with another man. It was obvious what she was doing. Apparently she was doing it to get money to buy drugs.'

Treanor knew he had to flee when one day she pulled a six-inch dagger from her knee-length boot. Gripping the decorated handle, she began stabbing the carpet. He took his daughters and moved to Glossop in Derbyshire, where he married.

'I really believe Jo is evil, pure and simple,' he said. 'That is why I took the girls as far away from her as possible.'

KILLS FELLOW TENANTS

Dennehy moved to Peterborough. She was looking for a room to rent when she met her prospective landlord, forty-nine-year-old Kevin Lee. His business partner Paul Creed recalled: 'She told us a story that she had killed her father due to her father raping her and having his child and losing the child … She also showed us multiple scars on her arms and stomach.'

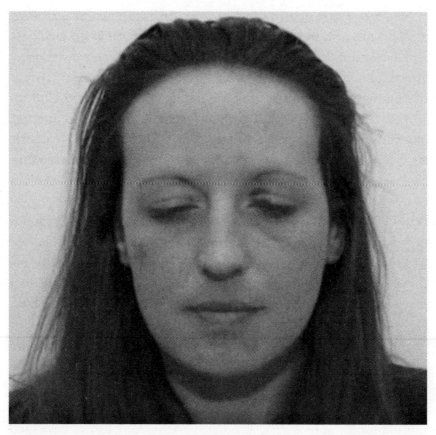

Dennehy told her prospective landlord she had killed her father because he had raped her and made her pregnant before she lost the child. She showed him multiple scars on her arms and stomach.

These were from self-harm. Creed was not keen on taking her as a tenant, but Lee decided to give her a chance. She lived rent-free in return for looking after his properties.

There was no foundation to the allegation of rape against her father. Nevertheless, she told another acquaintance that she had served thirteen years in prison for killing him, because he had been sexually abusing her since the age of six.

Dennehy had indeed served time, but it was for theft and drugs offences. She was also on probation for assault and owning a dangerous dog.

When her boyfriend, 7 ft 2 in Gary Richards, aka Stretch, had done some work for her landlord Lee but had not been paid, she said she would 'f***ing kill him'.

Stretch's flatmate, Carla White, met Dennehy three weeks before the murders and found her 'very rude and very arrogant'. After shaking hands, Dennehy told White to 'f*** off'. When White took offence at this, Dennehy put her hands around her throat, only letting go when White grabbed a hammer. This encounter seems to have excited Lee's interest in Dennehy. He compared her to Uma Thurman in the movie *Kill Bill*.

Lee wanted to clear the house so he could redecorate, so Dennehy took care of the matter for him. Thirty-one-year-old housemate Lukasz Slaboszewski thought he was going to have sex with Dennehy when he received texts luring him to a flat she had access to. Instead, he was stabbed in the heart and his body was dumped in a wheelie bin.

Fifty-six-year-old Falklands veteran John Chapman was high on drink and drugs when Dennehy came on to him. He too was stabbed, this time in the neck and chest, and his body was dumped ten miles away at Thorney Dyke. Although Lee had been trying to evict these two men, who were unemployed at the time, he had not envisaged the methods Dennehy would use.

THEN MURDERS LANDLORD

Then Lee, who seems to have become Dennehy's lover, received a text from Dennehy asking him to meet her, saying that she wanted to dress him up and rape him. In fact, she stabbed him in the heart and then dressed him in a black sequin dress before dumping his body in a ditch near Newborough. It was found face down with the buttocks exposed in what the prosecution described as a 'deliberately engineered ... act of post-death humiliation', adding: 'The way in which his body was dumped was part of the playing out of your sexual and sadistic motivation.'

After Lee's murder, Dennehy sang the Britney Spears track 'Oops I Did It Again' down the phone. Dennehy and Stretch then posed for photographs celebrating the killings. They also torched Lee's Ford Mondeo.

Lee's wife was already suspicious that her husband was having an affair. She noticed that one number appeared frequently on her husband's telephone bills and rang it. The number was Dennehy's. The police used it later to show that she was in the vicinity of Lee's Mondeo when it was set on fire.

'FUN' STABBINGS

Three murders were not enough for Dennehy. A few days later, she told Stretch: 'I want my fun. I need you to get my fun.' He then drove her to Hereford where she stabbed Robin Bereza and John Rogers, two men innocently walking their dogs. Mark Lloyd, who was unwittingly along for the ride, was terrified of Dennehy.

'If she had told me to put my head through the windscreen, I would have done,' he said.

When Lloyd discovered that the couple were wanted by the police, he said: 'I thought it was Gary who had done the murders because he's 7 ft 2 in and looks like Herman off *The Munsters*. She looks like butter wouldn't melt until she opens her bloody mouth.'

When they spotted Bereza, Lloyd said: 'I thought she was going to mug him but then it twigged on me. I thought, "You just want blood."'

She was now a murderer with ambitions.

'She wanted to be like Bonnie and Clyde,' he said. 'She wanted nine victims.'

Bereza was minding his own business when, he said: 'I felt a blow to my right shoulder. I turned around and saw this lady, she just stared straight through me. I kicked her and made contact. It had no impact on her. She just came straight towards me. I ran into the road. I put my hand to my jacket and saw all this blood. She tried to come for me again, I kicked her again; she still didn't react.'

The attack on Rogers was even more brutal. First, he said he felt a punch in the back, as if a neighbour or a friend was messing about. In fact, he had been stabbed.

'I turned around and saw the woman who stabbed me just standing there,' he said. 'She started stabbing me in the chest.'

He asked Dennehy: 'What's this all about?'

She told him he was bleeding before saying: 'I better do some more.'

Rogers recalled: 'I said "just leave me alone please, please can you leave me alone", but she didn't. She didn't seem to be showing any emotion. She didn't seem to be enjoying herself. She just seemed like she was going about business.'

He said he fell to the ground but Dennehy continued with unrelenting hostility: 'I was just waiting for it to stop. There was loads and loads of blood on the floor, on the ground. As I lay there I thought, "This is where I'm going to die."'

He had been stabbed forty times in his arm, chest, stomach and back. Dennehy left him for dead, but he survived.

SMILING AFTER ARREST

After two days on the run, Dennehy and Richards were captured by two armed officers when their green Vauxhall Astra was spotted parked in The Oval area of Hereford. Surrendering to the police, Stretch told the officers: 'I suppose I'm Britain's "most wanted".' In fact, that dubious accolade belonged to Dennehy.

Seeing a video of her daughter after she was arrested, Kathleen said: 'When I saw this footage of Jo it was like somebody I didn't know. She's standing there being charged, smiling and laughing. That's not the kind, loving Jo that was our baby.'

In custody, Dennehy was unrepentant. She told a psychiatrist: 'I killed to see if I was as cold as I thought I was. Then it got moreish and I got a taste for it.'

At the Old Bailey, Dennehy unexpectedly pleaded guilty to the three murders, against the advice of her lawyers – although she had bragged that she had killed eight people. She also pleaded guilty to two counts of attempted murder and preventing the lawful and decent burial of her murder victims.

When her barrister asked the judge for more time to reconsider her plea, she said: 'I've pleaded guilty and that's that. … I'm not coming back down here again just to say the same stuff. It's a long way to come to repeat what I have just said.'

She was sentenced to life with a whole-life tariff after writing to the judge saying she felt no remorse for the killings. Just thirty-one, Dennehy was only the third woman to receive that sentence. The other two were Myra Hindley and Rosemary West.

'WILL I BE A KILLER LIKE MY MUM?'

Stretch was found guilty of two counts of attempted murder, while Leslie Layton, another housemate of Dennehy's, was convicted of perverting the course of justice and preventing lawful burials. Stretch was sentenced to life, serving a minimum of nineteen years and Layton got fourteen years.

Dennehy and Stretch exchanged letters from jail, confirming their love for each other. She sued the authorities over being kept in solitary confinement in jail, but the case was dismissed after it was revealed that she had been plotting to escape by cutting off a guard's finger in order to open the biometric locks in the prison.

Meanwhile, John Treanor had to reassure his thirteen-year-old daughter, who had seen her mother's face in the news.

'Dad, is that how I'll turn out?' she asked. 'Will I be a killer like my mum?'

He explained to her that being a murderer was not something you inherited. 'She's truly terrified of turning into her mother. She went through a lot while living with Joanna. Now she's facing an even greater challenge,' he said.

At that time, their youngest daughter had no idea about her mother or that she was a killer. Dennehy had been nowhere near the child since she was an infant.

'Now I'm going to have to sit her down and try to explain the whole thing to her,' said Treanor. 'I'm dreading it. How do you tell a seven-year-old that their mother is an evil serial killer?'

DONATO BILANCIA
THE MONSTER OF LIGURIA

HUMILIATED AS A CHILD

In 1997 and 1998 there was a series of murders in Liguria, the north-western coastal region of Italy whose capital is Genoa. They were linked by the same murder weapon – a .38 Smith & Wesson pistol using wadcutter ammunition. However, there was no consistency in the MO. Some murders were motivated by theft while others had a sexual motive. Still others seemed to be purely random.

After six months the inveterate gambler Donato Bilancia was arrested. He had been suspected after an identikit picture of him had been circulated – the description had come from a victim who had survived by playing dead.

More clues came from a second-hand Mercedes Bilancia had bought. The transfer of ownership had not been completed, so fines for traffic infractions continued being sent to the old owner, who spotted that the offences had taken place near the murders and at around the same time.

When arrested, Bilancia confessed everything – including a couple of murders that the police had not linked to the other killings. His frank confession and his co-operation with forensic psychiatrists gave a complete picture of the making of a serial killer.

Born in 1951, Bilancia was frequently beaten for minor transgressions of the rules set by his father. As a result, he wet the bed and his parents then put the mattress out on the balcony to dry where it could be seen by the neighbours.

'I remember that I was dying of shame also because in the apartment in front lived a gentleman with one or two daughters, who were about my age and this was even more unbearable for me,' he said.

Further humiliations were to come. When he visited his cousins, his father would pull down his briefs to show them his undeveloped penis. 'At that moment, I twisted on myself, falling to my knees on the bed, dead with shame,' he said. 'This was the event that crucified me for the rest of my life.'

BEGINS LIFE OF CRIME

To get his own back he began stealing money from his parents which, as he grew older, he spent on prostitutes and gambling with cards. Then he embarked on a life of crime. Following several thefts, he was arrested in 1974 for carrying an unlicensed gun. He spent some time in a psychiatric ward and then served eighteen months in prison for robbery, followed by another six months for burglaries in France. After that, there were custodial sentences for armed robbery and unlawful imprisonment. And in 1985 he was also reported for illegal gambling.

Things seem to have got even worse for Bilancia when his older brother committed suicide by throwing himself and his four-year-old son under a train. Bilancia was then reported by a prostitute for sexual aggression and unlawful imprisonment and an assistant in a lingerie shop complained that he was a sex pest. Then in 1996 his presence was noted at the anti-Mafia trial taking place in the Genoese law courts.

REVENGE AT GAMBLING LOSSES

His murder career did not begin until 15 October 1997, when he was forty-seven – a late start for a serial killer. However, the first murder he admitted to did not involve the .38 pistol. He had lost heavily in a gambling den owned by retired businessman Giorgio Centanaro and, believing that the game was rigged, he waited outside Centanaro's apartment. When Centanaro came home at about 2 a.m. he forced his way in. He had the gun with him but decided not to use it as the noise of a gunshot would have attracted attention. Instead he forced Centanaro to strip to his underwear, then bound him with tape and suffocated him with a pillow, kicking him in the testicles to check that he was dead.

'I left the body in front of the apartment door,' he said. 'I wanted everyone to know he'd been murdered.'

Bilancia said there was 500,000 lire (about £230/$300) on the table, but he did not take it.

Next Bilancia went after Maurizio Parenti, a friend and partner of Centanaro's who also worked as a bouncer at the gambling den and had hooked Bilancia into the game. Bilancia stopped Parenti on the way home at about 4 a.m., saying that he had something to show him. Once indoors, Bilancia opened the plastic bag he was carrying and pulled out his gun. After handcuffing Parenti and putting tape over his mouth, Bilancia then emptied Parenti's safe containing 13 million lire (£6,000/$7,900) and five Rolex watches.

After beating Parenti with the butt of the gun, he shot him dead. Carla Scotti, Parenti's young wife of just three weeks, was also in the apartment so Bilancia bound her arms and legs and shot her too.

He took the watches he had stolen to Bruno Solari and his wife Maria Luigia Pitto, retired jewellers who then worked from home, but they did not want anything to do with stolen goods.

'I had to shoot them both because they could have identified me,' Bilancia said. Then he helped himself to some of their jewellery.

'There was their maid, but she was in another room,' said Bilancia. 'If she had seen me, I would have killed her too.'

NO FIXED MO

Wanting more money, Bilancia studied the movements of money-changer Luciano Marro. Entering Marro's office when he was sweeping up, Bilancio ordered him to empty the safe at gunpoint, then shot him numerous times.

Some years before, fifty-two-year-old night watchman Giangiorgio Canu had testified against Bilancia, sending him to jail, so Bilancia sought him out where he was working and killed him.

Two months later, Bilancia picked up Albanian prostitute Bodejana Almerina, alias Stela Truja, in Foce, Genoa's red-light district, and offered her a large amount of money to go home with him for sex. Instead he took her into the hills outside the city, then in an isolated spot he made her strip naked and get out of the car.

'She was pretty afraid and didn't want to get out, so I took her by her hand and I dragged her out,' he said. 'Then I made her fall on her knees and shot her in the head once. I left her there and went away.'

The next victim was Russian prostitute Ljudmila Zubskova. Again he took her to an isolated spot and made her get out of the car. Then, like Almerina, he made her get on to her knees and shot her in the head.

He then shot money-changer Enzo Gorni and emptied his safe of 30 million lire (£13,700/$18,000).

'I forced him to open up the safe and to give me all the money, but he tried to react and I unloaded the shot at him. ... Then I went away.'

Up until then Bilancia had been killing almost randomly. His next murder was planned. He noticed that the gates to the grounds of a local villa were not closed and went inside to reconnoitre.

IDENTIFIED FROM SKETCH

'I decided that it was suitable for my next homicide,' he said.

Nearby he met a twenty-four-year-old transsexual named Julio Castro, alias Lorena. After he got into the car, Bilancia drove him to the villa and, pretending that it was his, drove into the garden. He parked with the passenger door against a tree, so Lorena could not get out, and then demanded oral sex, but Lorena refused because Bilancia would not wear a condom. Ignoring his refusal, Bilancia was forcing him to perform fellatio when two cars turned up. They were driven by security guards Massimo Gualillo and Candido Randò.

The security men wanted to know what they were doing on private property. Bilancia said they were leaving and tried to keep Lorena quiet, but he kept yelling he was being sexually assaulted. One of the security men said that he had to check with head office so Bilancia decided that he had better stop that and shot them both.

In the melee, Lorena managed to escape and hide in the bushes. Seeing him, Bilancia shot him twice in the abdomen, but then he heard moaning from the security men. He reloaded his gun and shot them again and then he fired another three shots at Lorena, who continued fighting back. Finally, Bilancia hit him in the face with the gun butt and then left, believing he was dead. Lorena survived, however, and gave a description of the assailant to a police sketch artist.

The circulation of the drawing did not deter Bilancia. A few days later, Evelyn Esohe Endoghaye, alias Tessy Adobo, a twenty-seven-year-old Nigerian prostitute, was murdered. Again he took her to an isolated area, but this time he had sex with her before he dragged her out of the car by the hair. She tried to escape, but he shot her in the knee. When she fell to the ground he shot her twice in the head.

On 3 April 1998, he visited the apartment of Luisa Ciminello, another prostitute, with the intention of killing her, but when he drew the gun she burst into tears and begged for mercy, saying she had a two-year-old child. Bilancia found he could not pull the trigger and left Ciminello alive. She then identified her assailant from the sketch made from Lorena's description.

RAILWAY TOILET KILLINGS

Just over a week later, on 12 April, Easter Day, Bilancia got on to the train bound from Genoa to Venice. He then spotted thirty-two-year-old nurse Elisabetta Zoppetti sitting in first-class.

On 12 April, Easter Day 1998, Bilancia got on the train bound from Genoa to Venice. He then spotted thirty-two-year-old nurse Elisabetta Zoppetti sitting in first-class. Soon she was dead.

'I'd never seen her before,' he said. 'A few minutes later she went to the bathroom taking her handbag with her.'

He had a pass key with him and entered the cubicle. She started screaming, so he covered her head with her jacket and shot her in the head. Then he went through her handbag and stole her ticket as he had not bothered to buy one.

'I got the train because I wanted to kill a woman, even if I did not touch her,' he said. 'I didn't want to have sex with her. I just wanted to kill her as part of my criminal plan. I've got nothing left to say about that.'

Two days after that event, he picked up a young Slav prostitute named Mema Valbona, alias Kristina Kwalla, and reverted to his previous MO.

'I offered her a large amount of money for sexual intercourse at home in order to gain access to her quickly. Then I took her to an isolated area nearby Pietra Ligure's motorway exit, a place where I'd been before to check it out and considered it suitable for a killing. First we had sex together and immediately after I made her get out of the car. She was pretty afraid and didn't want to get out, so I dragged her out. Then I made her fall on her knees and shot her in the head. Then I left her there and went away.'

On 18 April, he lost a lot of money at the casino in Sanremo along the coast from Genoa. He then went to the station and jumped on a train.

'I saw a young woman,' he said. Her name was Maria Angela Rubino. 'I remember that I felt a sudden, irresistible urge to kill her. After a few minutes she went to the bathroom. I waited for a while and then opened the bathroom's door with my special key. She had no time to fight back. It took just a few seconds to kill her. I shot her in the head once, using her jacket as a silencer.'

But that was not the end of it.

'I remember that I felt pretty excited by her black underwear, so I locked the bathroom door and masturbated myself, using her clothes to clean up when I had finished.'

At the next station, he got out of the train on the wrong side, setting off an alarm. When asked what he was doing, he said he lived on that side of the tracks. Then he caught a cab back to Sanremo, where he had left his car.

WHY KEEP ME ALIVE?

Two days later, he wanted to fill up his car at a petrol station but he had no money with him, so he shot the fifty-one-year-old attendant Giuseppe Mileto numerous times, then took the day's takings – approximately two million lire (£920/$1,200). Then he went back to settle the bill he had left unpaid in a restaurant and afterwards he went back to the casino.

Although he confessed to everything after his arrest, Bilancia decided not to appear in court. Three forensic psychiatrists testified that he was sane at the time of the crimes and he was given thirteen life sentences with solitary confinement for three years. This was confirmed by the Court of Cassation, Italy's Supreme Court. In an interview with another psychiatrist, Bilancia asked: 'What's the point in keeping me alive?'

WILLIAM BONIN
THE FREEWAY KILLER

VIETNAM VETERAN

The endless anonymous freeways of California are the perfect place to pick up an innocent victim, kill them and dump their body. Three serial murderers have been given the nickname 'The Freeway Killer' – Patrick Kearney, Randy Steven Kraft and William George Bonin.

Kearney was arrested in 1977 after killing between twenty-one and forty-three hitch-hikers or young men he had picked up in gay bars. Kraft was convicted of murdering sixteen young men, but it is thought that he may have raped and murdered up to a further fifty-one boys and young men. He is also known as 'The Scorecard Killer' for the code list he kept of his victims. William George Bonin was the only one to have been executed for his crimes.

Bonin was born in Connecticut in 1947. Both of his parents were alcoholics and his father would gamble away the shopping money, leaving the family to starve. The children were left in the care of their grandfather, who was a convicted paedophile.

Bonin swapped this life for physical abuse at an orphanage at the age of six, graduating to a Connecticut juvenile detention centre when he was ten, for stealing licence plates. There he was sexually abused once more, as he was passed around the older boys.

In the hope of a fresh start, the family moved to California and it seemed to work. Bonin graduated from high school in 1965, then joined the US Air Force and got engaged to his girlfriend. He went to Vietnam as an aerial gunner and after risking his life to rescue a fellow airman he was awarded the Good Conduct Medal. This was perhaps inappropriate because while he was there he had raped two other servicemen at gunpoint. However, the matter went unreported at the time and he received an honourable discharge in 1968.

Back in California, he got married. Perhaps suffering from post-traumatic stress disorder, he told his wife of a recurring dream. He said he would be alone in a bar when a girl with no face would come up to him. After buying her a drink, he would take her to an isolated place, then rape her, kill her and bury her in a shallow grave. Unsurprisingly, they soon divorced.

STARTS ABDUCTING BOYS

Bonin moved back with his mother in Downey, some thirteen miles south-east of downtown Los Angeles. Soon after, he began abducting teenage boys. He would force them to perform oral sex on him, then he would sodomize them and torture them by squeezing their testicles. When he was eventually arrested in 1969 with a sixteen-year-old boy in his car, he told the officers that he was relieved to have been caught as he might have killed the teenager.

Examined in Atascadero State Hospital, he was found to have scars on his buttocks and head from earlier abuse. There was also damage to the prefrontal cortex of the brain, the area that restrains violent impulses. Despite two years' therapy, he was found to be untreatable and was sent to prison to finish his sentence. He was released in June 1974, when it was judged that he was no longer a danger to himself or others.

In September 1975 he picked up fourteen-year-old hitch-hiker David McVicker. When Bonin asked him if he was gay, McVicker asked him to stop the car but Bonin pulled a gun. In a deserted field he raped the boy and started to strangle him but relented when the boy screamed. Dropping him at his home, Bonin said ominously: 'We'll meet again.'

Two days later, he tried to run down a fifteen-year-old who rejected his advances. Admitting all charges, Bonin was sentenced to fifteen years in jail, but was out in three. Returning to his mother's home, he got a job as a truck driver and started dating a girl. He had a neighbour called Everett Fraser who regularly held parties, where he met twenty-two-year-old Vernon Butts, who dabbled in the occult and eighteen-year-old Texan Gregory Miley, who became his lover.

BUYS CAMPER VAN

Bonin then equipped himself with a green Ford camper van. On 28 May 1979, Bonin and Butts picked up thirteen-year-old hitch-hiker Thomas Glen Lundgren. He got in the back, but Bonin had removed the handles on the inside of the rear doors, so once a victim had entered there was no escape. When Lundgren's body was found, he had been strangled, his throat had been slashed, his body was perforated with stab wounds and his penis and testicles had been severed.

Later Bonin was arrested for molesting a seventeen-year-old boy. As he was still on probation he should have been sent back to prison immediately to serve the rest of his sentence, but he was released in error. When Everett Fraser picked him up from jail, Bonin said chillingly: 'No one's going to testify again. This is never going to happen to me again.'

Bonin still saw his girlfriend on Sundays, but on Fridays and Saturdays he cruised the freeways. On Saturday 4 August 1979, he and Butts picked up seventeen-year-old Mark Shelton, who had just left home on his way to a cinema in Westminster, Orange County. Screams were heard by his neighbours so it seems he was abducted by force. His torture included being sodomized with various objects including a pool cue, treatment which was so brutal that he went into shock and died. The two killers dumped his body while they went hunting fresh prey.

'HYPNOTIC WAY ABOUT HIM'

Butts was now hooked. 'After the first one, I couldn't do anything about it,' he said. Bonin was clearly in the lead, though. 'He had a hypnotic way about him,' said Butts.

The following day they picked up seventeen-year-old German exchange student Marcus Grabs, who was hitch-hiking around the United States. They took him back to Bonin's house, where he was stripped and bound before being sodomized and beaten. His naked body was dumped in Malibu Canyon. There was an electrical cord around one of his ankles and a rope around his neck. He had suffered over seventy stab wounds.

On 27 August 1979, fifteen-year-old Donald Hyden Jr was picked up on Santa Monica Boulevard. His body was found in a rubbish bin off the Ventura Freeway. He had been beaten around the head, strangled, sodomized by something the size of a fist and stabbed to death and there were also burn marks on his body. His throat had also been slashed and an attempt had been made to castrate him.

In the following month, seventeen-year-old David Murillo was cycling to the cinema when Bonin and Butts lured him into the van where he was bound, repeatedly raped and strangled, before his head was beaten in with a tyre iron. His naked body was dumped alongside Highway 101 on 12 September. Thirteen days later, eighteen-year-old Robert Wirostek was cycling to the grocery store where he worked when he was abducted. Two days after that, his body was found dumped alongside Interstate 10.

COOLING-OFF PERIOD

Part of the definition of a serial killer is that they take a cooling-off period. Bonin and Butts took five weeks off and then on 29 November they picked up an unidentified youth. They beat, sodomized and strangled him before dumping his body alongside Route 99 in Kern County. The following day, the naked body of seventeen-year-old Frank Dennis Fox was dumped alongside the Ortega Highway, five miles east of the intersection with Interstate 5. Along with the marks of beating, binding and sexual activity, there were green carpet fibres in his pubic hair – the same colour as the carpet in the back of Bonin's van, it turned out.

Ten days later, fifteen-year-old John Kilpatrick disappeared from Long Beach. His body was later found in a remote area of Rialto. Then on 1 January 1980, Bonin picked up sixteen-year-old Michael Francis McDonald in Rialto. His body was found alongside Highway 71 in San Bernardino County. He had been tortured and strangled.

Bonin took another month off, then on 3 February he was out with Gregory Miley when they picked up fifteen-year-old Charles Miranda, who was hitch-hiking along Santa Monica Boulevard. According to Miley, Bonin and Miranda had consensual sex in the back of the van while he drove and when it was over Bonin whispered to Miley: 'The kid's going to die.'

They overpowered the boy and tied him up. Bonin wanted to have his fun, so he pretended it was a kidnapping.

'What does your dad want for you?' he asked. 'How much do you think we can get as a ransom? Maybe a couple of thousand.'

Miranda said he didn't think he could get that much.

'How much money do you have?' asked Bonin.

'About $6,' Miranda replied.

Miley took the money and said: 'Why don't you let the kid go?'

But Bonin was adamant.

'No,' he said. 'He'll know us and he'll know the van.'

Miley attempted to rape the boy but could not sustain an erection so he sodomized him with the sharp objects Bonin kept in the back of the van for that purpose. Bonin then used a jack handle to twist a shirt around the boy's neck like a tourniquet, while Miley jumped on his chest. They left Miranda's naked body in an alleyway in downtown Los Angeles and dumped his clothing elsewhere.

Bonin then said: 'I'm horny. Let's go and do another one.'

'Oh, man, no way,' Miley protested. 'I don't want to do any more. I just want to go home.'

However, Bonin then spotted twelve-year-old James McCabe on Huntington Beach, who was on his way to Disneyland. According to Miley, McCabe entered the van voluntarily. As he drove, Miley said he heard crying sounds from the back and then he helped hold McCabe down while Bonin strangled him and crushed his neck with a jack handle. Miley joined in, he said, because: 'I felt like it.' After taking the money from the boy's wallet, they left his body beside a rubbish bin. Bonin later crowed that of all his victims McCabe had been the easiest to kill.

NEW PARTNER IN CRIME

On 24 March 1980, nineteen-year-old Ronald Gatlin was picked up in Van Nuys. The next day, his naked body was found in Duarte, near the junction of freeways 210 and 605. He had been sodomized and strangled with a ligature. There were wounds to the neck and the right ear that apparently had been made by an ice pick and the body showed signs of beating.

Then Bonin found a new partner in crime. At another party in Everett Fraser's apartment, he met seventeen-year-old William Pugh and gave him a lift home. On the way, Bonin told Pugh about picking up young male hitch-hikers then raping them, torturing them and killing them – cautioning Pugh that you should make sure that you had found a spot to dump the body before you picked the victim. Then he dropped Pugh off safely at home.

Pugh already had a long rap sheet full of petty crimes. On 20 March, he was with Bonin when they picked up fifteen-year-old Harry Todd Turner, a runaway from a children's home. According to Pugh, Bonin offered Turner $20 for sex and then tied him up, sodomized him brutally and bit his penis hard enough to draw blood. After that he told Pugh to beat Turner up, which he did, fracturing his skull in eight places. Bonin then strangled him with his shirt, as he had with Miranda, and dumped his naked body in an alleyway.

Two days later the naked bodies of fourteen-year-old Glen Norman Barker and fifteen-year-old Russell Duane Rugh were found along the Ortega Highway. They had ligature marks around their wrists and ankles and had been beaten and sodomized.

Again they had green carpet fibre in their pubic hair and Barker also had cigarette burns around his neck. His mother had cervical cancer and died before she could see Bonin brought to justice.

COPS REJECT SERIAL KILLER THEORY

Despite the similarities between this and other cases, the police were reluctant to say that a serial killer was at work but reporter J.J. Maloney at the *Orange County Register* spotted the trend. The newspaper dubbed the perpetrator the Freeway Killer and called in a forensic psychologist who said that he was a strong, clever white man in his late twenties or early thirties with a history of mental illness. Spot on.

He also remarked that the killer had suffered some sexual trauma in his childhood and had become bisexual, but could not accept the homosexual side of his character. The psychologist thought Bonin mutilated his victims because of the revulsion he felt, but in fact he delighted in it.

Even so, the police did not take up the idea of there being a serial killer at work, as a staggering number of bodies were dumped along the freeways every year. As there are commonly only four ways to kill someone – shooting, strangling, stabbing or bludgeoning – there are bound to be similarities between killings. They figured that the *Orange County Register* had cooked up the story to sell newspapers, but the *Register* stuck with it and soon the TV news took it up.

Bonin drove out to Orange County every day to buy the *Register*, to keep abreast of the investigation, and kept a scrapbook in the van full of cuttings on the Freeway Killer. The people he worked with remarked that he was obsessed with the case and fellow gays were outraged, complaining that the Freeway Killer was giving all gays a bad name.

On 10 April 1980, sixteen-year-old Steven Wood was picked up by Bonin after visiting the dentist. The following day his naked body was found by the Pacific Coast Highway and Long Beach Freeway, the marks on his body showing that he had been tied up, beaten, sodomized and strangled. His twenty-year-old brother Carl was so upset that he killed himself the next day.

Butts and Bonin went out on the hunt again on 29 April 1980, when they found nineteen-year-old Darin Lee Kendrick collecting trolleys in the parking lot of a supermarket. They lured him into the van with the promise of drugs and his naked body was found the following morning near the Artesia Freeway. On top of being sodomized and strangled, Darin had apparently been forced to eat chloral hydrate, which had left caustic burns on his mouth, chin, chest and stomach. He had also been stabbed through the right ear with an ice pick, causing a fatal wound to the upper cervical spinal cord.

KILLS MALE LOVER

Bonin had broken up with his girlfriend and seems to have then embraced his homosexual side, taking as his lover Lawrence Eugene Sharp, an eighteen-year-old from Long Beach. They went out on a date, but it made no difference.

'I just got up one morning and decided I was tired of him,' said Bonin. 'I just got tired of having him around, and so I decided that I should kill him.'

His body was dumped behind a petrol station in Westminster. He had not got off any more lightly than the others as he had been beaten around the face, sodomized and strangled.

Soon afterwards, Bonin abducted fourteen-year-old Sean King, then raped, tortured and strangled him and discarded his body. Following that he went to boast about the details to Butts, who had refused to come on the hunting trip with him.

Sean's body was not found immediately. After Bonin was arrested, he was read a letter that purportedly came from his mother, pleading with him to tell her where her son's body was so she could give him a decent burial. Bonin did so in exchange for a hamburger, which the cops went out and bought for him. The authorities went one better and did not try Bonin for Sean King's murder, as they had enough on him already. Unrepentant, Bonin even kept up a correspondence with King's mother while waiting on death row and never once said he was sorry.

NEW ACCOMPLICE

After the murder of Sean King, Bonin acquired a new accomplice – nineteen-year-old drifter James Munro, who went to live in his mother's house. He also landed a job at the same delivery firm as Bonin.

David McVicker, who had survived Bonin's attack five years earlier, had been following the media coverage and began to see parallels between what he had been through and what those who turned up dead had suffered. He even recalled his attacker saying, after the ordeal was over, that he was going to kill him but had decided he wanted to come back and use him again. When he called the cops they were forced to concede that a serial killer was on the loose and the forces in the various jurisdictions began to co-operate.

Then William Pugh was arrested for car theft and as part of a plea bargain he offered to tell the police who the Freeway Killer was. He did not tell them that he had been in on the murder of Harry Turner, only that William Bonin was collecting newspaper clippings on the case. Calling up Bonin's record, the cops found that he had convictions for assaulting teenage boys, including David McVicker.

When the police visited Everett Fraser and showed him a map of where the victims had gone missing, he was immediately convinced that Bonin was the killer.

UNDER SURVEILLANCE

Bonin was now put under surveillance and the very day the surveillance began Bonin and Munro went out on the hunt. Eighteen-year-old Steven Wells was standing at a bus stop on El Segundo Boulevard when he apparently agreed to have sex with the two of them. Bonin then drove Wells back to his mother's house. At first everything went well, but Bonin then offered Wells $200 if he could tie him up. Once bound, Wells was mercilessly beaten and sodomized before he was strangled.

They carried the body out to the van in a cardboard box and went to see Butts, who proudly showed Munro his collection of the ID cards of those they had killed. Bonin then showed Butts Wells's body.

'Oh, how nice,' Butts said. 'You got another one.'

Bonin and Munro dumped Steven Wells' body behind a petrol station in Huntington Beach and then went to McDonald's. Eating his burger, Bonin looked up at the sky and said, 'Thanks, Steve,' then looked down and laughingly repeated: 'Thanks, Steve, wherever you are.'

Later Bonin confessed to Munro that he was the Freeway Killer and that alone or with others he had killed forty-five people. Munro began to cry and Bonin comforted him, saying he was not going to hurt him unless he ran or called the police. But Munro was afraid.

William Bonin (left) with Vernon Butts, who police claimed had been the truck driver's accomplice in at least six of the 21 murders. Butts killed himself in jail by twisting a towel around his neck.

Bonin said that the only way Munro could learn to trust him was to let him tie him up. Amazingly Munro let him and then he begged him to spare his life, sounding like Wells had done. Bonin laughed and said again that he was not going to hurt him unless he ran away. Then he untied him.

The surveillance of Bonin started just too late to save Steven Wells' life. For nine days they followed him until, on 11 June 1980, he picked up a fifteen-year-old boy and took him to a deserted parking lot. By the time the police raided the van they were almost too late. Bonin was already in the process of raping and strangling his victim. The scrapbook of Freeway Killer cuttings and the ropes, tapes and implements in the back of the van were enough to tie him to the other killings.

'LIKED THE SOUND OF KIDS DYING'

Bonin did not confess at first. It was only when the letter from Sean King's mother was read to him and he was overwhelmed with the need for a hamburger that he confessed to King's murder and led the police to the body. However, the letter had not come from King's mother at all. It had been written by one of the detectives, which was why Bonin was not charged with his murder.

After that, Bonin confessed to the other killings, giving details of the torture and the murders in a matter-of-fact fashion. The police were outraged and sickened. He was formally charged with fourteen murders, eleven robberies and one count of sodomy, though another twenty cases were attributed to him. He also fingered Butts, Pugh, Miley and Munro.

Butts was charged as the accomplice in nine of Bonin's murders and killed himself in jail by twisting a towel around his neck, copying Bonin's murder method. Munro was arrested for Wells' murder, Miley was charged with two counts of murder, two of robbery and one of sodomy and Pugh was also picked up.

Interviewed by CBS, Bonin told TV reporter David Lopez that he had killed so many victims because he 'liked the sound of kids dying'. Nevertheless, he was terrified of facing the death penalty – which was the punishment called for by the jury in Los Angeles, after finding him guilty of ten first-degree murders. The judge concurred, saying that if the sentence was commuted to life by a higher court then each life sentence should run consecutively, so he would never get out.

At a second trial in Orange County, Bonin was convicted of another four counts of murder and given a second death sentence. There followed seventeen years of appeals, during which time Bonin wrote to one mother telling her that he loved killing her son the most 'because he was such a screamer'. He was executed by lethal injection in San Quentin on 23 February 1996.

Munro was sentenced to fifteen years to life for the second-degree murder of Steven Wells and Miley got twenty-five years to life for the murder of Charles Miranda. He received the same in Orange County for the murder of James McCabe – avoiding the death penalty by testifying against Bonin. However, in 2016 he was beaten to death by another prisoner. Pugh was jailed for six years for the manslaughter of Harry Todd Turner after his contribution to the capture of Bonin had been taken into account.

BEVERLEY ALLITT
THE ANGEL OF DEATH

FIRST MYSTERIOUS DEATH

On 23 February 1991, just two days after Beverley Allitt had started work as a nurse on Children's Ward Four at Grantham and Kesteven Hospital in Lincolnshire, seven-week-old Liam Taylor was brought in with a chest infection.

His doctor did not think his condition was serious but in hospital it could be properly monitored. The staff nurse said that newly enrolled state nurse Allitt would take good care of him, but when they returned two hours later they were told that he had taken a turn for the worse.

'I was feeding him and he suddenly threw up,' said Allitt. 'It went all over me. I had to go and change my uniform.'

The child was so sick, she said, that he had stopped breathing for a moment.

'He was choking on his vomit,' she said. 'If he'd been at home, you'd probably have lost him.'

The couple were upset but took an instant liking to the young nurse who was so frank with them and they were relieved and grateful when Allitt volunteered for an extra night shift to look after him. However, early in the morning Allitt called for an emergency resuscitation team as Liam had stopped breathing. The doctors managed to revive him, but there was bad news. The specialist told Liam's parents that, if their child survived, he would have severe brain damage.

'Normally, in children who have respiratory failure, their condition can be stabilized in a matter of minutes,' Dr Charith Nanayakkara said. 'In Liam's case, it took an hour and fifteen minutes.'

The chaplain was called to christen the child. Liam's parents then agreed to switch off the life support system, but Liam did not die – not immediately anyway. His parents took turns holding him until he finally perished seven and a half hours later.

The doctors could not understand how he had died. A post-mortem concluded that Liam had suffered an 'infarction' of the heart – that is, the muscles of the heart had died. This usually happened in patients in middle age or beyond, after a lifetime of heavy smoking or drinking, so the pathologist could not explain how it had happened to a tiny child.

INSULIN IN BLOOD

Then on 5 March, just three days after Liam had been buried, eleven-year-old Timothy Hardwick was admitted to Ward Four. He had been born with cerebral palsy and had suffered an epileptic fit. Again Allitt seemed to lavish care on the child and initially the doctors were pleased with his progress. Suddenly, when the ward was particularly busy, Timothy unexpectedly died. Given his chronic condition, no further investigation was made and no one called the police.

In the same bed just five days later, fourteen-month-old Kayley Desmond stopped breathing while in the care of Allitt. Then her heart stopped beating. She was revived and rushed to the intensive care unit at the Queen's Medical Centre in Nottingham, amid concern that she might have suffered brain damage when starved of oxygen. It was assumed that this had occurred when, as a bad feeder, she had inhaled milk and stopped breathing. No one spotted that under her right armpit there was a needle puncture with a small bubble of air behind it, as if someone had injected her ineptly. It was only seen when her X-rays were re-examined later. Nevertheless, Kayley made a full recovery.

Another ten days passed before five-month-old Paul Crampton was admitted to the ward with mild bronchitis. Responding well to treatment, he was due to be discharged four days later when suddenly he took a turn for the worse.

Sue Phillips, the mother of Becky and Katie Phillips, who were also on the ward, said: 'I heard Bev Allitt say: "I think I know what's wrong with him. He's hypoglycaemic."'

Paul was put on a glucose drip and quickly recovered.

'I thought how clever the nurse was to have realized what was wrong with him so quickly,' Sue Phillips said.

He had two more unexplained attacks of hypoglycaemia, a critical lack of sugar in his body. After the third attack, he was rushed to the Queen's Medical Centre, with Allitt in the ambulance, where the lab discovered that he had a high level of insulin in his blood.

PARENTS' GRATITUDE

The following day five-year-old Bradley Gibson was admitted suffering from pneumonia and during the night he complained of pain in the arm where his antibiotic drip was attached. He was attended by Allitt. On the second occasion, he suffered a cardiac arrest. For half an hour, the emergency resuscitation team battled to save him – successfully – and he too was taken to the Queen's. His parents went to the local newspaper, the *Grantham Journal*, to praise the doctors and nurses who had saved their son and the paper ran the story under the headline 'Our Miracle'. Three national newspapers picked up on it.

The day after that, two-year-old Yik Hung 'Henry' Chan was admitted after he had plunged from a bedroom window on to the

Beverley Allitt had been to Grantham College of Further Education with Sue Phillips. Allitt told Phillips she would look after her daughter Katie. 'She will be all right with me.'

patio below, suffering a fractured skull. Although he was dizzy and complaining of bad headaches, his condition quickly improved and the doctors were thinking about sending him home. However, when attended by Allitt the child started vomiting. Other staff saw he was blue, so the emergency team were called and he was revived with oxygen. When this happened a second time, Henry, too, was rushed to the Queen's.

Four days later, it was the turn of identical twins Becky and Katie Phillips. Becky had been admitted for observation after suffering from acute gastroenteritis. She was untroubled for the first two days because Allitt had been off duty. When she returned, Becky's mother Sue Phillips recognized her immediately, because they had been to Grantham College of Further Education together. Strangely, though, Allitt did not acknowledge her.

When Becky returned home she fell ill again and was taken back to hospital. The doctors suspected that the problem was with the milk the twins were being fed. Whereas the hospital used ready-mixed baby's milk, Sue mixed her own from powder. That evening Becky screamed and her eyes rolled in her head. Allitt did not want Sue to take Becky home but nevertheless she was discharged. However, despite a midnight rush to A&E, she died in the night. No reason could be found, though the doctor in A&E thought she might have contracted meningitis. The death certificate said 'infant death syndrome' – cot death.

As a precaution, Katie was sent to hospital for observation, only to be cared for by Allitt, who now offered Sue seemingly genuine words of comfort. Seeing Sue was tired, Allitt told her to go home and get some rest.

'You go. I will look after her,' said Allitt. 'She will be all right with me.'

Within half an hour of reaching home, Sue got a call saying Katie was having trouble breathing. She suffered a cardiac arrest, but Allitt was on hand to call for 'resus'. Emergency treatment saved Katie's life, but the same thing happened again two days later. Rushed to the Queen's, she was found to have suffered brain damage. She had cerebral palsy, paralysis of the right side and damage to her eyesight and hearing. What's more, five of her ribs were broken. This was put down to frantic efforts to resuscitate her. But Katie's mother Sue was so grateful to Allitt for saving her daughter's life that she asked her to be her godmother. As it was, the hospital's chaplain became Katie's godparent.

QUESTIONS RAISED

A few days later, six-year-old Michael Davidson was admitted after being accidentally shot with an airgun. After minor surgery to remove the pellet, Allitt helped prepare an intravenous antibiotic. When it was administered, the child stopped breathing. His face turned black and his back arched. CPR from Dr Nanayakkara had him breathing again before the emergency team arrived and after being resuscitated he recovered and was eventually discharged.

That same day two-month-old Christopher Peasgood was admitted with breathing difficulties. While he was put in an oxygen tent, Allitt suggested that his parents, who had lost a child to cot death two years earlier, should go and have a cup of tea. When they returned they found the emergency team in action. The boy was blue. A nurse had discovered that the alarm indicating he had stopped breathing had been turned off. Nevertheless, Allitt assured Christopher's parents that he would be all right, but he suffered another cardiac arrest during the night. Fearing that he was dying, the child was christened. The doctors wanted to send him to the Queen's but feared he might not survive the journey. However, Christopher's parents agreed to the move, figuring they had nothing to lose, and in the intensive care unit there he quickly recovered.

Christopher King was a month old when he was admitted for an operation, but he became inexplicably ill before going to surgery and had to be revived with oxygen. The operation was a success, but he had to be resuscitated four more times before he was sent to the Queen's. His mother Belinda was a nurse and she swore that she would never take Christopher back to Ward Four.

Seven-week-old Patrick Elstone had been playing and laughing when his parents had dropped him off for a check-up, but in Allitt's care he had stopped breathing – twice. He was rushed to the Queen's, but not before he had suffered brain damage. By then, the doctors at the Queen's were beginning to ask the question: Why were so many children coming into their care from Ward Four?

LIGNOCAINE FOUND

Asthmatic fifteen-month-old Claire Peck had been admitted to the ward on 18 April. She was put on a nebulizer that cleared her airways and she was discharged two days later, but after a coughing fit she returned on 22 April. Her mother Susan found Nurse Allitt unfriendly, even hostile, and the Pecks had been ushered away while their daughter was being treated. Left alone with the child, Allitt suddenly cried out: 'Arrest! Arrest!'

Doctors came running and revived the child, but as soon as she was left alone with Allitt the same thing happened again. This time the doctors could not save her. Susan Peck, holding the dead child, noticed that everyone else was upset but Allitt just sat there staring.

The authorities at first suspected that legionnaires' disease was responsible, so although no virus was found the ward was meticulously scrubbed. Initially a post-mortem showed that Claire had died from natural causes, but Dr Nelson Porter, a consultant at the hospital, was unhappy with the number of heart cases that had occurred in Ward Four over the previous eight weeks and ordered further tests. Lignocaine, a drug that was used to treat adults suffering from cardiac arrest, was found in Claire's body. It was never given to babies.

The police were called in and it was discovered, by checking the rotas, that Allitt was the only person who was present every time there was a medical emergency. Also, notes covering Paul Crampton's stay were missing. Allitt was suspended, but the parents of the Phillips twins had so much faith in her that they hired a private detective to clear her name.

MUNCHAUSEN'S SYNDROME

After Allitt's arrest a missing ward diary was found in her home. She was charged with four counts of murder and eleven counts of attempted murder, to which she pleaded not guilty at Nottingham Crown Court on 15 February 1993. In the court case, which lasted two months, the prosecution easily showed that Allitt had the means and the opportunity to commit the crimes – but what of the motive? Consultant paediatrician Professor Roy Meadow told the court that Allitt exhibited all the symptoms of Munchausen's Syndrome and Munchausen's Syndrome by Proxy. In the first condition, the sufferer seeks attention by self-harm or faking complaints. Allitt's extensive medical record confirmed that. Even while she had been out on bail she had been admitted to hospital complaining of an enlarged right breast. It was discovered that she had been injecting herself with water. She attended the court for just sixteen days, absenting herself for the rest of the time due to mysterious illnesses.

The second condition is usually exhibited by mothers, where they seek medical attention by complaining that their offspring is suffering from fictitious complaints or by inflicting actual abuse. Professor Meadow said that to suffer from both Munchausen's Syndrome and Munchausen's Syndrome by Proxy was extremely rare, but he came across around forty cases of the proxy condition a year.

Allitt was found guilty on all charges. In Children's Ward Four at Grantham and Kesteven Hospital in Lincolnshire, she had administered potentially lethal injections or attempted to suffocate twenty-three children in her charge, killing four and leaving a further nine irreparably damaged – all in just fifty-nine days.

DANGER SIGNS SINCE CHILDHOOD

In court, it became clear that Beverley Allitt should never have been allowed to become a nurse because she had shown disturbing symptoms of a mental disorder from an early age. One of four children, she sought attention by wearing dressings and casts over supposed wounds that she would allow no one to examine. Growing overweight as an adolescent, her attention-seeking became aggressive and her parents regularly had to take her to hospital for treatment for fictitious ailments. These included pain in her gall bladder, headaches, urinary infections, uncontrolled vomiting, blurred vision, minor injuries, back trouble, ulcers and appendicitis, resulting in the removal of a perfectly healthy appendix. The scar was slow to heal as she kept picking at the wound.

While training as a nurse she had a poor attendance record, frequently being absent with supposed illnesses. She was also suspected of odd behaviour, including smearing faeces on the walls of the nurses' home. Her boyfriend accused her of being aggressive, manipulative and deceptive. She falsely claimed to be pregnant and told people he had AIDS and she had accused a friend of his of rape, though she did not go to the police.

When Allitt returned to the dock for sentencing, the judge told her:

> You have been found guilty of the most terrible crimes. You killed, tried to kill or seriously harmed thirteen children, many of them tiny babies. They had been entrusted to your care. You have brought grief to their families. You have sown a seed of doubt in those who should have faith in the integrity of care their children receive in hospital. Hopefully, the grief felt by the families will become easier to bear, but it will always be there. You are seriously disturbed. You are cunning and manipulative and you have shown no remorse for the trail of destruction you have left behind you. I accept it is all the result of the severe personality disorder you have. But you are and remain a very serious danger to others.

He gave her thirteen concurrent terms of life imprisonment, which meant she would serve a minimum of thirty years and would only be released if she was considered to be no danger to the public. Committed to Rampton Secure Hospital, she admitted three of the murders and six of the attempted murders. Her earliest possible parole date is 2032, when she will be 64. Meanwhile, the families and the victims whom she disabled will have to live a lifetime with what she has done.

VLADO TANESKI
THE REPORTER WHO KNEW TOO MUCH

MURDER SCOOP

On 19 May 2008, Macedonia's biggest daily newspaper *Nova Makedonija* (New Macedonia) printed a story under the headline 'Serial Killer Stalks Kičevo Too'. Three women's bodies – naked, wrapped in telephone cable and stuffed into nylon bags – had been found around Kičevo, a poor mountainous town with a population of 27,000, about seventy-five miles south-west of Macedonia's capital Skopje. The previous year a serial killer had stalked Ohrid, just thirty miles away, though the MO was clearly different.

Nova Makedonija's story began:

> The people of Kičevo live in fear and panic after another butchered body of a woman from the town was found over the weekend. The local police, as well as the town populace, see the mysterious disappearances and terrible

deaths of Živana Temelkoska and Lubica Ličoska as the work of a single person – a serial killer.

Both women were tortured and murdered in the same fashion, which rules out the possibility that this could have been done by two different people. The Ohrid serial killer murdered three people but his victims were all street-based money exchangers and his motive was to rob them.

The motives of the Kičevo monster remain unclear. Both women were friends and living in the same part of town. Police have a few suspects who they are interrogating.

The latest body was found in a rubbish dump. It had been tied up with a piece of phone cable with which the woman had clearly been previously strangled.

It was bylined 'Vlado Taneski', a veteran reporter of twenty years who still used a typewriter and phoned in his copy, rather than send it by fax or even by laptop and email. There was usually little to report from Kičevo apart from local government incompetence or corruption, rising unemployment and petty crime, and then in November 2004 came a story Taneski could get his teeth into. Sixty-one-year-old Mitra Simjanoska, who some said was a woman 'of loose morals', went missing.

SUSPECTS JAILED

On 12 January 2005, her body was found dumped in a shallow hole in an abandoned construction site on the edge of town. She had been bound, brutally raped, strangled and then stuffed into a bag. The police quickly arrested two men in their twenties, Ante Risteski and Igor Mirčeski, who were charged with the murder of Simjanoska as well as that of Radoslav Bozhinoski, an old man who had been robbed and killed and horribly abused in the nearby village of Malkoetz. His penis and testicles had been squeezed with hot fire tongs and objects had been forced up his anus. It was reported that Risteski and Mirčeski had confessed to both murders, but in court

Mitra Simjanoska's body was found in a shallow hole in an abandoned construction site in Kičevo (pictured above). She had been bound, brutally raped, strangled and then stuffed in a bag.

they only admitted to killing Bozhinoski and said they had nothing to do with Simjanoska.

Under the headline 'Surgical Gloves for a Monstrous Murder', Taneski reported:

> In handcuffs and with searching eyes, 28-year-old Ante Risteski and his friend Igor Mirčeski, accused of a horrible double homicide in Kičevo and Malkoetz, walked into the courtroom. They stared vacantly at the ceiling and from time to time whispered, as if to themselves: it's all over and now we'll pay for our crimes.

They were sentenced to life imprisonment for the two murders. However, semen had been found on Simjanoska's body and the DNA matched neither that of Risteski nor Mirčeski.

INTERVIEWS VICTIM'S SON

Then in November 2007 fifty-six-year-old Lubica Ličoska went missing from the same part of town as Simjanoska. Taneski interviewed Ličoska's son Duko, who said:

> Lubica was a quiet and gentle woman. She fought poverty and worked as a janitor of apartment buildings to feed her family. Two days after the disappearance of my mother, I informed the police. I talked to the residents of the buildings where my mother used to work and searched around a bit for clues, but I couldn't find any traces of her. The police told me they are on the case.

Then locals remembered that in May 2003 another elderly woman, seventy-three-year-old Gorica Pavelski, had also gone missing from the neighbourhood. No trace of her was ever found. However, Ličoska's body was found dumped near the road from Kičevo to Gostivar. Like Simjanoska, she had been bound, raped, strangled and stuffed into a bag. But it appeared that she had been killed only days before, while she had been missing for three months. In the meantime she had been kept prisoner, while being tortured and raped. Taneski's article appeared in *Utrinski vesnik* (Morning Herald) on 6 February 2008.

> The new crime is Kičevo's top story. Rumours abound. While the police are working on the case, the majority of people in Kičevo think that this murder is related to the double homicide in Malkoetz and Kičevo, when two older citizens were killed for a very small sum of money.

How could that be when the convicted killers of Simjanoska were already behind bars?

Taneski speculated that Ličoska had been hit by a car and instead of taking her to hospital someone took hideous advantage of her defenceless state. The police, he said, were on their way to solving the case.

REPORTER ARRESTED

Then the body of sixty-five-year-old Živana Temelkoska was found on a rubbish tip outside town. Temelkoska had been bound, raped, strangled and stuffed into a bag in the same way as the others and during her torture she had been abused with a glass object and aftershave. She had numerous internal and external injuries, including five broken ribs and thirteen lacerations to the head, and again there was semen on the body. Temelkoska had gone missing from the same part of town as the others, just a week before she was found. Taneski was soon on the story, said Goce Trpkovski at *Nova Makedonija.*

> On 18 May, just after the gruesome murder of Živana Temelkoska, he called and pitched the story to us. He was very quietly spoken but also very persuasive. As a contributor we published his story as the main article on the crime pages the next day. ... To tell the truth, I didn't

believe the story – almost nothing happens in Macedonia, and suddenly we have two serial killers stalking our tiny country in a matter of months.

Taneski interviewed the detectives working on the case and reported:

Officials from the Ministry of the Interior say that they have several suspects, all of them from Kičevo. They were interrogated and released. There is confirmation that traces from the murderer have been found on both victims, and those are now being analyzed.

To keep the story running, Taneski told his editors that he was going to interview Temelkoska's family, who lived just down the street from his house. In fact, all of the victims had lived in his neighbourhood. But before he could do that, there was a break in the case.

'We heard that somebody had been arrested in connection with the case,' said Branko Zakev from the Skopje office of *Nova Makedonija*, 'but we didn't know who that somebody was. So we decided to call Vlado, who was our reporter in Kičevo, but nobody answered the phone. Then we called the Ministry of the Interior and they said, "You don't have a reporter in Kičevo anymore."'

KNEW TOO MUCH

The police had been reading Taneski's articles. In one, he said that Lubica Ličoska had been lured into a car after she had been told her son was injured. Taneski had also chided the police for pinning the murder of Simjanoska on Risteski and Mirčeski, as they were in jail when the other murders were carried out. But their innocence of that crime was only established when the DNA analysis was finalized. Finally, he said Temelkoska had been strangled with the same cable with which she was bound, but detectives had not released that detail to the media. It was something only the killer or someone close to the case could have known.

Lab tests showed that Taneski's DNA exactly matched samples taken from the bodies of Mitra Simjanoska and Živana Temelkoska. Only later was it shown that seven hairs found near Ličoska's body came from Taneski.

The source of the women's clothing found in his house and his summer cottage some miles away is disputed, but it is thought that Taneski dressed his victims up in his mother's clothes before he raped and strangled them.

Taneski had continued living in the family home, even after he was married, and his wife confirmed that his parents were the only people he ever got angry with. But his life fell apart when his father apparently hanged himself and his mother died of an overdose of sleeping tablets. Around the same time, Taneski was made redundant from his staff job on *Nova Makedonija*, though he continued writing for them as a freelancer while his wife left to take a job in Skopje.

DIED WITHOUT TRIAL

He did not drink or smoke and had few friends. Colleagues were shocked, always finding him mild-mannered. The worst they could say of him was that he occasionally plagiarized – a sin most journalists are guilty of.

Stoutly maintaining his innocence to the police and his estranged wife, Taneski was transferred to the jail in the nearby town of Tetovo. At 2 a.m., three days after he had been arrested, a cellmate found him on his knees in the lavatory with his head in a bucket of water. He had drowned himself. A signed note in his pocket referred the finder to a second note under the pillow on his bed. This read: 'I have not killed the women. I'm proud of my family.'

Taneski's boss at *Utrinski vesnik*, Daniela Trpchevska, said: 'Police said it was suicide; others – like me – don't think so. And I'm not a hundred per cent convinced that Vlado was the killer, either. After all, he never stood trial.'

However, the veteran reporter, a dedicated journalist, did go out on the best story of his life.

GUY GEORGES
THE BEAST OF BASTILLE

ALWAYS A PROBLEM

Born Guy Rampillon on 15 October 1962 in eastern France, Guy Georges was the son of black US Air Force cook George Cartwright and a local white girl named Hélène. Cartwright had a wife back in the US, while Hélène had another son from a previous relationship named Stéphane, who was white.

Guy was just an infant when Cartwright was posted back home to America. Hélène then took up with another US serviceman and planned to emigrate with him to California, taking Stéphane with her but leaving six-year-old Guy behind.

Her family refused to take him in, so he was handed over to the French social services, who gave him the surname Georges, after his father, and sent him to a foster home with thirteen other abandoned children. A withdrawn child, he began stealing food from the kitchen and tortured animals he caught in the surrounding countryside.

Georges had been a withdrawn child who tortured animals. Once released from prison, he moved to Paris where he lived in squats and turned to drink, funding this habit by working as a rent boy.

At the age of fourteen he tried to strangle one of the other children, a mentally disabled girl. Two years later he attacked another of his foster sisters and his foster parents had little choice but to send him back to the authorities. Fostered again, he attacked another of his foster sisters. This time he was arrested. Released after a week, he was rejected by his second foster family.

At seventeen he attacked a woman at a bus stop and ended up in prison. When he was released he attacked another woman, slashing her face with a knife and snatching her handbag. Arrested once again, this time he spent a year in jail. Once released, he moved to Paris, where he lived in squats and turned to drink, funding his habit by working as a rent boy. Meanwhile, he turned to rape.

BEGINS KILLING

On 16 November 1981, he attacked an eighteen-year-old neighbour as she returned home, raping and stabbing her. He left her for dead but she survived, while he served five months in jail for theft. Once released, he raped, stabbed and strangled another victim in a car park, but again she survived and he was sentenced to eighteen months in prison. When he was released, he raped and stabbed a twenty-one-year-old girl, again in a car park. This time he was sentenced to ten years, but due to good behaviour he was soon given daytime parole.

He seized the opportunity to return to Paris on 24 January 1991, where he spotted nineteen-year-old Pascale Escarfail, a student at the Sorbonne. He followed her home and as she was opening her front door he put a knife to her throat and forced his way in. After tying her up, raping her, slitting her throat and watching her die he travelled back to prison as if nothing had happened.

Within three weeks of his release in April 1992 he attacked another woman, though she escaped and went to the police. A further arrest did little to curb him because on 7 January 1994 he raped and murdered twenty-seven-year-old Catherine Rocher in an underground car park. Six days later, he attacked a broadcaster known as Annie L.

On 8 November 1994, he raped and murdered twenty-two-year-old Elsa Benady in the underground garage of her home in the 13th arrondissement. A month later, he attacked and murdered thirty-three-year-old Dutch architect Agnes Nijkamp in her own apartment in the 11th arrondissement. He liked to tie his victims up before he raped and killed them. The press began writing about the killer in east Paris, though he quickly became 'The Beast of Bastille' because most of his murders took place in the district around the site of the famous fortress and prison.

CAUGHT AFTER MANHUNT

While the definition of a serial killer includes the stipulation that they take a break between killings, it is hard to know whether there were other attacks in the seemingly fallow periods that have not been attributed to the same perpetrator.

Georges' next attributed attack was in June 1995, when he tried to kill a girl called Elisabeth O, but she escaped. She gave a description of her attacker but failed to identify Georges' picture.

Twenty-seven-year-old Hélène Frinking was not so lucky. She was raped and murdered in her apartment after returning from an evening out on 8 July 1995. However, the killer left a footprint. Then on 25 August 1995, he attacked Mélanie B in the Marais district.

He then took another break, resuming in September 1997 when he attacked and attempted to rape Estelle F, who fought back and escaped. On 23 September 1997 he broke into the apartment of nineteen-year-old student Magalie Sirotti, where he raped her and stabbed her to death. Five days after that, he attacked Valerie L in the stairwell of her apartment block. Then on 16 November 1997 he raped and murdered twenty-five-year-old Estelle Magd in her own home.

It was clear to the police that they had a serial killer on their hands and Georges was a prime suspect. He was sleeping rough at the time and after one of the largest manhunts in French criminal history he was caught in Montmartre on 27 March 1998. DNA evidence tied him to the rapes and murders of Pascale Escarfail, Catherine Rocher,

Elsa Benady and Agnes Nijkamp, along with another attempted rape. Confronted with this evidence while in custody, Georges confessed to these four murders, as well as another three – those of Hélène Frinking, Magalie Sirotti and Estelle Magd.

'I WILL NEVER SERVE MY SENTENCE'

Assessed by psychiatrists, he was found to be legally sane and fit to stand trial. While still on remand, he and three cellmates were caught trying to saw through the bars of their cell.

His three-week trial began on 19 March 2001. He then pleaded not guilty and retracted his confession, saying it had been beaten out of him. However, confronted with the DNA evidence and fifty witnesses, including four women who had survived being attacked and raped by him, he broke down in tears and begged forgiveness from his victims' families, adding: 'I ask forgiveness from my family, from my little sister, from my father, and from God, if there is one. I ask forgiveness from myself.'

After his lawyer told him that the time had come to talk, he answered 'yes' to each of the seven murder charges when they were put to him again, though he continued to deny the four other rapes he had been charged with, and he asked the court not to impose a life sentence.

'I am nearly forty years old,' he said, 'and I will never get out.'

Suicide was clearly an option and he sentenced himself to death.

'The sentence that you are going to impose on me is nothing. I will inflict a sentence upon myself,' he said.

He was given life and was told that he must serve a minimum of twenty-two years before he would be eligible for parole.

'Twenty-two years. That's nothing. Life is life,' he said. 'You can rest assured, I know that I will never leave prison. But I can assure you that I will never serve my sentence.'

ANTHONY KIRKLAND
NO PURIFYING FLAME

BURNING THE EVIDENCE

Among his many crimes, Anthony Kirkland ruthlessly hunted down his prey – small, young or down-and-out females. He was torn between lust and hatred, believing that women had ruined his life. Those he raped and killed he set on fire, claiming that he was purifying their bodies ready for burial, but clearly he was merely trying to destroy the evidence.

Born in 1968, Kirkland started how he meant to go on. During an argument at his home in Walnut Hills, Cincinnati, the eighteen-year-old Kirkland choked and beat his twenty-eight-year-old girlfriend Leola Douglas. It seems she had spurned his sexual advances. He then doused her with lighter fuel and set her on fire, killing her. He pleaded guilty to voluntary manslaughter and aggravated arson and was sentenced to seven to twenty-five years in jail.

Paroled after sixteen years, he was then released from parole a year later. Just three months after that, he was accused of breaking into a neighbour's house in Evanston and raping her at knifepoint, though he was acquitted by a jury later that year.

The following year, on 11 May 2006, the charred body of fourteen-year-old Casonya 'Sharee' Crawford was found in a secluded area off Blair Avenue in the Avondale district of Cincinnati, which abuts both Evanston and Walnut Hills. With his record, Kirkland was immediately a suspect.

He was a suspect again when the badly burned body of forty-five-year-old Mary Jo Newton was found behind an empty building in the 700 block of Wehrman Avenue in Avondale on 16 June 2006. She had gone missing some months earlier. Kirkland was brought in for questioning about both the Crawford and the Newton cases, but his attempt to destroy DNA evidence by fire seems to have worked. Unable to force a confession, the police were compelled to let him go.

KILLED AFTER REHAB

Twenty-five-year-old mother of two Kimya Rolison was visiting Cincinnati from California when she went missing. Raised in Southern California, she had moved to Cincinnati after marrying an older man, a Cincinnati native, at the age of twenty-one. But then she became addicted to crack cocaine and returned home with her two children to an apartment her family had helped her find, where she could start over. Her father and stepmother looked after her daughter and her son went into foster care while Kimya left the San Diego area and returned to Cincinnati, where she entered a six-week rehabilitation programme. She stayed in touch with her family by phone, but when the programme ended the phone calls stopped.

It was thought that she was murdered on 22 December 2006. Rolison had been in trouble with the law and was due in court in January 2007, but when she did not show up a warrant for her arrest was issued. Some bones were then found after a Labrador retriever unearthed a femur in woods near Pulte Street, North Fairmount, about four miles from Avondale. While trained cadaver dogs failed to find any more bones, the family pooch that had made the initial find found others. They were Kimya's and her body had been burned. The police later discovered that she had known Kirkland.

KILLER ASLEEP UNDER A TREE

While Kirkland does not seem to have killed again for two and a half years, he did not maintain a low profile where the police were concerned. On 14 May 2007 a SWAT team surrounded his house at 860 Ridgeway Avenue in Avondale, when he threatened to kill his eighteen-month-old son, but the standoff was concluded without injury. Three months later, Kirkland was convicted of two counts of unlawful restraint and sentenced to 115 days in prison, though he was released early.

On 17 September 2007, Reverend Walter Bledsoe sought a restraining order on behalf of his family, for reasons unknown. This was granted in December when Kirkland's sentence would have been completed. Meanwhile, on 26 September 2007, Kirkland was reported for soliciting sex from his girlfriend's thirteen-year-old daughter and in March 2008 he was convicted of importuning and sentenced to a year in jail, plus five years on parole.

Released after seven months, he moved into the Pogue Rehabilitation Center, a halfway house run by the Volunteers of America in the Over-the-Rhine district of Cincinnati, south of Avondale. As a designated sexual offender, he was required to register his address with the local sheriff's office.

At 11.30 p.m. on 27 February 2009, Kirkland got into a fight with another inmate of the halfway house. The police were called, but the other man refused to press charges. Nevertheless, Kirkland had to leave as he had violated the halfway house's no-fighting rule and he was escorted from the building.

Two days later he broke into his old house at 860 Ridgeway Avenue. He hid in the bathroom and attacked Frederick Hughes, stabbing him at least ten times with a pair of scissors. An arrest warrant was issued for felonious assault and aggravated burglary.

On the afternoon of 8 March 2009, thirteen-year-old Esme Kenney left her house to go for a jog round a nearby reservoir. When she was late returning, her parents called the police...

The next day his parole officer was informed that Kirkland had left the halfway house and started looking for him. Two days after that, another arrest warrant was issued for failing to inform the sheriff's office of his new address. A third arrest warrant was issued the following day for domestic violence, aggravated menace and violation of a protection order, after he was accused of threatening Roberta Baldwin, the mother of his child.

On the afternoon of 8 March 2009, thirteen-year-old Esme Kenney left her house in Winton Hills north of Avondale to go for a jog around a nearby reservoir. When she was late returning, her parents called the police, who began a search. At 11.30 that evening they found Kirkland asleep against a tree in the nearby woods. The police also found Esme's iPod and watch in his pocket. Given Kirkland's record, they feared the worst.

A few hours later, they found Esme's body hidden under brush about a hundred yards from where Kirkland had been sleeping. She had been violently strangled with a rope or a piece of cloth and the lower part of her body, around her upper thighs, had been set on fire. There was evidence of a sexual assault and it seemed she had been set on fire in an attempt to cover up the crime.

BURNING WAS FOR 'PURIFICATION'

Kirkland was charged with the aggravated murder of Esme Kenney, Casonya 'Sharee' Crawford, Mary Jo Newton and Kimya Rolison, along with the gross abuse of a corpse, aggravated robbery and the attempted rape of Kenney and Crawford. At the preliminary hearings he pleaded not guilty to all charges. The defence sought to have each case tried separately, but the prosecution wanted to have them tried together as it would make it easier to secure a sentence of death.

When his two-week trial opened, Kirkland changed his plea to guilty for the murder of Mary Jo Newton and Kimya Rolison and other charges relating to their deaths. Prosecutor Joe Deters dismissed Kirkland's claim that burning the bodies was his burial ritual for purification as 'a load of garbage'. It was to destroy the evidence of his sexual assault.

'Sometimes pure evil just exists. Most people can't get their arms around that,' Deters told jurors, calling Kirkland a monster. 'I think over the last two weeks, the state has … concluded that that's a fact.'

Deters also told the jury not to be fooled into believing Kirkland was anything but a cold, calculating, serial killer.

'Kirkland's not insane. Kirkland's not stupid. These guys do exist. They do exist,' he said.

Chief assistant prosecutor Mark Piepmeier told jurors that all four of the bodies were found in areas people treated like garbage dumps.

'In life, these women are sex objects to Kirkland,' he said. 'After life, they were nothing more than garbage.'

VICTIM'S FAMILY REQUESTS MERCY

Kirkland's attorneys presented no defence and the mountain of evidence the prosecution had against him included nine hours of statements Kirkland had given to the police, when he confessed in detail to the murder of four women.

The defence attorney said that Kirkland would enter an unsworn statement. That meant Kirkland could speak to the jury, but he wouldn't be under oath and nor could he be cross-examined by the prosecution. This denied them the opportunity of introducing details of his 1987 manslaughter conviction for burning Leola Douglas into evidence.

The Kenney family wrote to the judge urging that he impose the death penalty.

'I believe that Anthony Kirkland should be put to death because he is an evil, remorseless, sadistic murderer. No living person is safe,' aunt Elizabeth Kenney said.

'He deserves the strongest sentence possible,' wrote cousin Nikki Kenney. 'To do anything less would be unjust to all his victims.'

Another cousin, Brad Kenney, said: 'Maybe you … could have sat crying in the dirt where she was killed there with us and watched her mother pull singed pieces of Esme's hair out of the ground, desperate to preserve these few slim threads linking her daughter to this earth.'

But the family of Kimya Rolison asked the judge to spare his life. Though he had left two children motherless, stepmother Kathy Rolison said: 'We respectfully request that the convicted murderer be sentenced to life in prison.'

Kirkland was given two death sentences, one each for the murders of Casonya 'Sharee' Crawford and Esme Kenney. The judge also imposed two separate sentences of seventy years to life in prison for the murders of Kimya Rolison and Mary Jo Newton. While the conviction stood, there then began a long process of appeal against the sentence.

WALTRAUD WAGNER, MARIA GRUBER, IRENE LEIDOLF AND STEPHANIJA MAYER

THE LAINZ ANGELS OF DEATH

HUMANE KILLING

While Beverley Allitt killed children to draw attention to herself, in Lainz General Hospital in Vienna four nurses murdered as many as two hundred elderly and infirm patients who annoyed them. Allitt's murderous spree went on for a matter of weeks, but the Lainz Angels of Death managed to stay under the radar for six years.

In 1982, twenty-three-year-old Waltraud Wagner began work as a nurse's aide at Lainz General Hospital's Pavilion Five, which housed elderly patients, many of whom were terminally ill. Initially, she sought to make her patients comfortable and ease their pain and suffering, then in the spring of 1983 a seventy-year-old woman patient repeatedly begged Wagner to put her out of her misery. Wagner refused, but while she was off duty she reflected on the woman's appeals.

Plainly her death was inevitable, for no one recovered in Pavilion Five, and Wagner began to think that perhaps it was more humane to accede to the patient's request. So the next time the old woman begged for death Wagner gave her an overdose of morphine and watched the pained expression on her face turn to one of bliss.

Wagner had no regrets about what she had done. She was pleased that she had relieved someone whose life had run its course and when other patients begged her to end their suffering she obliged. Soon she got used to playing God.

Over the years, Wagner was joined on the graveyard shift in Pavilion Five by nineteen-year-old Maria Gruber, a single mother and nursing-school dropout, and twenty-one-year-old Irene Leidolf, who had a husband at home but preferred hanging out with the other women after work. Like Wagner, they came from large families in rural Austria with little higher education. While drinking in a bar near the hospital it was natural for them to discuss their patients and Wagner suggested to them that, in some cases, patients should be put out of their misery. It was the compassionate thing to do. The other two agreed. It upset them to see their patients suffering so much.

Wagner taught them how to administer the right amount of morphine that would be lethal but not arouse suspicion. They saw this as mercy killing and felt no guilt. Later the deadly team was completed by Stephanija Mayer, a divorced grandmother who had emigrated from Yugoslavia. She was twenty years older than Wagner but despite her seeming maturity she was happy to go along with the terminal procedures the others had established.

'THE WATER CURE'

Until 1987 they despatched only the most severely ill, but then the termination rate accelerated. They began to kill any patient they found annoying. These included patients who made a complaint, summoned the nurse during the night, snored loudly, soiled the sheets or refused their medication. These minor infractions would result in a death sentence, with Wagner joking that the patient concerned had booked 'a ticket to God' or had 'a meeting with the undertaker'.

To avoid questions about the amount of morphine that was being used, they began to despatch patients using insulin and Rohypnol. Then to cover their tracks more completely, Wagner introduced what she called 'the water cure'. Patients' heads would be tipped back, with their tongues depressed and their nostrils pinched, and then a jug full of water would be poured down their throats, filling their lungs. They would then drown. It was a slow and agonizing death, though virtually undetectable. Elderly patients frequently had fluid in their lungs when they died and the killing went on unimpeded.

NURSES LAUGH ABOUT KILLINGS

By 1988, rumours were rife that a murderer was at work in Pavilion Five, but the head of the ward Dr Franz Xavier Pesendorfer made no

In court: (from left to right) Stephanija Mayer, Maria Gruber, Irene Leidolf and Waltraud Wagner. They claimed they had killed elderly parents out of pity, but did they enjoy their power too much?

effort to investigate. The Angels of Death were eventually betrayed by their own hubris. In February 1989, while having a drink after work, they were discussing the death of elderly patient Julia Drapal. She had been given the water cure for refusing her medication and calling Wagner a slut, so clearly she deserved to die. A doctor seated nearby heard them laughing about it and reported the matter to the police. The four women were suspended while the bodies of those who had died on the ward were exhumed. Many were found with water in their lungs, which proved nothing, but others were found with high levels of morphine, insulin or Rohypnol in their bodies. After a six-week investigation, Wagner, Gruber, Leidolf and Mayer were arrested and charged with murder.

LIKE NAZI EUTHANASIA PROGRAMME

News of the killings stunned Austria. They brought to mind Nazi medical experiments at Auschwitz and other Nazi death camps. The mayor of Vienna called the four nurses the 'death angels'. They were seen as sadists, like the women who had guarded the concentration camps, which were still fresh in the memory of many Austrians.

Between them, the four women admitted killing forty-nine patients who were too demanding or troublesome. Wagner alone admitted thirty-nine murders. But later they retracted substantial parts of their confessions, claiming that they had killed only a handful of patients who were terminally ill, to alleviate their pain. Wagner admitted only ten assisted deaths and they were mercy killings, she insisted.

More bodies were exhumed and they were charged with the forty-two counts of murder. However, the state prosecutor said that the number of victims was much higher and would probably never be known. Some estimates put the number as high as two hundred.

In the month-long trial, the state prosecutor Ernst Kloyber evoked Austria's Nazi past. He told the jury:

> This was no mercy killing, but cold-blooded murder of helpless people, which reminds us of a period in Austrian

history none of us likes to remember … It is a small step from killing the terminally ill to the killing of insolent, burdensome patients, and from there to what was known under the Third Reich as euthanasia. It is a door that must never be opened again.

The judge dismissed Wagner's claim that they were alleviating pain, pointing to her use of the 'water cure'.

'These patients were gasping for breath for up to half a day before they died,' he said. 'You cannot call that pain relief.'

Wagner was convicted of fifteen counts of murder, seventeen counts of attempted murder and two counts of physical assault. She was sentenced to life imprisonment. Leidolf was convicted of five murders and also sentenced to life. Both immediately appealed. Mayer was sentenced to twenty years and Gruber to fifteen for manslaughter and attempted murder. It had been the biggest murder trial in Austria since the Second World War.

YOUTH CULTURE BLAMED

Dr Pesendorfer had been suspended when the four nurses were arrested in April 1989 and he was found culpable of failing to pursue rumours of mass killings in his department that had been circulating for at least a year. He defended his actions, saying he had alerted the authorities, doctors and supervisory nurses and had ordered post-mortems as soon as suspicions were raised.

'What more could I have done?' he said. 'The dead were not victims of the system but victims of crimes that could not have been anticipated and prevented.'

Other criticisms were levelled at the health service. Hildegard Fach, the head of the National Union of Nurses, said that the four women were merely nurses' aides and were not qualified to give injections. She said that regulations were routinely violated in Austrian hospitals, with nurses' aides allowed to give medication intravenously when their duties were supposed to be limited to cleaning, feeding and assisting patients. As a result, innocent nurses had been abused by the public. One even said she had been spat upon.

Commentators pointed out that the case spoke volumes about post-war society, which had become increasingly obsessed with youth and material well-being at the expense of any sensitivity towards the aged and infirm. A survey showed that twenty-five per cent of those questioned thought that euthanasia was justifiable in some circumstances.

A front-page editorial in the Viennese newspaper *Die Presse* said:

> The most recent investigation into what is 'holy' to the Austrians showed it quite clearly: Their own health is most important to the individual, but the general protection of human life – in the narrow, as well as the broadest sense – ranked behind protecting material goods. To damage an auto appears to be much worse than visiting injustice or harm on one's fellow man.

The four women admitted killing forty-nine patients who were too demanding or troublesome. Then they began to retract their confessions of murder, calling their actions 'mercy killings'.

GIVEN NEW IDENTITIES

Gruber and Mayer, convicted on lesser charges, were discreetly released in the 1990s and given new identities by the Austrian government, but in 2008 the release of Wagner and Leidolf caused outrage. The Austrian newspaper *Heute* carried the headline: 'The death angels are getting out.'

Even before their release, they had been let out to go shopping or visit the hairdressers. It was explained that this was part of a pre-release programme preparing them for life outside prison. They would have been released soon anyway, as in Austria those sentenced to life only serve fifteen years. They too were given new identities, so they could resume life anonymously.

'It's inhumane and immoral to execute a killer,' said one Viennese citizen, 'but it's not fair to their victims' loved ones when a killer can look forward to a nice life outside prison.'

BOBBY JOE LONG
THE CLASSIFIED AD RAPIST

RED FIBRE CLUE

On 13 May 1984 the naked body of an Oriental female was found in a remote area of southern Hillsborough County, Florida. She was lying face downwards with her hands tied behind her back and her legs spread so far apart that her pelvis had been broken. There was also an open wound on her face. It was clear that she had been deliberately posed that way. She had been strangled and dumped there forty-eight to seventy-two hours earlier.

None of the victim's clothing or personal possessions were ever found. However, her identity was discovered. She was Ngeun Thi Long, also known as Lana or Peggy, a twenty-year-old Laotian woman who worked as an exotic dancer in a joint on Nebraska Avenue in Tampa.

Tyre tracks were found near the body. The vehicle had tyres of three different brands and all were worn. Casts were taken and a piece of fabric was also found near the body. On it was a single red nylon fibre. From its shape, size and type, it was thought to have come from a carpet. As the body was found in an isolated area, it was very likely that it had been transported there in a vehicle which, very probably, had a red carpet.

Two weeks later, on 27 May, the naked body of a young white woman was found in a remote area of eastern Hillsborough County. Her clothing was found nearby and she had been dead between eight and ten hours. She was lying on her back and her arms were bound to her sides with a clothesline. There was a hangman's noose around her neck but her throat had been cut and she had suffered several blunt-instrument traumas to the head.

A composite picture of her face was released to the media and she was identified as twenty-two-year-old Michelle Denise Simms, a native of California. She had last been seen on the previous night, talking with two white males near Kennedy Boulevard, an area popular with prostitutes.

Again tyre tracks were found. One tyre was immediately identified as a Goodyear Viva, which had been put on with the white wall facing inwards. An expert in Akron, Ohio, identified another as an expensive Vogue tyre that is only fitted to Cadillacs. A red nylon fibre was again found, linking this to the Ngeun Thi Long case.

NUDE BODIES LINK

Other forensic evidence collected might help identify the killer. Semen was found on the woman's clothing which, in the days before DNA profiling, could be used to identify the perpetrator's blood type and hairs were found that could well have come from the killer. He was Caucasian.

On 24 June 1984, the body of another white female was found in an orange grove in south-eastern Hillsborough County. The victim was fully clothed, but the body was in a bad state of decomposition. She was identified as twenty-two-year-old Elizabeth B. Loudenback of Tampa, an assembly line worker, who had last been seen on 8 June. She had no criminal history but had been known to frequent the area around Nebraska Avenue.

Her boyfriend failed a polygraph test and appeared to be an excellent suspect. However, among the forensic evidence collected at the crime scene the FBI Laboratory found the same red nylon carpet fibre, tying her death to the two previous cases. But the evidence was not handled by the same forensic examiner, so the connection was not made until later.

On 7 October 1984, the naked body of a young black woman was found near the dirt entrance road of a cattle ranch on the Pasco–Hillsborough County line. Most of the victim's clothing was found dumped next to the body, but her knotted bra was hanging from the gate. Her head was in an advanced state of decomposition, but a post-mortem found a puncture wound to the back of the neck. However, a gunshot wound was found to be the cause of death.

She was identified as eighteen-year-old Chanel Devon Williams, who had previously been arrested for prostitution and was also known to frequent a gay bar on Kennedy Boulevard in Tampa. Last seen on the night of 30 September, she had been with another hooker who had found herself a client. The hooker and her client went back to the motel that they used to conduct their business and Chanel was told to walk slowly back there to check that her companion was okay. She never arrived.

The fact that Chanel's body had been found nude linked her murder to the first two cases. Forensic evidence was sent to the FBI labs and carpet fibres found matched those in the earlier cases. Brown Caucasian pubic hair was also found. There was semen on the girl's clothes, but the blood group did not match that found in the Simms case. That could have been because the women worked as prostitutes.

SERIAL KILLER ALERT

On the morning of 14 October 1984, the body of a white woman, naked from the waist down, was found in an orange grove in a deserted area of north-eastern Hillsborough County. Her wrists and ankles were bound and she was laid out on a golden bedspread. She had been struck on the forehead and strangled with a ligature. The victim was identified as twenty-eight-year-old Karen Beth Dinsfriend, a prostitute and cocaine addict who had disappeared from Nebraska Avenue earlier that morning. The same red carpet fibres were found, along with brown Caucasian pubic hair and semen. Hillsborough County sheriff's office then issued a warning that a serial killer was on the loose and they bought a personal computer to co-ordinate information gathered in the case.

The body count continued to mount. On 30 October, the mummified remains of a white woman were found in northern Hillsborough County. The body was so badly decomposed that it yielded little forensic evidence, other than that she was naked. Her identity was not established until after the perpetrator had been arrested and he only knew her as 'Sugar' – the street name of twenty-two-year-old Kimberly Kyle Hopps. She was last seen by her boyfriend getting into a 1977–78 maroon Chrysler Cordoba. This turned out be the killer's and strands of her hair were later found in it.

The next body was found scattered in Pasco County, just north of the Hillsborough County line on 6 November 1984. A shirt, a pair of panties and some jewellery were recovered, along with some of the victim's hair. Working with the Hillsborough County sheriff's office, Pasco County detectives identified the victim as eighteen-year-old Virginia Lee Johnson, who worked as a prostitute on Nebraska Avenue. Again the same red carpet fibres were found.

Then on 24 November 1984, the naked body of a woman was discovered at the bottom of an incline off North Orient Road in Tampa. Tyre tracks were found and it seemed that a vehicle had pulled over and the body had been tipped out. The victim was twenty-one-year-old nude dancer Kim Marie Swann, who was last seen leaving a convenience store near her parents' home on the afternoon of 11 November. The ligature marks around her wrists, arms and neck tied her murder to the other killings, so the Tampa Police Department contacted the Hillsborough County sheriff's office. The same red carpet fibres were found and the tyre tracks matched those from earlier crime scenes.

A serial killer was stalking women in and around beautiful Hillsborough County, Florida. The same red carpet fibres and tyre tracks kept showing up at the scenes of the crimes.

RELEASED VICTIM IDENTIFIES KILLER

However, before Kim's body was found, a breakthrough had been made in the case. On the evening of 3 November 1984, seventeen-year-old Lisa McVey was cycling home from work when a man jumped out of the bushes and pulled her off her bicycle. He had a gun and said he had a knife. After blindfolding her he pushed her into his car and then forced her to strip naked and perform oral sex on him while he drove around. Then he took her to an apartment where he repeatedly raped and sexually abused her over the next twenty-six hours.

Though Lisa was convinced that she was going to die, she kept her wits about her and while her abductor was not looking she dropped a hair clip so she could prove that she had been held there. Eventually her assailant mellowed towards her. Instead of calling her 'bitch' he began calling her 'babe'. It was said that he warmed towards her when she talked about the sexual abuse she had suffered at the hands of her father. They left the apartment to go to an ATM and under her blindfold she spotted the word 'Magnum' on the dashboard of his car. To her surprise he eventually stopped the car and let her go with the words: 'Take care.'

She went straight to the police and gave a detailed description of her attacker. The police discovered that only the 1978 Dodge Magnum had the word 'Magnum' emblazoned on the dashboard and they obtained a list of every 1978 Dodge Magnum registered in Hillsborough County. On the list was the name Robert 'Bobby' Joe Long, who was stopped while driving down Nebraska Avenue. He was co-operative and allowed officers to photograph him. Lisa identified him from his photograph and bank records confirmed that Long had taken cash from an ATM on the night of Lisa's abduction. He was put under surveillance.

'YOU GOT ME GOOD'

Meanwhile, among forensic evidence collected in connection with the kidnapping, the FBI found red carpet fibres that matched those at earlier crime scenes. Long was arrested coming out of a cinema. He quickly confessed to the abduction and rape of Lisa McVey but denied the murders. Meanwhile, his car had been seized. The fibres from the carpet matched those found at the crime scenes and the distinctive arrangement of the tyres also matched. In his apartment, detectives found Lisa's hair clip, along with items of women's clothing and naked photographs of the murder victims. Some of them even showed Long in the act of raping them.

Confronted with the physical evidence, Long confessed.

'Well, I guess you got me good,' he said. 'Yes, I killed them ... All the ones in the paper. I did them all.'

He realized the game was up when he let Lisa McVey live.

'I knew when I let her go that it would only be a matter of time,' he said. 'I didn't even tell her not to talk to the police or anything ... I just didn't care anymore, and I wanted to stop. I was sick inside.'

He went on to give a detailed account of each abduction and murder. Lana Long had got into his car because she needed a ride. However, the murder of Michelle Simms was more premeditated. The night before he had bought some rope, cut it into convenient lengths and put it all in the glove compartment. He then went looking for a victim on Kennedy Boulevard. Simms agreed to go with him for $50 and then he drove for about a mile before he stopped and pulled out a knife. He forced her to undress, reclined the seat until it was horizontal and then tied her up. After driving another twenty miles he stopped again and raped her. He then said he was going to take her back to Kennedy Boulevard, but on the way he stopped once more and tried to strangle her. She fought him off, so he hit her on the head and pushed her out of the car, then slit her throat. Then he threw her clothes out of the car and drove off. He claimed he had hit her on the head because he did not want her to suffer when he finished her off with a knife.

He had considered letting Elizabeth Loudenback go until 'she jerked me around'. He then strangled her with a rope, stole her purse and used her bank card before throwing it away. The gun he had used to kill Chanel Williams was the same one he had used to kidnap Lisa McVey, but with McVey he had emptied the bullets out because he had not wanted to hurt her.

He was strangling Karen Dinsfriend in an orange grove when he was disturbed by barking dogs, so he drove on to another place, where he finished the job. 'Sugar' – Kimberly Hopps – was dumped in a ditch. He did not even know her name, though he did know Kim Swann, who was drunk when he picked her up. He hit her a couple of times to keep her quiet.

He also admitted killing twenty-one-year-old Vicky Elliott, who was walking to her job on the midnight shift at the Ramada Inn. She accepted a lift, but when he tried to tie her up she fought him off with a pair of scissors. He drew a map showing where he had dumped her body. When the police found her remains, the scissors were in her vagina.

SCOURS CLASSIFIED ADS

Long's confession ran to forty-five pages. He also cleared up a long series of rape cases in Florida. He would look for houses with 'for sale' signs outside, then inveigle himself inside and rape the occupant if he found a female on her own – in some cases girls as young as twelve or thirteen. He also scoured the classified ad sections of the local newspaper. Looking through items to buy, he would call and arrange a visit at a time when the husband would be at work. If he found a woman alone, he would pull a knife, tie her up, rape her, then rifle the house. Those who resisted got punched. He also made the women talk to him while he was raping them, so he could imagine that they were 'getting into it'.

The newspapers began calling him the 'Classified Ad Rapist' or the 'Adman Rapist'. Even though the police knew how he was picking his victims, they could not catch him. It seems there were between fifty and a hundred and fifty victims.

It was thought that Long also raped twenty-year-old Artis Wick in Tampa on 27 March 1984. Feeling unsatisfied he went on to strangle her and it was then that he stepped from being a rapist to being a killer, though he never admitted to this murder. Another crime fits his MO. On 19 November 1984, a woman's dead body was found floating in the Hillsborough River. She had been strangled.

TROUBLED PAST NO EXCUSE

Naturally, Long's past was raked over by the defence in the hope of an insanity plea. It is true that he had had a troubled childhood. He was born with an extra X chromosome and developed breasts during puberty, so he was teased at school. He also slept with his mother until he was thirteen. Also during his childhood he had suffered a number of head injuries – falling off a swing, falling down the stairs and falling off a horse had all rendered him unconscious. At the age of seven he was hit by a car and spent a week in hospital and at twenty he had a serious motorcycle accident. Afterwards he became hypersexual, which led him to start his career as a rapist and resulted in the break-up of his marriage – though his wife never suspected.

Long was even accused of rape by his housemate Sharon Richards. However, there was not enough evidence to charge him. Later, during an argument, he hit her and was charged with assault. Although he was convicted, the verdict was later overturned on appeal and Long laughed at Richards as he left the court. He was later convicted of sending an obscene letter and photographs to a twelve-year-old, but was sentenced to just two days in prison and six months on probation.

Found fit to plead, Long faced a series of trials which earned him two death sentences and thirty-four life sentences, plus an additional 693 years in prison. The sentencing was followed by numerous appeals. Thirty years later, Long was still alive on Florida's death row.

INDEX

PICTURE CREDITS

Getty: 16, 29, 40, 56, 72, 82, 90, 128 (t), 137, 151, 185, 248

Shutterstock editorial: 66, 104

Shutterstock: 111, 121, 128 (b), 142, 164, 176, 195, 208, 236, 270, 278, 288, 295

TopFoto: 47, 215 (RIA Novosti / TopFoto)

Press Association: 254 (Topham / PA)

APA: 285

We have made every effort to contact the copyright-holders of the photographs within this book. Any oversights or omissions will be corrected in future editions.